The Swimsuit

The Swimsuit

Fashion from Poolside to Catwalk

Christine Schmidt

BERG

London · New York

English edition
First published in 2012 by
Berg
Editorial offices:
50 Bedford Square, London WC1B 3DP, UK
175 Fifth Avenue, New York, NY 10010, USA

Berg is an imprint of Bloomsbury Publishing Plc.

Library of Congress Cataloging-in-Publication Data

A catalogue record for this book is available from the Library of Congress.

British Library Cataloguing-in-Publication Data

A catalogue record for this book is available from the British Library.

ISBN	978 0 85785 122 2 (Cloth)
	978 0 85785 123 9 (Paper)
e-ISBN	978 0 85785 124 6 (ePDF)
	978 0 85785 125 3 (epub)

Typeset by Apex CoVantage, LLC
Printed in the UK by the MPG Books Group

www.bergpublishers.com

To Annette Kellerman

Contents

List of Illustrations

Acknowledgements

This book is dedicated to Annette Kellerman in recognition of her contributions to fashion, film and sport, and as a role model for women encouraging self-motivation and self-development. Moreover, it was John Hartley who started me on this quest which began with Kellerman—providing intellectual guidance and inspiration that contributed to how I shaped my arguments and this story of swimwear, and for which I am most grateful. I would also like to thank Bonnie English for her help, advice and encouragement in the completion of this book. Thanks are due to the staff at the Mitchell Library, State Library of Queensland, Fryer Library University of Queensland and, in particular, the Powerhouse Museum Research Library and Philippa Rossiter. The Australian National Maritime Museum, Powerhouse Museum Sydney and the David Jones Archives deserve a special mention for allowing me access to rich sources of archival material. And finally, thanks to my family—Arthur, Audrey, Phebe, my mother, and my brother, Michael—for their love and encouragement.

A Template for New World Fashion

The Swimsuit: Fashion from Poolside to Catwalk documents the modern swimsuit's trajectory from men's underwear and circus/performance wear to its unique niche in world fashion. It emphasizes the relationship between fashion, media, celebrity, sport and the cultivation of the modern body. In addition, the book offers new perspectives on national histories of the swimsuit and explains how traditional European haute couture has opened up to new markets and modes of living, bringing together influences from around the globe.

As a brief form of clothing, any study of swimwear is closely aligned to beauty, thinness and the fashion body—its changing shape and bodily ideals. The swimsuit is an equalizer stripping away the wearer's social markers; it results in the body itself being placed on centre stage and is linked to changing social mores and codes of morality and decency. Body exposure battles raged from the 1900s onwards with men and women demanding the right to reveal their bodies in streamlined swimsuits in public spaces. Arguably, the bared body has led to an increasing preoccupation with physical fitness, dieting and, more recently, cosmetic surgery to achieve a level of physical beauty suitable for wearing a swimsuit. Australian women including Annette Kellerman (early 1900s), Sue Becker (1960s–1970s) and Elle Macpherson (1990s–) have gained international reputations as experts contributing to the production of physical fitness programmes that instructed women on how to achieve a body worthy of public display.

This book will consolidate the links between swimwear and celebrity and examine the impact of stars including Annette Kellerman and Esther Williams upon this modern leisure industry. Tracing this fashion revolution over 100 years reveals that key contributors to the creation and popularization of the swimsuit, and the modern ideals of youth and physical beauty, transcended social barriers to gain notoriety and commercial success through unique personal styles and talent. These individuals, including stage and film stars, fashion models, sports celebrities and beauty queens, herald the democratization of modern fashion that was and is mediated through the entertainment industries. Importantly, these factors signal how the fashion system has evolved as a result of geographic, social and cultural influences, in particular the convergence and cross-pollination between individuals and global currents as fashion moves ever closer to ordinary life.

The Swimsuit tells the interesting story of a lost celebrity—Kellerman—who popularized the one-piece swimsuit in the early 1900s, and how famous swimwear and surfwear labels such as Speedo, Quiksilver and Billabong that originated in Australia developed out of a quintessential lifestyle of sand, sea and sunshine. While it reinforces the cultural mythology of a nation of bronzed, athletic swimmers and bikini-clad blondes, it relates the history of competitive swimming and surfing and the significance of sport to our understanding of swimwear's increasingly central place in contemporary globalized culture. Australia's influential role in the swimsuit's dynamic progress from the margins to the mainstream is placed within the context of developments in the United States, Europe and, more recently, South America.

Histories of the swimsuit trace how Parisian fashion designers such as Jean Patou and Coco Chanel in the early 1900s initiated the inclusion of sportswear to spring/summer collections, specifically for wealthy clients who vacationed at elite beach resorts and country estates. Since the 1920s, the swimsuit has been depicted in glamorous fashion images for magazines such as French and British *Vogue* as clothing an ideal woman, one of the elite few who may summer in Deauville or Antibes. Photographer George Hoyningen-Huené's stark neoclassical fashion images depict this woman as sophisticated, elegant and urbane. And it is also Paris in 1946 where the bikini makes an explosive launch modelled by Folies Bergères dancer Micheline Bernardini. Although the bikini was not immediately adopted by any nation, it suited the European jet set's relaxed attitude to skimpy swimsuits and nudity and, as a result, was seen on the beaches of the French Riviera from the 1950s and 1960s, and epitomized by film icons such as Brigitte Bardot.

The story continues across the Atlantic where the American West Coast manufacturers including Jantzen, Cole of California, B.V.D. and Catalina were a driving force behind the mass production of swimwear in the 1920s and '30s. Hollywood joined forces with these manufacturers simultaneously to spearhead studio publicity and promote stylish swimsuits endorsed by stars as a new form of accessible glamour. Moreover, films became vehicles for popularizing particular designs; for example, when Dolores Del Rio 'made fashion news by introducing the two-piece bathing suit' to audiences in her screen appearance in *Flying Down to Rio* with Fred Astaire and Ginger Rogers in 1933 (Tapert 1998: 144). The Golden Age of Hollywood saw a passing parade of beauties clad in equally stylish swimsuits and for some, such as Esther Williams, it is hard to imagine them fully clothed. Alongside this pin-up glamour, the American style associated with designer sportswear came into its own in the 1940s when, due to World War II, accessibility to Parisian fashion became limited. Unlike French couture with its 'grand style and the refinements of traditional fashion authority,' it was modern, practical and in tune with 'the lives of women of their era' (Martin 1998: 9); the swimsuit was naturally included in this wardrobe. Claire McCardell, arguably one of the most influential of a new breed of American designers, created a number of innovative swimsuits in wool jerseys that were both functional and reflected 'an honest delight in the body' (ibid. 31). Together with resort wear designers such as Tina Leser, she led the way for more casual wearable fashion. Similarly, as opposed to glamour studio shots, photographers such as Louise Dahl-Wolfe and Toni Frissell captured models wearing body-baring swimsuits in exotic location shots rejoicing in their athletic sensuality.

By the early 1960s, there was a further diversification of types or models. Teenage beach party movies featuring wholesome Californian surfer girls and boys in saccharine sweet summer adventures played alongside the more assertive grown-up action of the Bond girl. The memorable Ursula Andress in *Dr. No* striding from the sea in a daringly brief white bikini accessorized with belt and hunting knife foregrounded a new type of active glamour that was vigorous and youthful and removed from the sleek, sultry glamour of legendary film sirens such as Rita Hayworth and Marilyn Monroe. The look has endured and been replicated for new audiences in the 2000s with Halle Berry, once again, emerging from the waves—this time in an orange bikini with knife on hip in *Die Another Day*.

Moving through the decades of the twentieth century, the swimsuit was refined and integrated into the fashion system. National influences, in particular French and American (and more recently Brazil), pinned the swimsuit into position creating an evolutionary path mapped with beautiful women and sunny locations. Italian and French fashion designers and brands including Pucci and Eres (1960s), Dior (1970s), Chanel, Hervé Leger and a number of key ateliers from the 1990s have continued to make their mark on the luxury swimsuit. Cruise/resort collections and the swimsuit are now staple products of major fashion brands targeting wealthy travellers as they migrate to and from glamorous exotic locations around the globe. In 2004, IMG World (a global sports, fashion and media business) launched the inaugural Mercedes-Benz Fashion Week Swim in Miami to showcase swim and beach fashions from the best swimwear brands—in particular those from America, Australia and Brazil. The *Sports Illustrated* yearly swimsuit issue has added momentum to the swimsuit's popular appeal and increased the level of exposure for cover models including Christie Brinkley, Elle Macpherson and Tyra Banks. Similarly, swimsuit editorial is assured coverage on page one or three in newspapers, whereas other fashion stories are often omitted altogether, positioning the swimsuit as an ongoing newsworthy garment. One thing that is missing from the narrative of a garment that came in from the cold is the extent to which the swimsuit's history is also an Australian story. This book redresses the balance in order to show how a peripheral country may have a continuing impact on world fashion through innovation at the margins.

The study of swimwear reflects a fascinating aspect of contemporary fashion as the swimsuit, like blue jeans, has become an essential part of the history of sartorial popular culture. It challenges traditional socio-historical trends with aquatic performers, swimmers and those on the fringe, rather than the aristocracy, marked as early adopters. Consequently, it is a garment that conforms to dress scholar Joanne Eicher's description of the types of clothing worn by 'ordinary people' and an example of 'world fashion' that includes generic forms, such as jeans, in recognition of fashions that have not emanated from a central hub such as Paris (1995: 300). These garments represent a template for new world fashion initially fabricated for functional purposes (jeans, workwear; swimsuits, sport and leisurewear) that have come to symbolize freedom, individuality and rebellion. There is a belief that jeans are egalitarian, expressing honesty, neutrality and authenticity (Maynard 2004: 47–8)—all sentiments that are a fit with the swimsuit. Equally relevant, all jeans and swimsuits are not the same, and the nature of global attire—the types and complexities of a 'supposed universality of dress'—is challenged by marked differences in 'fabric quality, stitching and, to an extent, pattern' (ibid. 41), and more importantly, where it is worn and by whom.

The swimsuit and its position as a key global garment in today's fashion industry has been shaped by the important role of designers, multinational clothing corporations, syndicated fashion magazines, film, television and the Internet. This process of globalization can be seen as an integration and interconnectedness that 'transcends national and political boundaries, limits and viewpoints' (Kunz and Garner 2006: 5). However, there is an increasing focus on creating marketable and desirable national images and identities to compete in a global marketplace. Anholt (2007: 20) reports, 'Places with unusual or distinctive traditional or invented cultural products [to] "punch above their weight" in world affairs, and use their culture to communicate more of the real richness of their society to ever more distant audiences.' The concept of nation or place branding and how fashion can be linked to this identity is also covered in this book, which will use Australia as a case study to illustrate how fashion designers and brands have become synonymous with the country's identity. Over the last century, a number of Australian companies have achieved a global reputation as leaders in swimwear and surfwear design consolidating Australia's reputation as a nation of swimmers, surfers and beautiful women.

One garment sums up the fusion of fashion with modern popular culture: the swimsuit. This book provides an historical, sociological and cultural context in which to view how the swimsuit and the country, Australia, that significantly influenced its modern form migrated from the cultural and colonial periphery to the centre of international attention. I argue that the swimsuit and the spaces it occupies mark out a modern landscape where fashion, beauty, sport and leisure industries have worked together to capture a substantial market share worldwide. The book illustrates how the swimsuit is a democratic garment clothed in an authenticity and notions of egalitarianism that energize the fashion system, signposting the way forward in the twenty-first century. As such, the swimsuit is a global icon that does not fit into the traditional fashion-identity paradigm, where individuals build a variety of social surfaces with which to meet the world. Rather it symbolizes the decline of elitism that gave impetus to the growth of casual sportswear and a new world order stitched to a body-conscious aesthetic.

This story traces the rise of celebrity culture through a few extraordinary individuals—predominantly women—who transcended national boundaries to become globally renowned, thus creating a real-world understanding of this phenomenon. Their ability to create economic wealth as celebrity entrepreneurs across a number of industries (fashion, sport, entertainment, fitness) is underpinned by their talent and opportunism, and a drive to be makers and markers. Moreover, reconnecting the global impact of historical (Kellerman) and contemporary (Macpherson) individuals with branding Australia has entailed an investigation of how sport is itself a form of entertainment; the swimsuit has formed associations with both beauty and the fashion body and the high-performance sporting body.

Tracing the swimsuit's evolution through an Australian lens shows how a nation has captured a share of the global fashion market through place branding strategies. With a fresh approach, Australian designers, sportsmen and women, fashion and swimsuit models, and entertainers have made their presence known, capitalizing on the country's strength as a nation that fuses cultural traditions with sport and beach culture. *The Swimsuit* contributes significantly to our understanding of fashion in a new millennium, and demonstrates the fluidity of fashion as a result of geographic and cultural influences, and the convergence and cross-pollination between individual and global currents.

2

Testing the Waters: Morality and Undressing the Body

The swimsuit was and is closely aligned to underwear in terms of styling, and with the move from the boudoir to public spaces, it challenged moral codes and played off notions of the 'natural' uninhibited body against codes of civility and acceptable social conduct. In addition, the swimsuit 'articulated conflicts in moral and gender codes associated with sexuality' (Craik 1994: 131). It is a modern garment for a modern world stitched to bodily spectacle in spaces associated with leisure and pleasure, and sport.

From the late 1800s, people in Europe, the United States and Australia spent newly-acquired free time at beaches, baths and pools—democratic zones—and actively resisted the attempts of councils and government bodies to enforce modesty laws and restrictive, impractical swimwear. The introduction of topless swimsuits for men and the bikini for women were championed by beachgoers intent on enjoying a freedom from conservative dress conventions. Moreover, cabaret performers, sportsmen and women, and swimsuit models have contributed to naturalizing and popularizing this minimalist form of clothing, glamorizing a new physicality suited to display in a slimline, revealing swimsuit.

The transition from clothed to unclothed spans issues associated with the legal acceptance of minimalist swimsuits in public spaces and the increasing sexualization and eroticization of female and male bodies by mass media, particularly in men's and popular culture magazines from the 1960s and 1970s. In the 2000s, images of individuals and social groups that transgress perceived boundaries of propriety can be captured by professionals and amateurs with increasingly sophisticated technological devices and instantly transmitted around the globe via the Internet in the form of news online, blogs and social networking sites such as Facebook and Twitter, then filtered back through print media and television. For Australia, there is another layer of meaning stitched to an identity as a nation of swimmers that starts to unfold in this chapter and is investigated in depth in 'Going for Gold' (Chapter 5) and 'Branded Nation' (Chapter 7). Moreover, Australia's contribution to the swimsuit's popularization through the entertainment industries is discussed in 'Show and Tell' (Chapter 3) and beauty and physical fitness in 'Body Business' (Chapter 4).

REVELATIONS

There is evidence that beach culture existed in the ancient world, with the Greeks and Romans wearing simplified togas and embracing 'the pleasure of the sea' (Lenček and

Bosker 1998: 31). Costume and swimwear historians contend that the two-piece garments worn by young women for gymnastics depicted in Sicilian murals, circa AD 300–400, are precursors to the modern bikini.[1] There are similarities between the styling of these early clothing items and the contemporary bikini that show an early relationship between athletic activities and garments that expose the body. However, the murals belong to a period when 'fashion as we understand it hardly existed' in that 'the shape of garments remained unchanging' (Wilson 2003: 16). Fashion is connected to rapidly changing styles and is a characteristic of modern Western society and linked to early capitalism in the European city-states of the late Middle Ages—an urban rather than a beach creation. The swimsuit, where it would be worn, and its inclusion as fashionable, was still centuries away. Moreover, the demise of the Western Roman Empire in AD 476 and a new Christian ethos discouraged immodest body exposure or a narcissistic interest in the body and athleticism.

Prior to the mid-1800s in Europe, bathing and swimming was associated with health and medicinal treatments and the belief that fresh water had 'healing qualities' (Kidwell 1969: 5). Men and women swam separately and usually chose to swim naked (Craik 1994: 138). Although 'the common people had been congregating on the beach for centuries, along the Baltic, the North Sea, the English Channel, and the Atlantic' for recreational purposes (Lenček and Bosker 1998: 93), as did bathers in the Mediterranean, the beach was not colonized until the nineteenth century. Seaside holiday resorts connected to urban centres by rail and sea marked the prime coastal locations in Europe from Deauville to Étretat, and Scarborough to Brighton in England; in America, prime locations included Bar Harbor, Nantucket and Atlantic City. The beach experience was initially mapped out by the 'the social elites . . . the aristocracy of intellect and talent—artists, writers, philosophers, and their hangers on'—'though royalty and aristocracy legitimized bathing resorts' (ibid. 105, 137), and catered to all classes, often at different locations. In Australia, settlements clustered close to spectacular coastlines, and inhabitants were drawn to the idyllic beaches to frolic in the waves and escape the scorching heat.

With the advent of swimming as a popular pastime and the introduction of mixed bathing, there was social pressure to adopt clothing for the sake of modesty. The standard costume for men was a heavy one-piece design that covered the arms and torso, and thighs (see Figure 2.1), while the typical women's costume consisted of a yoked dress that was pleated, long-sleeved, and belted. Drawers that extended to the ankle were attached to the dress to ensure that the body was not exposed. These garments were generally made in wool or cotton and were cumbersome—restricting movement in the water (Kidwell 1969).

By the 1870s, the bathing suit for men was sleeveless and had come to resemble underwear in styling. Women's bathing suits had, by comparison, become more elaborate. They included corsets, stockings and shoes, and could weigh up to thirty pounds when wet. These bathing designs, which originated in England and Europe, were adopted in the United States (ibid. 6). Maxine James Johns's doctoral thesis investigating the history of women's functional swimwear compares the sea-bathing suits of the Americans,

Figure 2.1   Swimsuit 1906. David Jones Limited.

English and French. Johns reports that in the United States and France, 'mixed sex groups' bathed together but costumes completely covered the body, whereas in England the bathing suits were lighter and less attractive but bathing was segregated (1997: 36–7). Australian women also procured 'capacious woollen seaside' ready-made costumes of uncertain manufacturing origins (possibly locally produced or imports) during this period and engaged in mixed bathing. These garments were worn with oilskin caps and merino woollen socks (Maynard 1994: 104, 120–1).

Prior to the nineteenth century, the beach and sea were 'untouched by modern civilization' (Lenček and Bosker 1998: 101) and bathed in legends and myths that captured the imagination of Romantic poetics such as Byron and Shelley. It is argued that members of the Romantic movement 'actually invented swimming in the postclassical era'. Their interest in swimming was not underpinned by an interest in exercise, athleticism or practical techniques but as a method of experiencing a new bodily freedom (ibid. 104). Swimming can be traced to prehistoric times with early stroke developments attributed to people from the Pacific Rim and Native Americans. Of note, it was introduced as an organized sport from 36 BC in Japan (Raszeja 1992: 28). However, it not until 1785 that swimming schools appeared in Europe (Paris), and Lenček and Bosker (1998: 176) report, 'The nineteenth century belonged to the British' who 'surrounded by water . . . were ideally situated to promote swimming', and the English contributed to the advancement of swimming as a competitive sport, holding the first swimming carnival in the West in 1837. Australia was also placed to play a role in this nascent sport, introducing swimming events from 1846. The common swimming technique and style practiced at this time was breaststroke; it was Native Americans competing in an 1844 London race who introduced a radically faster stroke—the front crawl. It was not adopted immediately and was dismissed as barbaric and splashy compared to the more genteel action of the breaststroke. However, with an increasing focus on speed, in the 1870s Englishman Arthur Trudgen introduced a novel hybrid version of this Native American stroke that combined a scissor-kick with a front overarm movement. Australian swimmer Richard Cavill adopted and improved on this stroke, combining it with techniques learnt from Sydney-based Solomon Islander Alick Wickham to create the Australian crawl—a precursor to the contemporary freestyle stroke, the fastest of the primary four strokes (freestyle, breaststroke, butterfly, backstroke). England produced a swimming model that would be perfected in the colonies by ambitious Australians intent on making their mark, as they would on the design of functional performance swimwear.

Australians were early adopters of swimming for sport and leisure. A swimming enclosure was constructed in 1828 next to the Domain in Woolloomooloo Bay on Sydney Harbour. By the 1830s, middle-class women embraced recreational swimming and, as James Cumes (1979: 156) reports, this 'was a period in which aquatic sports were organized and became a significant part of the recreation and public entertainment'. The battle to expose the swimsuited body in public spaces started in 1833 when the New South Wales government passed an Act stating that bathing was prohibited 'near to or within view of any public wharf, quay or bridge, street or road or other public resort within the limits of towns . . . between the hours of six in the morning and eight o'clock in the evening' (Raszeja 1992: 32). An offender incurred a fine of one pound and as a result most citizens observed the Act. Veronica Raszeja, in an honours thesis researching the rise of women's competitive swimming in Sydney, explains that by the mid-1800s, the combination of shorter working hours and increased leisure (more than their British counterparts), together with a burgeoning population of free men and women (as opposed to convicts), led to the development of swimming baths in Sydney. The baths were segregated and provided women with the opportunity to pursue their interest in aquatic sports with relative freedom from conventional constraints. By the 1870s, there are records of competitive women's swimming events that were open to the public.

Due to Australian women's pursuit of swimming as a sport from the early 1800s, there was a split between recreational bathing and swimming as a form of exercise and competitive sport. It was impossible for women to swim in the ornate and billowing bathing suits, so women who swam adopted a men's style of one-piece swimsuit. The term bathing costume refers to swimwear's earliest form when people bathed as opposed to swam. Kidwell (1969: 5) defines bathing as 'the act of immersing all or part of the body in water for cleansing, therapeutic, recreational, or religious purposes', and swimming as 'the self-propulsion of the body through water'. Costume or suit, words used in conjunction with bathing, are terms that originated in England and were imported to America and Australia to describe what people wore at beaches or baths in urban locales (Gwynn 2003).

The swimming costume worn by these women evolved in ways similar to the men's, and Raszeja points out that, unlike the hindering bulky costumes worn by women engaging in land sports such as hockey, tennis, bicycling and athletics, swimmers were able to circumvent social dress codes due to the 'long acceptance of the sport and its required need for a specialized form of dress' (ibid. 42). An added advantage was that unlike land sports, which caused obvious sweating and associated notions of strength and muscularity, spectators would not have been aware of the physical stamina or effort involved in competitive swimming races, and the swimmers 'retained a feminine image of gracefulness and non-exertion' (ibid. 43). In 1902, the first New South Wales State Ladies' Swimming Carnival was held at the St Georges Baths in Redfern 'in the presence of the trousered sex' and swimmers received the support and admiration of the crowd (ibid. 55). This was the year when beach bans on daylight swimming were lifted, although there is evidence that there was 'a relaxation of the rules in the last decade of the 19th century and . . . many sinful folk of Sydney Town were defiantly breaking curfews' (Cockington 2005: 16). William Gocher, editor and publisher of the *Manly and North Sydney News*, is credited with influencing the Sydney councils' decision to rescind the by-law through bathing in daylight hours after publicly announcing his intention to do so, and by 1903 Sydneysiders were legally free to engage in mixed bathing at the many stunning local beaches.

Social and fashion commentators James Cockington and Alexandra Joel refer to the continuing battle fought by Australians to bare their bodies in public and the resistance to conventional social mores and constraints by conservative moralists often referred to as the Mrs Grundys in society (Joel 1984, 1998; Cockington 2005). As early as 1907 there was a series of public protests challenging the laws councils tried to enforce—in particular, that men and women were required to wear a skirt from the hip to the knees to ensure modesty was preserved. Referred to as the 'Bondi Burlesque' (*The Great Aussie Cossie* 2007), men paraded in embroidered ladies' petticoats, ballet skirts and sarongs, openly mocking the establishment and demanding the right to wear functional swimwear. Eventually, this led to local councils rescinding the laws. By 1911, the Australian Surf Suit was the standard costume and was thick enough to be worn without V trunks, known as 'athletes' drawers . . . bikini swimbriefs that were also popular among runners and circus performers' (Craik 1994: 138). In 1912, a Surf Bathing Committee was formed to report to the Legislative Assembly of New South Wales on the status of beach culture and resulted in a recommendation that bathers would be required to cover their bathing costumes with 'an overcoat, mackintosh, or other sufficient wrapper or clothes' when mixing with nonbathers on and off the beach (Crombie and National Gallery of Victoria 2004: 178). The beach population chose to ignore this ruling and continued to enjoy the liberating and sensual pleasure of the beach experience.

DECENT EXPOSURE: UNISEX STYLE

In the early 1900s, all sources refer to the type of costume worn by women in Europe and the United States as adapted forms of daywear with only a 'small number of progressive women' and 'expert swimmers' wearing a functional one-piece style of the competitive athlete (Kidwell 1969: 18; Colmer 1977; Lenček and Bosker 1989). Swimsuit design polarized opinion and over the next twenty years it was possible for women to purchase either functional one-piece or two-piece Canadian swimsuits in sensible knitted wool, cotton and silk, or 'natty little tunics in good black Italian' woven textiles (*The Draper of Australasia* 1914). Early trade and mail-order catalogues gave limited space to the promotion of the swimsuit, and it was not until around 1920 that beach culture gained momentum and people flocked to beaches to paddle and parade at the water's edge. Swimwear manufacturer entries are found from the early 1900s, and by the 1920s there were a number of Australian knitting mills producing fashionable bathing suits in unshrinkable wool and in bold colours.

During this period, Australians had established their right to swim in daylight hours in suitably practical swimwear. Populations were concentrated around beaches and, unlike most European and American beachgoers, who had to travel distances to the seaside, most Australians were only a short tram or train journey away from some of the world's best beaches. Due to temperate weather conditions, beach life prospered with swimmers, surfers, paddlers and promenaders taking to less cumbersome, practical swimwear. As a result, the whole family could be outfitted for a day at the beach. Quentin Bell discusses the 'theatre of fashionable operations' moving into the 'open-air' leading to the development of a 'new kind of clothes' (Bell 1976: 166)—and at the beach, a new order. The Daisy Bather family (Figure 2.2) illustrates how this environment was colonized. The family members wear similarly styled swimsuits, with only the mother's embellished with contrast borders and a modest additional overlay. The young master gazes into the distance, foot firmly planted on his beach spade, flanked by his parents and siblings, waves crashing behind, enjoying 'the democracy of the sea' (Wells 1982: 13).

The Draper of Australasia.   October 31, 1923. 45

DAISY BATHING COSTUMES

'DAISY BATHERS''

Figure 2.2 Daisy Bathing Costumes. *The Draper of Australasia* 31 October 1923. Collection: Powerhouse Museum Research Library, Sydney.

Manufactured from raw material to finished article, under model, up-to-date conditions, the "DAISY" Bathing and Swimming Costumes are guaranteed to be perfectly hygienic.

Sold Exclusively to the Wholesale and Shipping Trade.

In the 1920s, the dress-style bathing costumes for women were phased out and re-placed with androgynous unisex swimsuits that emphasized the desirability of a lean, boyish figure and marked the acceptance of the undressed body in public. By late in the decade and in the early 1930s, sun worshipping reached a boiling point and the trend was to expose more of the body through cut-outs in the back, under the arms and on the sides of swimsuits—detailing that enhanced the benefits of sunbathing (Figure 2.3). The new styling is the subject of Australian poet Kenneth Slessor's 1933 poem *Backless Betty of Bondi*, which describes the enthusiasm for the shrinking swimsuit, its wearers and its spectators.

Oh, make the great Pacific dry,
And drive the council speechless,
Remove the breakers from Bondi
The beach, and leave us beachless,
The fair, the bare, the naked-backed,
The beer, the pier, the jetty—

TAKE ANYTHING AT ALL
IN FACT,
BUT LEAVE
OH LEAVE US BETTY

(Slessor 1983: 32)

Figure 2.3 Low-back swimsuit Sargood Gardiner Ltd, Sydney. *The Draper of Australasia* 22 May 1934. Collection: Powerhouse Museum Research Library, Sydney.

Although there was public acceptance of body-baring swimsuits, it was tempered by the resistance of local governments to men exposing their chests and circumvented by manufacturers in the United States and Australia. Many styles were designed for easy roll-down, with Jantzen creating the Topper model, a zipped two-piece which allowed for the top section to be removed (Lenček and Bosker 1989: 70–71), as did the Melbourne-based Botany Knitting Mills Black Lance label with the Buccaneer style (Figure 2.4). This advertisement was accompanied by the racy slogan, 'As modern as the moment after midnight' (*The Draper of Australasia* 1935), reinforcing the novelty value of this style of swimsuit.

On the French Riviera, men wore ribbed swimming trunks with fishnet beach shirts that 'were a natural where shirtless bathing' was still prohibited (Hochswender 1993:

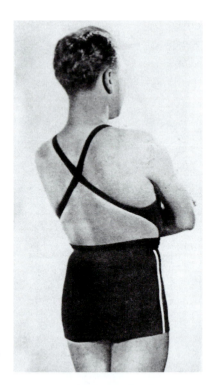

Figure 2.4   Black Lance Buccaneer detachable top swimsuit. *The Draper of Australasia* 31 December 1935. Collection: Powerhouse Museum Research Library, Sydney.

35). Council regulations in Australia had not been altered since the 1907 skirt scuffle, and in 1936, Eric Spooner, a local government minister in New South Wales, was determined to force men to comply and wear the concealing traditional one-piece swimsuits. There was resistance, public protests and a stalemate, and beach inspectors refused to impose the by-law. By the late 1930s, the battle was over, and men strode confidently surfside to battle the elements bare-chested in dapper high-waisted trunks with contrasting belts. Similarly, in the United States, the bans that demanded 'no gorillas on our beaches' were lifted, and men were 'free to hang their swimsuit tops on a hanger' (Lenček and Bosker 1998: 21). However, for women there were still a few battles to be fought.

PEEPHOLES TO THE FUTURE

During this period, women's swimsuits had so many portholes the two-piece that emerged in the mid-1930s was not unexpected, although the styling was modest, exposing the midriff but leaving the navel concealed. While the introduction of two-piece swimsuits was relatively seamless, 1946 marks the birth of the bikini. Two French designers presented their individual creations in the summer of this year. The least pro-vocative or revealing was Jacques Heim's Atome. Louis Réard, an engineer, introduced his simple design which he called the bikini. It is believed that both designers were inspired by the atomic tests at Bikini Atoll—the explosiveness of atomic testing and its symbol-ism (Alac 2002; Lenček and Bosker 1989; Rymer 1996). The bikini signposted a new era in the swimsuit's evolution: the briefest—and most significant—exposed the navel. The design, essentially two triangles of cloth for each the top and the bottom, provided minimum concealment and was sold in miniature boxes, 'emphasizing not only how small the costume was but how scandalous it might seem' (Alac 2002: 39). Lenček and Bos-ker (1989:92) report that 'Americans were horrified by the spectacle of so much bared flesh, rejecting this skimpy costume as naughty, French and un-American'. The bikini was adopted by only a daring few. Réard launched it at one of the first bathing contests held post-World War II, where 'shapely misses from the Folies Bergères compete for the crown' (Rymer 1996).

Conventional fashion models refused to wear such a revealing costume, so the bikini was modelled by dancer Micheline Bernardini. Similarly, the year before in Australia, a Tivoli nightclub showgirl, Patricia Nyland, wore a bikini on George Street in Sydney and was snapped by a photographer for the *Daily Telegraph* newspaper. It was a publicity stunt to promote an upcoming event at the Roosevelt Cabaret and proved a successful method of capturing press coverage. There is no mention of who designed this bikini—however, it does illustrate that Australians were experimenting with daring swimsuit styles. In both instances, it was cabaret performers who were the first to wear the bikini in public, just as it was circus and vaudeville performers who first wore the one-piece swimsuit in the late 1800s. This supports the idea that the swimsuit filtered into the fashion system through less conventional channels.

The bikini was not immediately adopted by any nation, and the one-piece continued as the dominant swimsuit design for women. Swimsuit historians consistently jump to the 1960s as the decade in which the bikini gained social acceptance, a result of the youth revolution that equated nudity with liberalism (Alac 2002; Batterberry and Bat-terberry 1977; Lenček and Bosker 1989; Glynn 1978; Rymer 1996). Lenček and Bos-ker (1989: 92) report that Americans were conservative, thus slow to adopt the bikini, preferring the safety of less-revealing one-piece swimsuit designs. The French bathing suit modelled at the Sydney department store Mark Foy Limited in 1946 is described as 'daring and NOT likely to be worn on the Victorian beaches this summer', however, the author wryly comments that 'each succeeding reduction in size is being greeted by loud protests, only to be accepted in the end'. Adding the prediction that 'the sweet young things will get their own way' whether or not the new style may be desirable, older generations find it objectionable, or wearers have the body that 'lends itself to the pocket-handkerchief dimensions of the modern swimsuit'. Concluding with the comment that 'Australians have never taken kindly to censorship of films, morals, or of anything else, and resent any attempted dictation as to what they shall wear or how they should conduct themselves' (*The Draper of Australasia* 1946). That a conservative department store such as Mark Foy chose to display the new style of swimsuit on a fashion model (see Figure 2.5) (although it does cover her navel and is modestly accessorized with a cape) demonstrates the willingness of Australians to flout convention and adherence to an American preference for the one-piece swimsuit at this time.

A number of Australian beaches, particularly Queensland's Surfers Paradise, eagerly embraced the bikini, although not without determined sections of the community actively campaigning against acceptance of the brief design. Nyland's 1945 public appearance in a bikini resulted in a court case, an eight-shilling fine, and difficulty obtaining work beyond a lingerie model or magician's assistant (Ward and Cockington 2004: 4). Queensland designer Paula Stafford was designing and selling bikinis from as early as 1946, and she recognized the value of using the controversy surrounding tussles between beach inspectors and bikini wearers when model Anne Ferguson was ordered to cover up at Main Beach by inspector Johnny Moffat, while wearing a Stafford creation. Stafford promptly produced more stock and invited authorities to view five of her designs on girls on location at the beach (Cockington 2005: 87–89). As a result of beautiful models wearing Stafford's swimsuits on Gold Coast beaches and the accompanying

Figure 2.5 French Bathing Suit, Mark Foy Ltd Sydney. *The Draper of Australasia* 10 September 1946. Collection: Powerhouse Museum Research Library, Sydney.

sensationalistic newspaper reportage ensured success for the bikini with local and national swimsuit wearers.

One style of swimsuit, introduced in 1964 by Austro-American anti-establishment designer Rudi Gernreich, stretched conventional boundaries of how much flesh could be exposed in public: the topless Monokini design. Gernreich believed that once fashion came from the streets, clothes were no longer just clothes, but a form of communication that could challenge gender stereotypes and advance sexual equality. The Monokini received 'extraordinary press coverage' (Martin and Koda 1990: 113), and was perceived as one of the last frontiers in the battle to bare all. Although Gernreich believed he was freeing women from the bonds of fashion, the response to the Monokini was more witty entertainment than women's liberation—a freakish joke at women's expense. Unlike the Monokini, the Scandal Suit introduced by Cole of California in the same year, daringly used see-through net to reveal tantalizing glimpses of the body while technically covering it. The styling was copied by other American West Coast swimsuit manufacturers and 'high-fashion designers . . . dedicated to the notion of bringing high style to the water front' (Lenček and Bosker 1989: 127), and while less scandalous, it was infinitely more wearable than the Monokini or an 'itsy-bitsy' bikini.

SPREADING THE IMAGE: LET ME HEAR YOUR BODY TALK

By the 1970s, both the one-piece and the bikini were popular. The bikini reached a new level of minimalism when the Tanga appeared on the beaches of Rio de Janeiro around 1974. In the same year, Gernreich created a similar design naming it the Thong. The introduction of such extreme body-baring designs caused anxiety for many wearers and triggered a revival of less-challenging one-piece swimsuits. An iconic image of Christie Brinkley in 1975 in a Tanga crouching in foaming surf leaves little to the imagination, and appropriately appeared in 'a paper that portrayed the world as a man's dream, *Sports Illustrated*' (Alac 2002: 152). Launched in 1964, the swimsuit issue of *Sports Illustrated* was devoted to providing readers with images of celebrity fashion models and movie stars posing suggestively in daring swimsuits, usually in exotic locations. The models appear robustly healthy, veering toward the Amazonian rather than waif-like fashion ideal epitomized by Twiggy (1960s) and Kate Moss (1990s). Whereas revealing the legs (1920s), back (1930s) and navel (1960s) had been revolutionary as well as an evolutionary process, the focus in the 1970s shifted to the thighs and buttocks.

Brinkley's suggestive pose and almost nonexistent bikini bottom drew little adverse commentary, in part due to its inclusion in a men's magazine, and because the pose blatantly positions Brinkley as an object of male desire. By contrast, fashion photographer Deborah Turbeville's swimwear shoot (Bath House Series) for US *Vogue* in the same year incited many readers to anger, with some US states banning the sale of the issue. Although the models are modestly attired in sporty maillots rather than Tangas, it was suggested that the five models portrayed a lesbian scene with the model in the foreground purportedly masturbating (Angeletti and Oliva 2006: 237). Thus, a tableau vivant constructed with questionable or ambiguous sexuality, combined with the notion that these women do not appear posed for the male gaze, challenged traditional concepts of eroticism. In addition, the swimsuit, unlike other items of clothing, does not have the ability to elaborately reveal or conceal the body—'the under-clothed body is a moving target' (Craik 1994: 152).

Men were not exempt from the male or female gaze. At the 1972 Munich Olympic Games, swimmer Mark Spitz's lean, muscular body was a perfect backdrop for his Speedos—the briefest swimsuit style for men to date. The company had reduced the size of the swimming trunks by the 1970s to minimize water drag and in the process made 'Speedo the fastest . . . and also the sexiest' (Killoren Bensimon 2006: 228). A 1973 *Rolling Stone* magazine cover featured Spitz in a glam swim cap reminiscent of a Busby Berkeley aquacade showgirl, and dubbed him 'America's Latest Pin-Up', and 'a pelvic heartthrob'. The objectification of Spitz's body extended to milk advertisements splashed across billboards. Wearing 'a pair of brief competition briefs,' Spitz appealed to 'both women and the gay community' (Cahill 1973: 22). However, as the ultimate male swimmer of the decade, he 'represented something more than a vacant Hollywood convention' (Martin and Koda 1990: 131).

Back at the beach, by the late 1970s, body exposure battles were waning, and in Australia, the southern end of Bondi Beach was officially claimed as a top-free zone for women. Spectators were no longer tantalized by thoughts of the concealed body's secrets as the layers had now dissolved to reveal often more than was ideal or desirable.

Let's get physical
I wanna get physical
Let's get into physical
Let me hear your body talk, your body talk,
Let me hear your body talk

(Newton-John 1981)

Australian pop icon Olivia Newton-John's hit song *Physical* from her 1981 album of the same name encapsulates the 1980s cult of fitness with aerobics, jogging, and body building for both men and women. In the video for this platinum music-chart hit, a lithe, fit Newton-John wears a T-shirt over a high-cut leotard, similar in styling to the then-fashionable maillot swimsuit, together with leggings and a sweatband. Initially, the gym is populated with muscled, intently self-absorbed men in Speedo-style micro-trunks, only to be replaced by overweight sweaty males in unflattering boxer shorts, struggling to negotiate the gym equipment. The video cuts back to the original buffed and appealing men, and we see Newton-John, who is ready for a round of tennis. But she faces rejection from these beauties who depart hand in hand leaving her to the unfit, though interested men. The beautiful, gym-toned male body contrasts sharply with 'the no-nonsense "wash and go" masculinity, which dominated the nineteenth and twentieth centuries', to reveal 'the "new man" whose narcissistic preoccupation with his appearance became the stuff of advertisements and men's magazines from the 1980s' (Entwistle 2007: 146), and who, at this point in time, was implicitly gay.

This decade marks the sexualization and eroticization of the male body through advertising campaigns for brands such as Calvin Klein, particularly by photographers Bruce Weber and Herb Ritts. Steele observes that Weber 'created the most famous erotic photographs of men ever used in mainstream advertising' with his portrayal, in 1982, of sexy men wearing only Calvin Klein underwear. Previously, men were less objectified than women, due in part to 'a lingering Puritanism or homophobia' [Steele and Fashion Institute of Technology (New York) Museum 1997: 126]. Male bodies and men's undergarments were commodified and packaged for mass consumption, and 'in addition, to overt connotations of erotic underwear and glamorous icons', swimwear and sportswear were influenced by 'sports photography and fitness' (Craik 1994: 149). While American rapper Marky Mark (Mark Wahlberg) was modelling underwear for Calvin Klein, in Australia, with less ambiguous masculinity, Grant Kenny, Ironman and Olympic canoeist, in regulation Speedos, ran, swam, and white-water rafted his way through cereal commercials and penned a publication advising others how to achieve, *Fitness for Gold*. The male swimsuit stitched to sport created an alternative form of (heterosexual) male exhibitionism that was also fused to a self-absorbed interest in physical fitness.

A new breed of fashion models also emerged in this decade who would in time be referred to as 'Glamazons' [Steele and Fashion Institute of Technology (New York) Museum 1997: 135]: women with a steely inner strength, expressed through finely tuned, muscular bodies. Australian supermodel Elle Macpherson exemplified this new athletic body aesthetic, and her signature style was intrinsically connected to the swimsuit and *Sports Illustrated*, a magazine that, although 'frankly exploitative,' favoured a 'genuine sports type, something subtly differentiated from a pornographic ideal, yet equally and aggressively erotic' (Martin and Koda 1990: 131). Macpherson's swimsuits spanned the spectrum from conventional one-pieces and bikinis to daring and playful styles such as an asymmetric design that exposed her right breast, referencing both Gernreich's Monokini and the mythic Amazonian warrior woman depicted in Roman statues. The swimsuit is 'nothing more than an artful framing mechanism for an exquisitely tone and sculpted physique' (Lenček and Bosker 1989: 131), and Macpherson—'The Body'—is a symbol of an era where the body became the site of fashionable construct.

By the 1990s, body exposure debates shifted focus to tanning and resultant skin damage. The Australian government and medical professionals advised citizens to avoid excessive sun exposure, and 'in 1991 the sale of sunscreens in Australia totalled $21 million dollars' (Maynard 2000: 146). In *Nothing to Hide*, an Australian swimsuit documentary, the future prediction was a return to neck-to-knee swimwear—a direct result of campaigns exposing the dangers of the sun and risk of potential skin cancer (Rymer 1996). The rash top or rashie, in addition to all-in-one wetsuit styles, gained popularity, particularly for children, in this decade, and is now part of the regulation school uniform for children participating in swimming and water sports. However, for summer

2009, the Australian government launched a national skin cancer campaign directly targeting 13-to-24-year-olds, as statistics indicate that this group has been choosing to ignore the warnings, continuing to spend long periods in the sun without hats or protective clothing (*Evaluation of Skin Cancer Campaign* 2009). In 2008, in an article in *The Sydney Morning Herald* article titled 'How Flesh Became the New Black,' Munro reports that at St Kilda's beach, young girls 'oiled up and crisping nicely' wear miniscule bikinis (Munro 2008), defying the government directives to cover up for health reasons. Modesty for many is no longer an issue and swimsuit wearers continue to embrace sunbathing, although the orange-tinged fake tan has gained popularity in the 2000s.

PROHIBITION IN THE NOUGHTIES

As the first decade of the twenty-first century draws to a close, it would seem that, generally, citizens have extensive personal choice in what they wear in public spaces. Codes of morality and decency that have clothed dress in terms such as 'proper' and 'improper' and been enforced by religious and government authorities (Ribeiro 2003: 12–18) appear to have diminished control. The swimsuit has been subject to regulations and bans, with designs such as the Monokini being denounced by the Vatican as 'the by-product of the "industrial-erotic adventure" that "negates moral sense"' (Lenček and Bosker 1989: 123). And, in 2012, 'less is more' does not just apply to the swimsuit but to race-wear and eveningwear, in particular. Does this mark the end of aesthetic, social, political or religious constraints on what we wear? Surprisingly, no.

The Burkini (also spelled Burqini), created by Sydney-based Aheda Zanetti in 2003, is a head-to-toe Islamic swimsuit design for women, and in August 2009, it was banned from a French public pool as, 'ostensibly' it 'constituted a "hygiene problem"' (Totaro 2009). Although officials stated they were 'simply abiding by rules . . . because larger items of clothing are believed to carry higher levels of bacteria' (ibid.), the ensuing public debates and temporary bans in other countries suggest that certain garments, even when the body is concealed, still have power to spark controversy. Zanetti commented, 'I believe that they just don't want Muslims to integrate' (Robinson 2009). The ban is not the first in France; President Nicolas Sarkozy and lawmakers recommended a partial ban on the burqa in public places such as at schools, at hospitals and on public transportation. In 2010, Muslim girls were not permitted to wear headscarves in state schools, nor were other students allowed to wear 'conspicuous religious symbols including Sikh turbans, large Christian crucifixes and Jewish skull caps'. Sarkozy is reported as saying that the burqa ban is an issue 'of a woman's freedom and dignity and did not have to do with religion', and the French Parliamentary Commission was assessing whether 'full veils pose a threat to France's constitutionally mandated secularism' (Bittemann 2010). Consequently, on 11 April 2011 France banned women from wearing face veils in all public spaces, and those flouting the law risk fines and citizenship lessons (Chrisafis 2011).

And, one week later in Australia—where the Burkini to date has been received positively and was used in an advertising campaign in 2007 to reshape the lifesaver image and 'show how a once traditional Aussie pursuit has evolved to embrace modern multicultural Australia' (Addington 2007)—celebrity chef and 'domestic goddess' Nigella Lawson caused a frenzied response in newspapers and blogs, which generated over 100,000 items on a Google search for this story, when she wore a Burkini to swim at Bondi Beach. Known for her voluptuous body and figure-hugging cashmere sweaters, Lawson, covered in this head-to-toe unflattering albeit modest outfit, raises another aspect of the ongoing debate. Madeleine Bunting comments, 'At the heart of both stories is an obsession with women's bodies and how they should and shouldn't be displayed—and the fierce patrolling of different social conventions governing them' (2011). While Islamic women in France protest for the right to cover up, there were allegedly public protests in Sydney and Los Angeles condemning Lawson's choice of near total concealment as offensive and retrogressive (Gordon 2011). Arguably, Lawson could have been equally condemned for wearing a bikini, as her curvy middle-aged figure would most likely been scrutinized and critically picked to pieces and deemed flawed and imperfect. From a fashion perspective, Lawson's Burkini endorsement has not led to increased sales for the company that created them (Modestly Active), perhaps for several reasons. Although Lawson is recognized as an arbiter of style and an iconic English rose, the Burkini design lacks aesthetic appeal, and most beachgoers, who benefit from anonymity as noncelebrities, can enjoy a freedom to wear next to nothing without the world watching or caring—if not located in a country imposing the mandatory covering of the body due to religious requirements.

Meanwhile, the male Speedo swim trunk has also been the object of bans in the United Kingdom at a water park in Alton Towers. In this instance, the Speedos were deemed too brief and revealing and the ban was 'to prevent embarrassment among fellow members of the public and to maintain a family-friendly atmosphere at the resort' (Kennedy 2009). Conversely, 60-year-old Long Island, New York, lifeguard Roy Lester lost his job for refusing to wear Speedos 'on the grounds of public decency' and believes 'there should be a law prohibiting anyone over the age of 50 from wearing Speedos' (Gosper and Woolnough 2011). In Australia, where Speedos originated, there is not 100 per cent support for the design either. Over the last decade and into the present, the debate about whether men should wear Speedos or boardshorts continues. A blog discussing the pros and cons, originally posted in 2004, continues to receive heated and diverse responses. In particular, the view that if a man, no matter his age, is fit, he should feel comfortable sporting Speedos (AntBlog701 2004). De Brito reports that Speedos and boardshorts 'happily co-existed' until the 1980s when 'saturation advertising from surfwear companies gradually made it uncool for teens to wear what's essentially an Australian icon'. Further, due to an increasingly fat population, 'boardshorts have become a more "tasteful" option with Speedos viewed as "unseemly"' (de Brito 2008). Whereas less is more for women, even if they are on the weighty side, for men, 'unless you are on the Australian swim team or closely resemble a trim, taut and terrific underwear model, please refrain from wearing the budgie smuggler' (Wilson 2007).

The tasteful/seemly debate was further spurred when Tony Abbott, leader of the Opposition in the Australian House of Representatives, was photographed in Speedos at a surf club carnival, which caused an intense public reaction. Then Prime Minister Kevin Rudd commented, 'If there was a referendum tomorrow between budgie smugglers and boardies, I think I'd be voting for boardies.' He primly added, 'I think there are certain things the Australian people should be protected from and one of those things is national political leaders so attired' (quoted in AAP 2009). And on the political front in France in 2006, presidential candidate Ségolène Royal was exposed to intense scrutiny and debate when snapped in a turquoise bikini on holidays. The online articles and comments about Royal's body and bikini worthiness were generally positive. However, although it was suggested that the shots were staged to increase her popularity with voters, it is believed that the images were damaging to her campaign, positioning her as lightweight (Bremmer 2006). Abbott continues to be lampooned in the press, caricatured in Speedos and swim cap, and for politicians of both sexes, as well as high-profile celebrities a la Nigella Lawson, the swimsuited body is a minefield, exposing them to almost instant ridicule via the Internet.

Whether the body is fully or barely clothed, and even when the wearer is presumably suitably clothed for a space and event, public opinion is influenced by local, national, religious, political and social customs as well as a fashion system that continue to focus the lens on the body beautiful.

3

Show and Tell: Popularizing the Swimsuit

Beyond the undressing of the modern body, and ongoing fashion threaded to changing codes of dress that reveal and conceal the body, the swimsuit has been popularized and filtered into the fashion system through unique individuals and their performances in vaudeville, film and television, and documented in newspapers, fashion, film and women's magazine—and more recently, on the Internet. From the 1930s, Hollywood's contribution to the popularization of poolside glamour swimsuits by screen goddesses such as Dolores del Rio, Betty Grable, Rita Hayworth and Marilyn Monroe has been well documented; however, the mythological mermaids, underwater ballerinas and glamour swimmers of the theatre and sport have also played an important role in the swimsuit narrative—which begins in Australia—and are the focus of this chapter.

Central to the swimsuit's evolution from an adapted version of the existing daywear in the last quarter of the nineteenth century to the unisex one-piece of the 1920s is Annette Kellerman (1886–1975), an Australian long-distance swimmer, diver, vaudeville performer and silent-movie star. Kellerman learned to swim and dive at the renowned Farm Cove Baths (run by the Cavill family), one of the floating baths situated around Sydney Harbour in the 1890s. By the age of 16 (1902), she held the women's record for swimming 100 yards in 1 minute 22 seconds, in addition to the mile championship of New South Wales, which she completed in 33 minutes 49 seconds (Walsh 1983: 548). Kellerman regularly competed—and won—against men and was encouraged to train, proving capable of swimming long distances. Swimming historian Murray Phillips points out that this is one of the few sports where women can compete equally with men (Morice et al. 2002). Kellerman enjoyed performing, and when the family suffered financial difficulties and moved to Melbourne, she was able to support them with the funds she received from swimming record distances for a woman, of between five and ten miles. She extended her repertoire to include performing underwater displays at the Melbourne Aquarium with its fishy inhabitants. Here Kellerman developed her mermaid persona through water ballet sequences that she continued to refine throughout her career.

Sydney's swimming elite, including the Cavill brothers and Snowy Baker—one of Australia's best divers, who would later teach Olympic swimmer and Hollywood's first Tarzan, Johnny Weissmuller, to dive—believed Kellerman had the potential to be the first woman to swim the English Channel (Gibson and Firth 2005: 10). There was to be a commemorative Channel swim to celebrate the original crossing by Englishman Captain Webb in 1873, and with their encouragement and the support of her father, Kellerman travelled to London in 1905 to try her luck. Kellerman swam the Thames from Putney Bridge to Blackwell, a distance of twenty-six miles, as a publicity stunt that led to the *Daily Mirror* sponsoring her to swim the English Channel (Walsh 1983). She made the first of three unsuccessful attempts on 24 August 1905; it would be another twenty-one years before Gertrude Ederle from the United States would succeed at this challenge.

Kellerman was a natural self-promoter and the *Daily Mirror*, dubbing her the 'Australian Mermaid', engaged her to undertake a series of beach swims averaging forty-five miles per week. The *Daily Mirror* (publication commenced in 1903) was in a unique position as the first pictorial newspaper in England to provide photographic images of Kellerman's extraordinary swimming feats. Documenting these events ensured her celebrity status and exposed the public to the uncorseted female form in a one-piece swimsuit. The newspaper continued to exploit her popularity, encouraging Kellerman to set new records for a female swimmer. Swimming twenty-four miles from Dover to Margate, she broke all previous records and was greeted by the largest crowd gathered to support a swimming event to date (Gibson and Firth 2005: 25–30).

As a result, a number of swimming clubs around England engaged Kellerman to perform swimming and diving acts for their members. Gibson and Firth report that diving was new to England and a novelty for audiences, who were captivated by Kellerman's skill as a diver and incredulous at how she 'could fly through the air so gracefully' (ibid. 42). She was a fearless and spectacular diver and showed a purity of form and style in her diving technique. Here was a disciplined body that could transcend earthly boundaries. In an analysis of Leni Riefenstahl's use of divers for the film *Olympia*, Crombie observes that it represented 'the transcendent presence of an elite athlete', describing their bodies 'as supra natural, the modern-day gods and goddesses of a classical Greek lineage who draw their power and harmony from the universal of nature' (Crombie 2004: 81). The Australian Mermaid, documented by a popular newspaper thirty years earlier with perhaps less mythic symbolism than Riefenstahl's Olympians, was in effect, an accessible goddess.[1]

Although Gibson and Firth (2005: 27) report that Kellerman's image graced the front page of the *Daily Mirror* for eight consecutive weeks to become 'the first female athlete to benefit from this kind of publicity', my searches of the *Daily Mirror* archive have not unearthed such photographs. However, there are a small number of images that capture Kellerman swimming or endorsing Cadbury's cocoa (see Figure 3.1), foregrounding early sponsorship deals that prefigure powerful associations between athletes, popular media and commercial products. In addition, the newspaper was clearly documenting Kellerman's aquatic tour and popularizing the lady swimmer as a romantic 'Channel Mermaid', thereby ensuring her ongoing bankable appeal as a public performer.[2] As a result of the publicity, a performance was arranged at the exclusive Bath Club for the Duke and Duchess of Connaught (Queen Victoria's third son). It was deemed unacceptable for Kellerman to appear before royalty in a revealing men's one-piece swimsuit, which was her standard attire for both distance swimming and diving. However, she had no

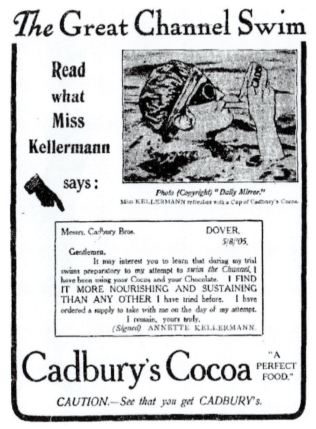

Figure 3.1 Cadbury's Cocoa advertisement. *Daily Mirror* 17 August 1905, page 1. Mirrorpix.

intention of donning the heavy and cumbersome garments of a conventional women's bathing costume so accordingly devised a method of retaining a streamlined design by stitching a pair of stockings to the legs of the swimsuit. The effect was striking, and Kellerman created a trademark style (Figure 3.2) that is consistently identified by costume historians as the inception of the modern swimsuit for women.

In 1905, Kellerman travelled to Europe to compete in an annual swim along the River Seine. She was the only woman competing against seventeen men and placed third in the race. Returning to London, she was hired to perform a twelve-minute aquatic spectacle at the Hippodrome as part of a variety programme that featured a combination of circus and variety acts. The stage was built in the form of a circus ring with the audience seated on three sides and the platform where performances took place could be raised and lowered by hydraulic pistons to reveal a large water tank. The roof would slide open so divers could leap into the tank from approximately sixty feet (Longman 2003). The acts were intended for families and, in particular, women. They offered clean

Figure 3.2 Annette Kellerman, *How to Swim* 1918.

entertainment as opposed to burlesque and music hall traditions that primarily catered to a male audience. Kellerman's act was essentially a series of dives and a demonstration of swimming strokes, with her athletic body packaged in a woolly one-piece swimsuit. This form of bodily spectacle appealed to women and children who would have found her natural unaffected Australianness charming, while the *cooee* girl's charms did not go unnoticed by the men.[3]

VAUDEVILLE AND MASS URBAN ENTERTAINMENT

As Kellerman's star rose, America and the vaudeville circuit beckoned. Vaudeville in the early 1900s was a popular form of mass entertainment that included a variety of acts to cater to audiences with diverse tastes. The acts 'had to be simple, cheap and easy to understand, designed to delight men as they represented the majority of the audience' (Fields 2006: 1). Erdman (2004:51) claims that vaudeville contributed to the development of American popular culture by knitting together audiences to create 'a modern audience of national proportions'. These audiences 'were not passive observers' and could make or break an act, thus influencing the type of performers offered by the booking managers (Kenrick 2003). Kellerman's act was a headliner and a huge success brokered by regular editorial in newspapers and magazines, ensuring she remained in public view. 'According to the *Philadelphia North American*, her main appeal was her bathing suit clad body' (Erdman 2004: 93), and there is no doubt that the bathing suit angle was a huge draw for audiences, representing novelty and spectacle. However, Kellerman had more to offer, and headliners 'had tons of personality and extraordinary stamina' as they often had to perform five shows a day (Kenrick 2003). She was a skilled performer who engaged and enchanted audiences, cooee-ing before dives and entertaining with a varied and challenging routine—she was 'vaudeville's first aquatic glamour girl' (Erdman 2004: 254). There were a number of female vaudevillians who wore skimpy costumes or bathing suits, and although this was part of Kellerman's allure, her act genuinely required this style of clothing, thereby legitimizing the swimsuit as suitable active attire for women beyond the theatre setting in public spaces.

In 1906, Kellerman accepted an offer to appear at the White City Amusement Park in Chicago, a forerunner to contemporary theme parks. Her next engagement was at the Wonderland Amusement Park at Revere Beach in Boston, and it was here that the profile of the swimsuit gained momentum. Kellerman was allegedly arrested at Revere Beach for indecency while preparing to swim along the coastline in her Australian men's swimsuit.[4] Due to media interest surrounding Kellerman's sporting achievements and physical prowess, she came to the attention of a Harvard professor, Dr Dudley Sargent, who was conducting the first research project focused on physical fitness in women. The criterion was someone who radiated health and physical beauty. Sargent measured over 10,000 women, using the measurements of the Venus de Milo as a guideline, and in 1908 he declared that Kellerman most closely resembled this mythical beauty, resulting in her being named the 'Perfect Woman'.

Her act was magical, artistic and ideal entertainment for modern urban mass audiences, and her allure was heightened by costumes that left little to the imagination. Kaplan and Stowell's investigation of the relationship between fashion and the theatre in the late 1800s and early 1900s reveals an alternative source of influence to the Parisian ateliers in the form of West End actresses and their stage wardrobes. Kaplan and Stowell suggest that the stage costume was 'not merely reflecting but anticipating and creating fashion' (1994: 8–9). Dress scholar Christopher Breward supports this idea in his analysis of four London actresses who performed at the Strand's Gaiety Theatre: Kitty Lord, Constance Collier, Marie Tempest and Mary Moore. Through events such as the Ascot Races, promotional posters and picture postcards, these actresses represented a form of accessible glamour that influenced both theatregoers and the more general public (2005: 107–108). Actresses were fashioned and groomed for stardom and celebrity. In addition, Marlis Schweitzer notes that in America 'with a demographic and geographic reach much greater than the individual department store, the legitimate theatre and vaudeville, its popular counterpart, were well-positioned to shape modern American consumer culture, especially tastes in fashion' (2009: 51).

The women most influenced were 'the shopgirls, milliners, dressmakers, typists, stenographers' (Breward 2005: 117), who Nead argues were 'not a simple list of female types', but working women in modern jobs with disposable incomes to spend on leisure activities such as the theatre. Other forms of leisure consumption available were tabloid newspapers and magazines where images of actresses created a 'transitional medium between the stage through which fashion and celebrity were apotheosized' (Nead 2005: 123). Actresses worked hard to invent a public image that cast them in a flattering light, manufacturing a persona which 'was part and parcel of who they were or who they had become' (Tapert 1998: 13). How they dressed was integral to fashioning the notion that they were beautiful and glamorous.

The costumes Kellerman wore for her performances could not be worn to the races or to afternoon tea, but they could be worn for a picnic at the beach or lake, and unlike the West End or Broadway actresses, her public image was centred on her being a wholesome, unaffected beauty—an outdoor girl. While Erdman suggests her skills 'were eclipsed by her appearance' (2004: 93), I contend that Kellerman's skills, her body, and the swimsuit she wore were an integrated package, heralding the cult of physical fitness, healthy leisure pursuits and personal achievement for all—a democratic modernity with which shopgirls, telephonists and milliners could identify. If an Australian woman could reinvent herself as the 'Perfect Woman' and 'Queen of the Mermaids' for an international audience and survive the vaudeville circuit for over twenty years, others could reinvent their lives by focusing on their personal goals and development. Kellerman was an active, earthy celebrity who believed that girls can do anything, and that we can all realize our dreams.

SILENT MOVIES

'~ ~ as quick as ~ ~ by telephone ~ ~ the message is delivered'

(Sullivan 1924)

The moving picture, which would supersede vaudeville, was a dynamic medium that could disseminate the modern ideals Kellerman's body represented—a new sporty physicality. Moreover through her promotion of the one-piece swimsuit, Kellerman led women and the fashion market towards styles that would reflect this modern look. Kellerman was a swimmer who wanted to be an actress and star in fantasy films about mermaids and sirens and shot in exotic locations. According to Gibson and Firth (2005: 116–17), the initial reaction from major Hollywood studios was unpromising. Presumably, the response of Carl Laemmle, head of Universal Studios was, 'What! A woman fish on screen!' James Sullivan, Kellerman's husband and manager, was undaunted and managed to convince Laemmle that Kellerman's notoriety as the woman 'who had given the world the one-piece bathing suit' and lectured to thousands of women in Europe and America about physical beauty was made for movies. Not only were movies ideal vehicles for adding another layer to Kellerman's mermaid persona, the novelty of seeing Kellerman performing aquatic scenes in glittering costumes would ensure capacity houses and public support for this new and spectacular form of film.

Kellerman made her first mermaid movies in 1911, *The Mermaid* and *Siren of the Sea*, which were followed with *Neptune's Daughter* in 1914. While primarily a tale of revenge, the latter shares some ideas with Hans Christian Andersen's *Little Mermaid*, such as the mermaid's magical transformation to human form and falling in love with a human king.[5] Kellerman plays Neptune's daughter Annette, whose younger sister has been captured in a fisherman's net and died. Seeking the help of a sea witch, Annette takes human form in order to kill the land king whom she holds responsible for her sister's death. However, she falls in love with the king while he is disguised as a peasant; on discovering his true identity, she is unable to follow through with her plan and returns to her underwater world. Seeing her pining for her lost love, her father, King Neptune takes pity and, transforming her once again to human form, returns her to the human world and the king.

Kellerman had realized her dream to star in underwater fantasy films, and it opened to rave reviews all over America. Unlike many early silent movies that were shot on studio sets, *Neptune's Daughter* was filmed on location in Bermuda, enchanting audiences who saw 'real mermaids and diving in exotic locations' (Gibson and Firth 2005: 124). A large glass tank was built to shoot the underwater scenes; however, the specifications were modified and the glass was not the required thickness. It was not until a scene with Kellerman and Herbert Brenon (director and actor) was being filmed that the mistake was discovered. The glass cracked creating a hole that sucked both actors and fish out onto the set. Both actors survived, although they required hospitalization, and Kellerman's foot was badly injured and scarred. Hollywood at this time was a dangerous place where actors performed risky stunts that quite often resulted in injury. Kellerman was unfazed by the accident, fearlessly diving from heights never before attempted by a woman, and undertaking stunts which included jumping into alligator-infested pools and tightrope walking in windy conditions, seventy feet above shallow water with sharp rocks just below the surface.

Challenging the boundaries between self and the world by exposing her natural form, Kellerman peeled back the clothing to reveal a natural, unadorned physical beauty, adding a mystical layer to her public persona. Audiences had not seen underwater film sequences before and the novelty of viewing a scantily-clad mermaid was integral to making Kellerman a star. Her performances were centred on her body and tailored to her water skills. Fairy tale stories romanticized and filtered her unclothed body through a fictional layer, neutralizing any suggestion of indecency. *Daughter of the Gods* (1916) was her next movie and the first film to cost over a million dollars to produce. It was considered a masterpiece at the time due to the creative and artistic cinematography and the daring exotic costumes. The publicity surrounding its release included cardboard cut-outs of Kellerman in the theatre foyers with details of her physical measurements. All female patrons were supplied with a paper tape measure and encouraged to 'compare their vital statistics with those of the Perfect Woman'. In a number of film stills,

Kellerman is featured apparently in a body stocking, essentially appearing unclothed, which lead one reviewer to comment, 'Clothes may make the man but they don't make a daughter of the gods, at least not the sort Annette depicts' (ibid. 146–8). Kellerman maintained a focus on her body and the movie-going public was happy to gaze.

Queen of the Sea (1918) followed themes similar to those of Kellerman's earlier films, with an exotic mermaid seeking romance with a handsome prince or king while avenging some injustice. At some stage, in reverse of the Little Mermaid's metamorphosis, the character is transformed from human to mermaid and Kellerman performs a graceful and creative aquatic ballet. The film still from *Queen of the Sea* (Figure 3.3) highlights the fairy tale aspect and drama of these fantasy movies. Kellerman, encased in her mermaid costume with fishy tale, held high in the air by a muscular, primitive man (a curious mix of caveman and Nordic Viking) represents a transitional figure transgressing the boundaries between human and nonhuman.

The voice, an integral part of feminine charms in both the underwater merfolk world and the human world, was relinquished by the Little Mermaid as part of her bargain with the sea witch, and beyond the technical parameters of moviemaking for Kellerman's films, forcing both the Little Mermaid and Kellerman to rely on their bodies to express their thoughts and desires. The Little Mermaid did not succeed in her attempt to achieve immortality, or win the prince; however, she had life experiences that allowed her to challenge the traditional values of her underwater world and the metropolis, transcending to

Figure 3.3   Film still—*Queen of the Sea* 1918. Hilton Cordell Productions.

meet new and unknown territory with the daughters of the air—spirits seeking immortal souls through 300 years of good deeds. Similarly, Kellerman used mermaidenry to promote the modern woman as athletic and glamorous, albeit in this image she is constrained and immobilized on land by her costume.

Like many movies of this period that were created on fragile nitrate film, nearly all of Kellerman's movies have been lost, with the exception of *Venus of the South Seas*, which was produced and directed by her husband, James Sullivan, in 1924. Kellerman plays Shona Royale, the daughter of a South Seas pearl trader, and demonstrates her strength and fearlessness when she discovers and apprehends one of the pearl divers stealing pearls in a dramatic underwater scene captured in the film still seen in Figure 3.4. Additionally, the mermaid fantasy scenes are romantic, glittering and magical, in part due to Kellerman's ability to hold her breath under water for long periods seemingly effortlessly. Kellerman (Figure 3.5) was in the vanguard, a feminist who had the ability to make independent choices and challenge traditional women's roles through taking on the masculine role of the saviour in her films. She was no simpering heroine awaiting rescue by a strong, dominant male; she was determined to be both hero and heroine.

These films made Kellerman a star and, according to Richard Dyer, author of *Stars*, an integral part of constructing stars is the concept of audiences accepting them as 'truly being what they appear to be', legitimizing and authenticating this quality through the belief that their performances reflect the real person in a spontaneous and believable

Figure 3.4   Film still: underwater fight scene—*Venus of the South Seas*. Grapevine Video.

Figure 3.5 Film still: mermaid sequence—*Venus of the South Seas*. Grapevine Video.

way (Dyer 1991: 132–39). It is hard to imagine the silent movies made in the early years before the Hollywood star system of the 1930s and '40s producing this response. The primitive techniques and the stylized gestures actors employed to compensate for the lack of dialogue, combined with the overriding novelty of watching moving images, did not project authenticity. Nonetheless, Kellerman playing herself energized the screen with her natural vitality and charisma. Without the benefit of stunt doubles or sophisticated special effects, she performed dramatic dives, underwater fight sequences and magical mermaid scenes, fabricating characters that expressed who she was—the Australian Mermaid and Diving Venus, a woman with a unique star quality.

Lipovetsky proposes that stars reveal characteristics and communicate an on-screen personality that audiences come to associate with the actors, 'the little-changing individuality that the public encounters over and over in all his or her films' (Lipovetsky 1994: 182). Kellerman's movies are thematic, centring on fairy tales and mermaids who wear little clothing—acceptable in their exotic underwater habitats, if not the real world. Her characters are often named Annette, underpinning her box-office popularity and close association with a unique form of mermaidenry. By the time she made her last movie, in 1924, most women were wearing pared-down one-piece swimsuits similar to those worn by Kellerman since the early 1900s. Women such as Kellerman, and the media attention they attracted, influenced social acceptance of the exposed female body in swimsuits. Innumerable articles and photographs were published to satiate the appetites of fans who, according to Gibson and Firth (2005: 153), were eager to know as much as possible about Kellerman—'what she thought and what she ate'. And her fame was not confined to America and Europe, reaching remote locations such as Takata, New Zealand. Composer Juliet Palmer, whose grandmother accompanied silent movies on the piano in the local theatre, told of her memories of 'the underwater world of Australian silent film star, Annette Kellerman' (*Flotsam & Jetsam* 2002). Kellerman became an international identity who communicated ideals associated with an athletic physical beauty and the one-piece swimsuit through the magic of the moving picture.

HOLLYWOOD ACTIVE GLAMOUR

The popularity of water pageants gained momentum in the 1920s and 1930s, particularly in America, with the birth of synchronized swimming, initially termed water ballet, which entailed formation or rhythmic swimming. Then followed Aquacades, professional shows initially created by impresario Billy Rose, with the first in Cleveland, Ohio, in 1937; it then travelled to New York and San Francisco in 1939. It was 'a true spectacle—a Broadway musical in swimsuits'—a floating amphitheatre that 'featured water ballet, divers, hundreds of swimmers and two Olympic champions, Johnny Weissmuller and Eleanor Holm' (Kerper Jr. 2002: 16–17, 24–28). In Hollywood, dance director Busby Berkeley created memorable productions featuring regiments of chorus girls in synchronized geometric arrangements both in and out of the water. The film *Footlight Parade* (Bacon et al. 1933) included an exotic water sequence and musical number titled 'By a Waterfall' that featured kaleidoscopic pattern formations and complex diving sequences, including lines of girls mimicking a zipper opening and closing. The costumes were spectacular and Berkeley developed new camera techniques such as personal close-ups of individual chorus performers.

Water spectaculars peaked in the 1940s and 1950s with 'America's Mermaid', Esther Williams. Williams was an elite swimmer and Olympic hopeful in the 1930s (the 1940 Tokyo Games were cancelled due to World War II), who became the 'swimsuit's pin-up girl'. After starring in Rose's San Francisco Aquacade opposite Johnny Weissmuller in 1940, Williams made her mark in Hollywood as a glamour girl—'the undisputed princess of the pool' for whom 'an entire sub-genre', the aquatic musical, was invented (Morton 2003: 88). Her career as a movie star took off in 1944 when she starred in *Bathing Beauty* opposite comedian Red Skelton; eight years later, inspired by a script entitled *The One-Piece Bathing Suit*, about the life of Annette Kellerman, Williams played the lead in the film adaptation, *Million Dollar Mermaid* in 1952 (LeRoy et al. 1989). Extravagant Berkeley water ballet sequences were a highlight and Williams, like Kellerman, is dazzling and adept at gliding gracefully and skilfully under water. Shot in Technicolor with glittering costumes created by Helen Rose, the movie is remembered for the splashy, colourful water scenes rather than Kellerman's life story, with kitsch references to her Australian origins such as a boxing kangaroo. However, Berkeley's vision of Kellerman's Big Show at the Hippodrome cemented her role as the inventor of water ballet – an enduring form of popular entertainment.

Williams's movies did not directly reference mermaids or fairy tales, although images such as that in Figure 3.6 reinforce associations with exotic underwater worlds and creatures such as seahorses. Her films were more about girls who swam their way through aquatic spectacles on their way to romance and success (Buzzell and Cummings 1989; Walters et al. 1992). MGM's 'million dollar mermaid' character was a sparkling beauty from the pages of a modern fairy tale of Hollywood glamour, and equally sparkling and desirable were the glamour swimsuits she wore. A Diving Venus upgrade, Williams glittered and shimmered in gold Lastex swimsuits encrusted in sequins and gold flakes—a design West Coast manufacturer Cole of California simplified for the mass market, encouraging wearers everywhere to embrace their inner starlet. Images of Williams, who was lauded for having one of the best swimsuit figures at that time,

Figure 3.6   Esther Williams swimsuit shot. Esther Williams.

were also regularly featured on the cover of magazines such as *Photoplay*, ensuring that women had access to a popular model of desirability and feminine beauty.

Fantasy mermaid films did not entirely fade from the screen, with *Mr Peabody and the Mermaid* released in 1948 (Pichel, Johnson and Fowler Jr. 1988). Unlike Williams's movies, which centre on sporty water ballets, this film is about the mid-life crisis of a 50-year-old male, Arthur Peabody, and the innocent and desirable youthfulness of Lenore, the mermaid he catches on a fishing trip while holidaying in the Caribbean. Ann Blyth as Lenore is captivating, and in the eyes of Peabody, represents an ideal woman, one who cannot speak, a characteristic shared by Andersen's little mermaid. Similarly, *Splash* (1984), with Daryl Hannah and Tom Hanks, draws loosely on the Andersen story to produce a light-hearted romantic comedy. The mermaid narrative takes amphibian beauties from pristine worlds of aquatic innocence to the bright lights of the human world in search of their dreams, and entails a personal quest that requires reinvention and assimilation into different worlds. Mermaids are glamorous fantasy characters defined by their affinity with water and an exotic, unclothed beauty. Elizabeth Wilson suggests that, historically, glamour had early magical associations with the occult and wizardry, evolving into a quality connected with charismatic individuals or outsiders whose glamour was expressed through dark emotions including 'desire, fear, loss and an acknowledgment of death'—a glamour achieved through suffering that was cleverly concealed through work and effort (Wilson 2007: 97–101). Kellerman and Williams epitomize this dark glamour skirting an alien watery world and risking all for their dreams. These women and their ability to move gracefully between land and water underline and shape the swimsuit's desirability.

TWENTY-FIRST CENTURY: SMALL SCREEN AND REAL-WORLD MERMAIDS

A century on from Kellerman's global status as 'Queen of the Mermaids', Australia has new mermaid celebrities: eco-activist, professional mermaid and actor Hannah Fraser, and Claire Holt, Phoebe Tonkin and Cariba Heine, stars of the television programme *H2O: Just Add Water* (Shiff, Budds and Walker 2007). The TV mermaids are teenagers navigating the transition from child to adult (a universal narrative), and exploring newly acquired watery superpowers that include the ability to freeze or boil water. There are also the problems they encounter when it takes just a few drops of water for them to metamorphose into mermaids. *H2O* originally screened on Network Ten (Australia), then the Disney Channel, and 'is [now] broadcast in more than 120 countries to an audience of 250 million' (Tucker-Evans and Sourris 2009). A significant aspect of this television series is its geographic location and Australianness. The programme's executive producer, Jonathan Shiff, commented, '*H2O* celebrates the Gold Coast and doesn't pretend it's America.' He continued, 'We painted a positive lifestyle, a warm experience, there's beaches, cafes, fishing: the characters walk through a tropical jungle, so we are overtly Australian' (quoted in Cordaiy 2007). Whereas Kellerman took the Australian mermaid to the rest

Figure 3.7 Hannah Fraser. Hannah Fraser by Michael Gleissner.

of the world, performing in a variety of locations, these actors have brought the mermaid home to sell both the programme and Australia to a global community.

Fraser's career as a professional mermaid spans fashion (swimsuit model); performance (Sydney and Melbourne aquariums); film (*Heart's Atlantis*); television and magazine advertisements; music video clips (*Beautiful*); and environmental activism (Surfers for Cetaceans). Performing for live audiences swimming with sharks and other sea creatures, Fraser adds realism to mermaid mythology and in Figure 3.7 shows her ease in an underwater environment like her predecessors Kellerman and Williams. Moreover, referred to as 'an eco-warrior—an ocean activist', she 'uses her unique link to the ocean to inspire and educate people on the importance of marine life' (The Next Eco-Warriors 2009). As an amphibian beauty with a quest to protect sea creatures, Fraser contributes to the ongoing narrative and identity fused to an idyllic world, similar to the *Little Mermaid's* 'benign paradise, something of a parallel universe, but with more leisure and natural beauty' (Tatar 2002: 303). And, like Kellerman, Fraser is a woman with drive, ambition and individuality who transcends traditional notions of femininity, pursuing a quest to change the world.

These modern mermaids seek immortality through careers in film, television and fashion. What unfolds is a story of Australian amphibian beauties who have become global identities, spirited and adventurous, as opposed to mute and naïve. Unlike the formulaic glamour of Hollywood screen sirens, mermaidenry and the magic of fairy tales draw on a magical, unconventional, active glamour. The swimsuit is also associated with this island paradise and these mermaids. Often dismissed or overlooked as a fashion garment, the swimsuit, popularized by actresses over the last century, has cemented public interest and acceptance of the undressed body. When worn by individuals such as Kellerman and Fraser, and mediated through the entertainment industries, it embodies a dream-like quality embedded in a unique (female) Australianness.

–4–

Body Business: Beauty Made to Measure

> For their part, the mass media no longer present any unified model, any single ideal of
> Beauty . . . Our Explorer of the future will no longer be able to identify the aesthetic ideal dif-
> fused by mass media of the twentieth century and beyond. He will surrender before the orgy
> of tolerance, the total syncretism and the absolute and unstoppable polytheism of Beauty.
> (Eco and McEwan 2005: 428)

There is no one beauty model, or perhaps ever was. One contemporary ideal is the athletic beauty, and when seen through an Australian lens, it reveals the transition from the
'Perfect Woman' in 1908, Annette Kellerman, to 'The Body' in 1989, Elle Macpherson,
to Miss Universe 2004, Jennifer Hawkins. Physical culture has played a significant role
in shaping the ideal body and can be traced back to antiquity. In modern times, Australians have been players in striving to produce women and men who embody a healthy,
sporty beauty ideally matched to the swimsuit, and with an emerging new world order,
there is a niche for a body-conscious aesthetic fused to these values.

MEASURING UP TO THE CLASSICAL IDEAL

The ancient Greeks encouraged an ethos of masculine beauty that valued youthful,
muscled, athletic bodies and recognized that such beauty may be achieved through pro-
longed exercise in the gymnasium. The organic beauty of the body captured in sculptures and paintings adhered to a proportional canon that 'embodies all the rules of
correct proportion among the parts' (ibid. 72–75). The naked male body represented an
idealized form of Greek beauty, and historian Anne Hollander observes, 'Among Greeks,
modesty was an appropriate function of clothes for women but not men.' She continues
that drapery was worn for effect and to heighten the beauty of the male body as opposed to concealing it from view (1993: 6). 'The consummate beauty of physical form
for which the Greek—especially the Athenian athlete—was famed' (Sandow and Mercer
Adam 1894: 2) became a focus for modern physical culturists from the late 1800s.

One of the most influential was Prussian strongman Eugen Sandow (1867–1925), a
physical culture expert who developed physical training methods based on the ancients'
approach to bodily exercise. Sandow was determined to educate the broader public,
espousing the value of aspiring to a heroic physical ideal seen in 'the figures of Apollo
and Michelangelo's David, immortalized in stone and bronze' (Daley 2003: 18). He
was equally athlete and entertainer and 'deliberately turned his body into a marketable

commodity' and 'prepared his body for public consumption' (ibid. 16). Sandow was a consummate self-promoter and entrepreneur, creating a business empire initially built on music hall performances that in turn led to world tours, a physical culture institute, and, from the 1890s, books [*Sandow on Physical Training* (1894) and *Strength and How to Obtain It* (1897)] and a magazine [*Physical Culture* (1898); the name changed to *Sandow's Magazine of Physical Culture* (1899–1907)]. Greek Classicism was a constant reference point for Sandow and 'he began each performance standing still allowing his audience to take in the perfect symmetry of his physique' (ibid. 16), one to which others could aspire to through adherence to his exercise regimes. Travelling to Australasia in 1902 with a vaudeville troupe, Sandow appeared before audiences wearing only leopard trunks, more Hollywood Tarzan than classically Greek, entertaining and astonishing with his toned, muscled body. Physical culture was not only for men, and Sandow also targeted women, believing they could achieve an idealized beauty and female perfection similar to that of the Venus de Milo through a milder form exercise than their male counterparts. He advises, 'In women we do not look for strength, still less for the robust muscles of an Amazon' (Sandow and Mercer Adam 1894).

In the Antipodes, there were no local men at this time, like Sandow, exhibiting their perfectly formed physiques in the public domain. Instead, Australian chorus girl and vaudeville performer Pansy Montague would uphold the virtues and ideals of feminine classical beauty in the *pose plastique* tradition when she performed in Melbourne, Sydney and New Zealand in 1905. The Modern Milo (and later, La Milo), as she was called, impersonated famous characters from Greek mythology such as Venus, Diana, Sappho, Psyche and Hebe, and 'presented her act in a brightly lit garden scene . . . posed on a plinth like a statue in the park'. Montague's performances were considered artistic as opposed to risqué, and as shown in Figure 4.1a, her resemblance to the original sculpture is uncanny—'the armless Venus de Milo achieved by "ingenious stage arrangements" of black velvet' (Callaway 2000: 70). This form of posing belonged to a popular form of entertainment—living statuary, which 'was an international craze' (Daley 2003: 89). Montague's measurements were of particular interest to the public and were regularly publicized and compared to those of the Venus de Milo. Women could analyse and compare their bodily form to 'her beauty and it was implied its dis-integration into a series of measurements and fragmented traits could be reduced to a formula and was therefore attainable' (Erdman 2004: 106). La Milo 'achieved international pin-up status' with Australasians 'able to enjoy this new performer and performance before London theatregoers' (Daley 2003: 89–90). Moving from the periphery to the centre stage in the United Kingdom, Montague was 'a lionized ideal of feminine sexuality' (Erdman 2004: 106), and along with Kellerman, measured up to a classic beauty. Together, they set a precedent for Australian women to be perceived as perfect women—of a particular type—athletic, toned, natural beauties—women who travelled abroad to make their mark on an international stage.

In *Physical Beauty ~ How to Keep It* (1918), Kellerman asks the questions, "what is the ideal form?" and "does anyone have a truly perfect figure?" She contends that the

Figure 4.1a   Pansy Montague—La Milo. Resources Manager (Stock and Services) Plymouth City Council.

Venus de Milo, who was popularly considered the ideal, 'if realized in flesh, would be [a] rather fat and loosely built type of woman'. She continues that all marble records are the product of human makers, and 'like all things human are imperfect', and as such 'only a graven image of one man's ideas of feminine beauty' from 2,000 years ago. Rather than perfection, Kellerman believed in the classical model, suggesting that the Venus de Milo most closely resembled the contemporary feminine ideal 'with a firmly knit and muscular body'. Her own body measurements had been compared to those of Venus and Diana and represented 'a fully developed modern woman' with a body shape the average woman could achieve through a series of daily exercises (Kellerman 1918: 47–49). Kellerman refers to the popular health and fitness publication *Physical Culture Magazine* (1899–1955), and Milo Hastings's method for comparison of the male and female body through the use of a measurement table that mathematically calculates the degree of femininity and difference between the male and female body through the addition and division of various body parts (Table 4.1). Applying the formula comparatively to the measurements of the Venus de Milo and the average measurements of a group of athletic Wellesley College girls, she argues that the contemporary woman was

BEAUTY OF CARRIAGE AND GRACE OF MOVEMENT FIND EXPRESSION IN THE HANDS AND FEET.

Figure 4.1b   Annette Kellerman. *Physical Beauty ~ How to Keep It* 1918.

more feminine than the woman of ancient Greece, in that the waist-to-hip ratio is greater and 'more widely different from that of man'. Figure 4.1b demonstrates Kellerman's assertion that physical exercise and the resultant muscular development does not make women more masculine, and the modern woman embodied 'a form more charmingly feminine than the classic Venuses' (ibid. 51–53).

Kellerman and the Wellesley College girls' BWR (bust-to-waist ratio) and WHR (waist-to-hip ratio) percentages are similar to the Venus de Milo as opposed to the Venus de Medici. The Venus de Medici has a less pronounced BWR and WHR difference, thus a more masculine shape. (For men, the standard is generally a 90 per cent WHR.) Kellerman's assertion that the modern athletic woman reflected the ideal modern body without a loss of femininity was central to her argument, and foregrounds a conflict for women—finding a balanced marker or measure of attractiveness to which to aspire to in their quest for physical beauty. Kellerman aspired to the more athletic form of the Venus de Medici, reflecting a common dissatisfaction women still have with their bodies and desire for improvements. Since the early 1900s, the obsession with body size, proportions and type has not waned, but rather escalated, and Table 4.1 has been extended to illustrate a changing feminine ideal—taller with an increase between BWR and WHR

Table 4.1 From Venus de Milo to Jennifer Hawkins: Body Measurements (inches): Schmidt 2011

The Model	Venus de Milo	Venus de Medici	Pansy Montague	Annette Kellerman	Average Wellesley College Girls	Marilyn Monroe	Twiggy	Elle Macpherson	Kate Moss	Sarah Murdoch (nee O'Hare)	Jennifer Hawkins
Bust	33	33.6	37.5	33.1	31.4	37	32	36	32	34	35
Waist	26	27.3	26	26.2	24.6	23	22	25	24	24	26.5
Hip	38	36.6	42	37.8	35.2	36	32	35	35	34	36
BWR	79%	81%	69%	79%	78%	62%	69%	69%	75%	71%	76%
WHR	68%	75%	62%	69%	70%	64%	69%	71%	69%	71%	74%
Height	5.4	5.3	5.8	5.4	5.7	5.55	5.6	6.0	5.7	5.10	5.10

Measurements for contemporary models, in particular Kate Moss, vary slightly depending on the Web site and an arbitrary decision was made on the final measurements included in the table.

ratios. What unfolds is an average of 73 per cent BHR and 69 per cent HWR, and a feminine form that regardless of body weight and measurements ('weight classes') can be attributed to Marilyn Monroe, Sophia Loren, Twiggy and Kate Moss, and commonly accepted feminine ideals (Gruendl 2007). Pansy Montague and Marilyn Monroe represent extreme womanly curves, particularly the WHR, and interestingly the Wellesley College girls' measurements are similar to those of Kate Moss rather than the ancient or early twentieth-century Venuses. Australians, Macpherson and Hawkins are examples of a contemporary body type that is tall and athletic. For the average woman, all of these iconic celebrity bodies have provided complex guidelines to a desirable body shape, though achieving this in a swimsuit, without corsets or clothes, requires a strict diet, a fitness regime, and increasingly in the twenty-first century, cosmetic surgery.

TRAINING THE BODY

The early 1900s was a transitional period for feminine beauty and bodily ideals. Victorian and Edwardian women had aspired to achieve womanly curves of full proportions, a plumpness that was accomplished through a hearty appetite and then sculpted into shape with body contouring corsets. In a study of feminine beauty at this time, Valerie Steele refers to Baroness Staffe and her 1892 book, *The Lady's Dressing-Room*, which describes an unacceptable female figure as 'an angular form and a want of flesh that displays the skeleton under the skin are considered a disgrace in a woman' (Steele 1985: 221–2). For women with a continuing interest in health and the pursuit of active sports which originated in women's colleges in the late 1800s (see Warner 2006), the issue of body image and modifying those shapely curves into a more muscular and lean frame through diet and exercise was a high priority. Steele observes that the 'ideal modern beauty' was more an image than the reality, as the body cannot change radically to embrace a new aesthetic immediately (Steele 1985: 224). Of note are Montague's and Kellerman's figure types, as they too were transitional, neither Victorian plump nor 1920s boyishly slim. Over 400 years, women had come to rely on their undergarments to mould their bodies to an accepted form and to conceal their imperfections. The more body-revealing fashions that emerged in the twentieth century were less forgiving and required the body itself to provide the necessary structural silhouette.

Women were poised to embrace, for some the pleasure of, and for others the anxieties of, revealing their bodies in a swimsuit, a garment that by the 1920s was a streamlined, modern design that could not be worn with a corset. The modern swimsuit exposes the raw beauty and vulnerability of the body stripped of defined social and cultural markers, and the media played a significant role in normalizing this new natural look. Greek Classicism and mermaids were ideal reference points to tap into women's desires for fairy tale romance, glamour and exoticism of the less-clothed body. Headliners Kellerman and Montague received regular editorial and promotional advertising in magazines and tabloid papers; they also performed publicly on the vaudeville circuit and, for Kellerman, in silent movies. As a result, women had the opportunity to measure themselves against these legendary beauties and buy into a twentieth- and now twenty-first-century phenomenon and aesthetics connected to a preoccupation with the body—how to reshape, define and attain a body worthy of public display.

While Sandow came to the Antipodes promoting physical culture and its health benefits for men and women, Kellerman took her message to women in the United States and Europe. Lecturing to 'hundreds of women' (Gibson and Firth 2005: 87) in all the cities she toured, she extolled the virtues of exercise and a healthy diet. Kellerman rejected the corset in the early 1900s; she was adamant that lacing, padding and squeezing the body into a desired shape was immoral, and a form of 'enslavement and degradation'. A woman should aspire to 'genuine physical beauty' and unlock her potential to enjoy life (Kellerman 1918: 21–24). Kellerman was confident that her body was beautiful in its natural state (although not ideal), and consequently happy to have others gaze upon her in public in revealing and clingy wool swimsuits. Her 1912 self-published book, *The Body Beautiful*, promised women that through a series of simple daily exercises in the home and a sensible diet, every woman could achieve a level of physical beauty and experience the self-assurance that comes with having a healthy body.

In common with other physical culturists at this time, Kellerman was inspired by Grecian sculptures and paintings, in particular Diana Watts's research and images in the publication *Renaissance of the Greek Ideal*. Watts insisted, 'The modern human being has drifted so far away in physical form from the Greek as to fail to realize the differences' (1914: 2). By mimicking the poses of classical statues, Watts surmised that the positions the poser adopted could only be achieved 'with muscles exquisitely trained to elasticity, exceptional activity, and balance' (ibid. 8). Kellerman developed her own set of exercises similar to those that may have been practiced in an ancient gymnasium in an endeavour to achieve a feminine form similar to that of the Venus de Medici. Unlike Watts, Kellerman's exercises were less mythic and more practical, encouraging women to take control of their bodies and their lives in the privacy of their homes, with the aid of household furniture (see Figure 4.2). Kellerman's early publications prefigured twentieth-century magazine formats that, as Craik observes, offered 'advice, information and instruction specifically for women (practical techniques of being female), while on the other hand, they offer images of femininity, fashion, beauty (techniques of desire and femininity)' (1994: 50).

Combining the dual influences of antiquity and modern science, men and women were drawn to bodily development and the idea of disciplined daily practice that required a solid dose of self-involvement and an opportunity to focus on themselves. It was a trend fused to the advance of consumer culture, a new sense of purposeful and individualized body work driven by 'the new media of motion pictures, tabloid press, mass circulation magazines and radio extolling the leisure lifestyle, and publicizing the norms and standards of behavior' (Featherstone 1991: 172). Kellerman's notoriety as an entertainer followed by publications and lectures about the benefits of physical fitness placed her in the vanguard of this twentieth-century movement, and, importantly, she

AN INTERMEDIATE FORM OF THE DIP AND PUSH-UP EXERCISE.

Figure 4.2   Annette Kellerman: *Physical Beauty ~ How to Keep It* 1918.

targeted ordinary women, providing practical solutions and advice that could lead to a healthy, if not glamorous, life.

By the 1960s, the feminine ideal had evolved in a circular fashion from the androgynous *garçonne* look of the 1920s, to the 1940s and 1950s hourglass shape of Marilyn Monroe, to the slim, boyish body exemplified by British fashion model Twiggy. As a result, women's obsession with attaining a waif-like frame and a fear of fat, a phobia that afflicts American women in particular, intensified (Seid 1994: 3). Twiggy at '98 pounds represented the boundary beyond which no ambulatory person could go; however, her image became one that women thereafter aspired to meet'. According to Seid, 'The new emphasis on fitness was just a variation on the theme of slenderness' (ibid. 6–7). Australian women were not immune to the revival of this body ideal or fashion tailored to this body type, although Maynard notes that the 1962 Australian Wool Board parade held at the Melbourne Olympic swimming stadium illustrated a uniquely Australian style that blended fashion, sport and the athletic body. The models, wearing wool fashions, were ferried on small boats through a festive, balloon-laden pool while Olympic swimmer Dawn Fraser 'in a pure wool bathing suit, did a spectacular dive and demonstration swim', reminiscent of Kellerman's performances in the early 1900s (Maynard 2000: 129). The swimsuit and swimmer continued to be a touchstone for Australians, influencing how fashion was viewed and adapted on the margins.

Continuing a focus on athleticism as much as slimness, Australia produced another, mostly forgotten, fitness guru in the 1960s, Sue Becker. A radio and television personality, Becker developed a workout programme that proclaimed, 'Exercise is not only good; it's fun as long as it's boomphy' (Becker 1971: 7). The ABC (Australian Broadcasting Commission) television daytime programme and subsequent book, like Kellerman's early publications, targeted women in the home, and with her practical, no-nonsense persona, Becker had a positive and realistic approach to achieving fitness and long-term health, if not the feminine ideal at this time. In the early 1970s, moving to the United Kingdom, the *Boomph with Becker* show was televised on the BBC, transmitting another Australian physical culturist's philosophy abroad (Figure 4.3).

Figure 4.3 *Boomph with Becker* 1971. Becker Family.

In the 1980s, while Olivia Newton-John got physical, US actress Jane Fonda encouraged women to exercise their way to perfection. Fonda was a leading exponent of aerobics and regular, strenuous workouts to attain and maintain a reed-thin body. Although the twin benefits of exercise are popularly acknowledged as increased health and beauty, when practiced to excess, the result can be emotionally and physically damaging. Fonda has admitted to obsessively over-aerobicizing as well as struggling with bulimia and anorexia for thirty years in an attempt to attain a near-perfect body (Zahn 2005). Women's desire to achieve a fashionable feminine ideal—an ideal that is constantly evolving and changing—is not new. However, by this decade, with high-cut bodysuits, leotards and swimsuits staples of everyday wardrobes, anxiety levels escalated. Feminists argue that exercise, dieting and eating disorders illustrate how women are controlled and oppressed by patriarchal societies, their bodies fetishized and compared to the feminine ideal (see Grimshaw 1999 and Markula 2001 for an overview), and certainly these are issues of concern. Another viewpoint articulated by Fonda acknowledges that a woman's beauty is 'an accomplishment, something one does actively and autonomously' (Grimshaw 1999: 95), and indeed 'women need to obtain the feminine look to successfully manipulate the power source—the men' (Markula 2001: 240). However, Fonda and similar fitness gurus set an arduous benchmark for many women—at the cost of health and well-being.

Pioneers Annette Kellerman and later Sue Becker foreground an Australian approach to fitness regimes and pedagogical dissemination that was passed on to a new generation which included fashion model Elle Macpherson and elite athlete Lisa Curry. An Olympian swimmer, Curry released a series of health-and-fitness books for women that encouraged readers 'to strive not simply for thinness', claiming 'a fit person has an abundance of energy and vitality, glowing good looks and high self-confidence' (1990: 4). In 1994, Macpherson, with a body deemed ideal, released a workout video with trainer Karen Voight sharing her vision of how to attain a healthy, fit body with women around the world. The enduring message from these women is the importance of health as much as a size zero, and empowerment for women through physical activities such as swimming and home workouts.

CONTESTING BEAUTY

From the early 1900s, through associations with the aesthetic purity of Greek Classicism and the mythological goddess of love and beauty, Venus, an emphasis has been placed on the artistic nature of women's physical beauty, minimizing accusations of sexualizing or commodifying women. The idea that women can be measured and then judged as beautiful flourished and led to the rise of the modern beauty contest. Daley's research on the modern body and leisure in New Zealand revealed that there were local beauty contests in Australia and New Zealand held as early as 1906, and they were part of an international trend. Magazines such as Sydney-based *Lone Hand* (1907–21) and local newspapers advertised for contestants and reported the results of competitions and pageants (Daley 2003: 84–99). A one-off Miss Australia contest was sponsored through *Lone Hand* in 1908, with entrants from New South Wales, Victoria and Queensland competing for the title. The winner was Victorian Alice Buckridge. According to Saunders and Ustinoff in a study of Australian beauty and the Miss Australia quest, the contest's primary goal was 'to attract customers: whether they were newspaper readers, patrons at an amusement venue, or visitors to a country fair' (Saunders and Ustinoff 2005: 4). Early competitors' measurements were compared to both the Venus de Milo and women such as Kellerman by a panel of experts, and winners could revel in their new fairy tale status as the most beautiful woman regionally or nationally. Integral to the beauty contest was the swimsuit, a garment that could reveal optimal flesh and justified as essential for judges to assess that contestants measured up to the feminine ideal. The first official Miss Australia Quest competition was held in 1926, and the winner, Beryl Mills, was lauded as a fine example of Australian womanhood. Mills was physically fit, a competitive swimmer and university educated. In short, she possessed beauty and brains. A key focus of any competition was the quest for the perfect woman, and although the Miss Australia Quest stressed the importance of education, no entrant who reached the finals was unattractive. Contestants such as Mills 'represented the kind of modern femininity that Australians could proudly claim and defend . . . not just physical beauty, but also youthful vigour and vitality' (ibid. 11). In addition, the winner was 'both representative of a country's finest form of womanhood, as well as the country itself' (ibid. 9).

Throughout Miss Australia Quest's history, the swimsuit category has been a source of debate, and excluded from some of the pageants in an attempt to focus on other aspects of the entrants' qualities, in particular their ability to fundraise for charities. However, in the early years, the swimsuit 'was used to determine the important aspect of "beauty of figure"' (ibid. 73). The year 2000 saw the demise of this contest and the title of Miss Australia is now associated with the global Miss Universe and Miss World beauty contests. Jennifer Hawkins is often referred to as the all-Australian beach girl and was crowned Miss Universe in 2004, continuing an ongoing celebration of body, beauty and feminine spectacle packaged in a swimsuit. Moreover, in recent years a number of Australian entrants have appeared in a swimsuit for the national costume segment of the pageant; and since 2009, Western Australian swimwear brand Kooey has been a major sponsor of Miss Universe, reinforcing the idea that Australia has taken the crown for its swimwear. In 2010, the Miss Universe Australia entrants included a police officer, a truckie and a waterski champion, demonstrating that the modern beauty contestant is not only outdoorsy, but also capable of taking on professions usually associated with men—without losing their femininity or desirability. Measuring up to a feminine ideal is not confined to beauty contests, and whether beauty contestant, fashion model, actor or, more recently, athlete, the ideal's essential ingredient is captured by Esther Williams's comment, 'The gene pool the best pool of them all' (Morton 2003).

For those individuals who have won the genetic lottery and beauty contests, there is the potential to segue into careers in film, television and fashion—a stepping-stone to fame and fortune. Hawkins illustrates how this has escalated in the 2000s. Since taking off her Miss Universe crown, her career has flourished; she has performed across different media in roles that range from being the international face of Lux, 'following in the famous footsteps of Sarah Jessica Parker, Giselle Bündchen and Linda Evangelista' (*Jennifer Hawkins* 2006), to a television host on *The Great Outdoors* and a host of Channel 7's *Make me a Supermodel*. Hawkins has extended her business interests to include a swimwear label called Cozi, launched for Myer department stores, the company she also represents as an ambassador, having received a seven-figure contract. A press release in the *Daily Telegraph* glibly reinforces the economic potency of merging beauty, a celebrity body and commerce: 'She made her name as the most beautiful woman in the universe—now it seems Jennifer Hawkins is destined to rule the world' (Toy 2008).

Before the rise of the beauty queen businesswoman, a number of highly successful fashion models led the way, making the transition from fashion and swimsuit model to entrepreneur. The 1980s and 1990s saw the rise of the supermodel. Models from around the globe including Christy Turlington (US), Claudia Schiffer (DE), Naomi Campbell (UK) and Linda Evangelista (CA) ruled the runways and regularly graced the covers of international fashion magazines. At the same time, models including Cheryl Tiegs, Christie Brinkley and Australia's Elle Macpherson represented 'a commercial and high-fashion crossover phenomenon' (Koda and Yohannan 2009: 102), who made their mark as a result of the fashion industry's expansion 'into multi-tier conglomerates aimed at infiltrating every level of the marketplace' (ibid. 134).

Vogue Australia told its readers, 'The key to success is a good body, narrow as an arrow, curved where a girl should be curved' (November 1982). With a tall, broad-shouldered athletic frame, Macpherson was a model who exemplified this new body aesthetic. In 1989, *Time* magazine dubbed her 'The Body', a title closely associated with the swimsuit, glamorous athleticism and a healthy Australianness. While other supermodels were muses for iconic fashion brands such as Chanel and Dior, Macpherson profited from her superbody through regular editorial swimsuit modelling for the popular men's magazines *Sports Illustrated* and *Playboy*, for which she confidently posed as a centrefold in 1994. Gawenda reports that while 'strikingly tall, and, while not exactly Rubenesque, she has a bust and a waist which taken together form a healthy, exuberant femininity'. He continues, 'She is not a mysterious beauty', but rather a type to be found on any Australian beach (1989). Macpherson set a precedent for an Australian ideal or aesthetic that contributed to an international reputation for fashion models who are toned and athletic, as opposed to waif-like—a stark contrast to the Kate Moss heroin chic of the early 1990s. Sarah O'Hare and Jodhi Meares joined Macpherson as iconic fashion and swimsuit models in this decade, reinforcing associations with Australia as 'an outdoorsy nation' inhabited by beautiful women with a 'beach-going lifestyle' (Weiss 1999).

Macpherson has made movies (*Alice*, *Sirens*), made television guest appearances (*Saturday Night Live*, *America* and *Australia's Next Top Model*) and been the host of

Britain and Ireland's Next Top Model (2010–current), and has been earmarked to host a new US series called *Fashion Star* that will compete against *Project Runway*, hosted by Heidi Klum, and *The Fashion Show*, hosted by Iman. Her business ventures include the Intimates lingerie line, manufactured by New Zealand company Bendon, which is sold globally and generates £40 million per annum, and a range of beauty products with 'The Body' brand name; she is also on the board of surf-fashion label Hot Tuna. As a result, Macpherson is 'a model who has established a long-standing brand that transcends her fame' (Rose 2007). And, as a result of the continuing exposure of haute couture to broader audiences often facilitated by the inclusion of celebrity models and actresses, Macpherson walked the runway for Louis Vuitton at Paris Fashion Week 2010. Designer Mark Jacobs commented, 'His aim had been to create a collection that appealed to a wider market' (Abraham 2010), and the response to Macpherson's inclusion (which has over 200,000 Google search results) reflects her ongoing popularity and ability to garner public interest and admiration. The predominant focus of reports was the return of womanly curves and a celebration of the sexy as opposed to waif beauty, a circular and fickle conversation.

From Australia, Sarah Murdoch was another successful fashion export in the 1990s, with notable swimsuit editorial for fashion magazines such as *Vogue*, and like Macpherson, she was a regular for *Sports Illustrated*. She was the face of Wonderbra in 1997, and although not a fashion designer, Murdoch was pivotal in the revitalization of the Bonds underwear brand, steering its image as the underwear of choice (cottontails) for old ladies, towards a desirable product for a new generation of teenagers and young women. Murdoch also branched out into film (*Head Over Heels*) and television (*Friends*, Channel 9 *Today* host), before joining Foxtel in 2008 as the executive producer and host of *Australia's Next Top Model*. Murdoch's production company, Room 329, was also contracted to produce a series of documentaries, the *Pride of Australia*, celebrating Australia's unsung heroes ('Sarah Murdoch Joins Foxtel' 2008).

In the 2000s, models-turned-talk-show-hosts are a popular choice for reality TV programmes stitched to fashion, such as the *Next Top Model* franchise and *Project Runway*, with some hosts also branching out as fashion designers creating their own labels (Klum for Jordache). In Australia, model Jodhi Meares's post-television career as a popular host of *Australia's Next Top Model* for cycle three and four transitioned to fashion designer focusing on swimwear, a clever choice in view of her highly-acclaimed reputation as a swimsuit model and Australia's reputation as a leader in swimwear design and manufacture. Meares launched a swimwear label, Tigerlily, in 2000 that was acquired by international surfwear company Billabong in 2007; Meares was retained as creative director, affirming the brand's and Meares's commercial viability. The boundaries continue to blur between makers and markers, producers and wearers, in an increasingly democratized and flexible fashion system.

For all these women, their bodies have been an entrée to forging, extending and mediating entrepreneurial careers that include fashion design, acting, hosting and producing programmes for film and television. Theirs are modern success stories that represent 'new ideals and life-styles based on personal accomplishment, entertainment, and consumption' (Lipovetsky 1994: 189), and also illustrate how empowering beauty can be when used to reinvent oneself—repackaged for popular media and the fashion industry. According to Melissa Campbell, women like Macpherson and Murdoch (she also mentions Kylie Minogue), represent an image of 'international Australian femininity' and 'appear to be in control of the objectifying' and 'signify something about Australia as they entertain the world'. That something? 'Exciting and desirable' (Campbell 2003), qualities that can be traced back to early Australian beauties Kellerman and Montague. Sarah Murdoch's famous 1999 *Sports Illustrated* image, where she is adorned in a sand bikini, articulates the symbiotic relationship between this natural Australian feminine ideal, the swimsuit, and the swimsuit's natural habitat, the beach—iconic imagery that has been successfully sold to a global community.

THE CULT OF THE BODY

Lipovetsky observes that there is

> . . . an increase in commercial activity linked to a growing preoccupation with the body. After the theatricality of clothing, we have the narcissistic cult of the body: it has its fashions, aesthetics, dietetic, and athletic model . . . From this point on, seduction is incarnated less in attention-seeking clothing than in the imperative of youthfulness, beauty, thinness, and vigorous good health . . . In the era of consummate fashion the aesthetics of the body has become a matter of psychology and performance. (1994: 244)

The Australian women discussed who have contributed to the body business are members of a unique group of superindividuals with the ability to create cultural visibility and economic value using their physical beauty, often via products intimately connected to, and used to enhance or preserve, the body. Through careers in the entertainment and creative industries, they fabricate a look that other women can aspire to and monitor through a number of popular magazines, Web sites and blogs dedicated to constantly scrutinizing and dissecting celebrity bodies. For example, Britney Spears was lampooned by the press for exposing her less-than-toned body in a bikini for her MTV comeback concert in 2007.

Comments from viewers revealed that it was not her wearing the bikini that was a problem, it was that 'she isn't fit enough to be wearing (or not wearing) what she is' (Noveck 2007). Spears is by no means fat, and the debate sparked by the film clip centred on body image and the unforgiving nature of swimsuits. Criticism of Spears's or any other celebrity body demonstrates how important the body is in building a successful, ongoing career in the entertainment industries. Discussing 'the beauty of consumption', Umberto Eco explains, 'The mass media is totally democratic' offering contrasting models of beauty from svelte to voluptuous' (Eco 2005: 425); however, there is no room for flaws, whatever the type. Spears fell foul of the system by daring to ignore the strict bodily guidelines, paying the price with innumerable articles and blogs cruelly criticizing her demise from sexy to loser. Spears is no ordinary individual and has indeed bounced back, reinventing herself through body shaping, naturally or medically. (There are rumours of liposuction, breast implants and rhinoplasty, and in March 2011 she admitted she would consider plastic surgery in the future). With her single 'Hold it Against Me' ranking number one on iTunes and the most successful first-week track for a female artist to date (OMG 2011), Spears has been assured that fans approve of the song. Although there are criticisms in the blogosphere of less-than-energetic dance performances, for the moment, she is back on top, and like her new perfume Cosmic Radiance ('Be the Brightest Star in the Universe'), Spears seeks ongoing popularity.

There is no question that body issues, eating disorders and anxiety about ageing and the accompanying loss of beauty are increasing social problems, and in Australia, the government is recommending that 'fashion, media and advertising industries adopt a voluntary code of conduct that would present healthy, realistic and natural images of the human body'. Youth Minister Kate Ellis launched this initiative together with Sarah Murdoch at a press gathering at Parliament House Canberra. Murdoch, standing beside a blow-up image of herself destined for the Australian *Women's Weekly* cover (November 2009) all-natural and unairbrushed, was an additional promotional tool. This event overshadowed the Minister of Families Jenny Macklin's announcement that the nation would be offering a formal apology to 500,000 forgotten orphans and fostered children pre-1970 (*The Age* 2009), highlighting the sheer newsworthiness of celebrities, natural or otherwise. Subsequently, *marie claire* magazine featured Jennifer Hawkins naked and unretouched on the February 2010 cover to support the Butterfly Foundation, a charity for young eating disorder sufferers. Like Murdoch, Hawkins is a beautiful woman, with less to conceal than most, and a number of blogs were critical, commenting that it is hardly a stretch for her to forego airbrushing. In addition, both women host reality television programmes that implicitly encourage young women to reduce their weight to fit a fashion industry standard for thin models. Conversely, Murdoch and Hawkins appear healthy and naturally slim as opposed to gaunt, and are role models for how to extend careers creatively and commercially beyond the catwalk. Moreover, these women generate much-needed funds for charities and embody the concept of beauty with a purpose. And the centuries-old debate of natural versus artificial beauty continues.

Over ninety years ago Kellerman wrote:

'Fat' is a short ugly word. But 'stoutness', 'plumpness', 'fleshiness', 'obesity', 'embonpoint', are only soft-pedal euphemisms. It is fat just the same, just as clumsy, as unhealthy, as ugly and awkward when spelled with ten letter as with three. (1918: 24)

It is an attitude to body weight that has escalated over the ensuing decades. Since Kellerman's time, the modern body has been empowered through self-discipline whether due to strenuous exercise and a healthy diet, or more extreme methods such as British fashion model, actor and swimsuit designer Elizabeth Hurley's adherence to a dinner of 'a slice of toast and marmite and an apple' for a week to flatten her stomach (Barron 2007: 453), or partial redesign via cosmetic surgery. For astute fashion and swimsuit models, and film, television and sports celebrities, the value of a perceived ideal body presents an opportunity for economic success. The body is a focus for celebration of its ability to transform and shape up, although this is challenged by the neuroses and anxieties many suffer in the process. Self-determined and motivated individuals intent on controlling their bodies and their destinies are altering the future where the body is tailored to fit fashions such as the swimsuit. And, in Australia, while conforming to global trends in body ideals, there is a sense that the local model has been fine-tuned and underpinned by an athletic, sporty aesthetic.

Fashion commentator Suzy Menkes described the feminine ideal in 1996 as 'a body . . . moulded by gymnastics to the peak of its power. It has broad shoulders, swelling athletic thighs and buttocks', continuing that 'its development has become a metaphor of self-discipline and self-development'. Menkes reports that it is an approach that harks back to the 'glorification of the body and the cult of the male-only gymnasium in ancient Greece', and for women 'the sporty takeover of the fragile figure' (1996). The reference to Greek Classicism illustrates a cyclic return to a bodily ideal, one admired since the early twentieth century, and just as these ideals span waif to Amazon, the media cyclically endorses either or both. *Vogue* Australia heralded the 'return of the curve' in 1999, and in 2008, *The Australian* reported, 'Stick models go out of fashion', with subsequent debates about the curvy figure highlighted by Tahnee Atkinson's *Australia's Next Top Model* win in 2009 win over 'waif-thin competitor Cassi Van Den Dugen'. Described as having 'an ample bosom and a sexy bottom' (Kelly 2009: 164), although only an Australian size 8 (UK 6, US 4), Atkinson represents one beauty ideal that continues to be attributed to Australian fashion models, including Miranda Kerr; she was referred to as one of 'a cluster of slightly more curvy models' on the runway for Prada in 2010 (Krum 2010). Conversely, Karl Lagerfeld declared that 'the world of fashion was all to do "with dreams and illusions, and no one wants to see round women"' (marie claire UK 2009), adding that the backlash was driven by 'fat mummies sitting with their bags of crisps in front of television, saying thin models are ugly' (Connolly 2009). However, what unfolds is the complexity of shaping up and fitting in with an elusive, fluid feminine ideal. Australian women fashion models and entertainers (past and present) are more typically viewed as curvy or Amazonian, although a number are increasingly edging towards waif-like, as Lagerfeld's fashion view of the ideal body gathers momentum in the 2000s.

News on the fashion frontline in 2011 was that there is a new level of interest in women who do not conform to model proportions. Although referred to as plus-sized, which is hardly flattering or inclusive, it does suggest that the fashion industry is attempting to cater to real women. French *Elle* led the way, featuring Australian Robyn Lawley (AUD Size 14–16) on the cover of the April 'Body' issue, followed by *Vogue* Italia in June with Lawley, Tara Lynn and Candice Huffine. *Vogue* Australia followed suit in the September issue with a ten-page spread of Lawley titled 'Belle Curve'. The reaction has been extraordinary and 'went viral worldwide . . . with hundreds of magazines, blog sites and newspapers' commenting on this shift (Huntington 2011). As the debate continues, and fashion magazines create sections to target this untapped market ('Curvy'—*Vogue Italia*), women around the world are kept abreast of trends via the Internet, and actively engage in discussions that add another layer of cross-fertilization and interactivity to the fashion system. Beauty and its measure—the pursuit of perfection in increasingly different shapes and sizes—slips and slides across the body, and Australian women continue to be at the vanguard with aspirational models or ideals for others to emulate.

Going for Gold: Sport and Fashion

The swimsuit is a modern garment fitting with a new century and 'the democratic-individualistic universe affirming the primordial autonomy of individuals' (Lipovetsky 1994: 62). The raw potential of individuals unfettered by compliance to existing fashions—with a desire for change—can make them makers and markers of fashion trends. According to Kidwell, the trickle-down theory of fashion does not apply to the swimsuit, and that it 'entered the fashion pages by a different route as a result of women who went against popular opinion and swam' (Kidwell 1969: 30). Importantly, swimming is a sport that women have equally contributed to alongside men, wearing the same garment. The Olympics was and is the meeting place for the sporting elite, and the quest for gold in swimming resulted in performance swimwear honed to produce the fastest times. Australia has produced a significant number of Olympic swimmers and was home to the Speedo brand from its inception in the 1920s; this chapter traces this journey, which has increasingly led to a fusion between sport and fashion.

DAUGHTERS OF THE GODS

Kellerman was not Australia's only aquatic export in the early 1900s. Beatrice Kerr, referred to as the 'Forgotten Mermaid', was the Australasian amateur swimming champion of 1905. A consummate swimmer and diver, it is reported that she performed the 'show stopping Monte Cristo Fire Bag Trick', which entailed being fastened in a canvas bag saturated with petroleum, set alight and thrown into the water. Within ten seconds, Kerr would spectacularly surface in a spangled swimsuit (Nelson 1991: 74–76). Kerr followed Kellerman to England in 1906, determined to challenge her to a series of diving and swimming races; Kerr was confident she could outperform her competitor. Kellerman judiciously chose to decline and retired from competitive swimming soon after to focus on the vaudeville circuit and the entertainment industry. Historian Angela Woollacott maintains, 'Both Kerr and Kellerman's careers were built on sensationalism, based on their remarkable physical accomplishments and their daringly revealing costumes' (Woollacott 2001: 192). Together these women established an international reputation for Australian female swimmers, promoting the pursuit of active sport and acceptance of the one-piece swimsuit. They were performers who transcended the sporting arena to entertain with novelty acts; unfortunately for Kerr, her career was overshadowed by the charismatic Kellerman and Kellerman's extraordinary self-promotional skills.

At home, Australian women were competing in functional men's one-piece swimsuits in swimming races and carnivals at this time. However, acceptance for this type of revealing clothing in public spaces was from far from seamless. Rose Scott, an early feminist and vice president of the Sydney Ladies' Swimming Club (SLSC, founded in 1901/2), was a firm believer in women's rights to physical freedom to engage in competitive sports, with the proviso that it occurred in a segregated, male-free space. The formation of a central controlling body for women's swimming, the New South Wales Ladies' Amateur Swimming Association (NSWLASA, similar to the already-existing men's club NSWASA, New South Wales Amateur Swimming Association), led to a bitter division with the SLSC with Scott suggesting, 'There was not the need for the women to become "like men", that is, to become seriously competitive' (Raszeja 1992: 64). Scott's insistence that public competition 'posed a threat to desirable images of femininity—modesty and moral inviolability' resulted in a return to the private sphere (ibid.). The advantage was women continued to wear streamlined swimsuits that led to swimmers such as Fanny Durack and Mina Wylie setting world-record times. The private/public debate escalated as the 1912 Olympics drew closer, and the decision was made to allow Durack and Wylie to compete for their country. The most controversial aspect was wearing their flimsy swimsuits (as opposed to actually competing) in the presence of men; this led to Scott resigning in protest from the SLSC and the NSWLASA.

Durack and Wylie were elite athletes who had the honour of being the first two Australian female swimmers to represent their country at the Olympic Games (1912), as that was the first time the Games included women's swimming events. Not only did they win the gold and silver medals respectively in the 100-metre freestyle race, but they were also the first Australian swimmers, male or female, to win gold. Frederick Lane won the 200-metre freestyle event at the 1900 Olympics; however, as it was pre-Federation, he competed as a member of the British team. Warner reports that at the first modern Olympics, held in 1896, women were not allowed to compete in any events, and at the 1900 Games, there were a meagre twelve female athletes; this decreased to eight at the 1904 Games. By 1908, the number of women had quadrupled, with thirty-six competitors. Tennis, golf and archery were the first sports to include women, with officials believing the fairer sex should be confined to recreational and leisure sports (Warner 2006: 84–89). According to Raszeja, individual sports such as tennis and golf were 'largely elite, fashionable pastimes', whereas swimming was the first sport to avoid categorization as a suitable activity for marriageable young women or importantly masculinizing (Raszeja 1992: 6–7).

The 1912 Games saw a change in the number of women competing, and it may have been the result of the 'more enlightened views' in the Scandinavian countries (Warner 2006: 90). It is significant that no American women swimmers competed (1920 would be their first Games for swimming), and it was the Australian contingent who won the women's swimming event. This demonstrates that Australians were ahead of their counterparts as a result of a progressive approach to women engaging in swimming as a competitive sport, and the early adoption of swimsuits (styled on the men's swimsuit) that were skirtless and sleeveless. Warner comments that American women did not dare to wear this style of costume in their home country much before the 1920 Olympics in Antwerp (ibid. 96–97). And indeed, 'the Stockholm affair marked the beginning of a new phase' for Australian swimmers—'with champions lauded and praised by the press for their contributions to the image of a nation' (Raszeja 1992: 74).

Australian swimming stars emerged in discrete blocks throughout the twentieth century, with women strongly contributing to individual and medley medal tallies, and also leading—with Durack's first place—Australia's gold medal tally in 1912. Durack was followed by Clare Dennis in 1932; Dawn Fraser, Lorraine Crapp, Faith Leech; and Sandra Morgan in 1956; Fraser in 1960 and 1964; Lyn McClements in 1968; Shane Gould, Gail Neall and Beverley Whitfield in 1972; Michelle Ford in 1980; and Susie O'Neil in 1996 and 2000. In the twenty-first century, the Athens 2004 and Beijing 2008 Olympics saw Australian women swimmers winning the majority of Australia's gold medals, highlighting the significance of their near-century contribution to the national medal tally. In Athens, Jodi Henry and Petria Thomas won individual gold medals; they were also on winning relay teams—the 100-metre freestyle and 100-metre medley events—with Alice Mills, Libby Lenton, Giaan Rooney and Liesel Jones. In Beijing, Stephanie Rice and Liesel Jones won two individual gold medals, Libby Trickett (nee Lenton) won one, and the relay teams won the 200-metre medley and 100-metre freestyle events. Although Australia's early champion lady swimmers and their successors have not been memorialized in poems or statues, as winners were in ancient Greece, they are indeed daughters of the gods.

SPEED ON IN YOUR SPEEDOS

Olympic swimming events are especially significant for a sport-obsessed nation such as Australia that has produced a long line of champion swimmers. The 1912, 1920, 1924, 1928 and 1932 Olympics profiled some early great Australian swimmers, including Durack and Wylie (1912), Andrew (Boy) Charlton (1924,1928), Frank Beaurepaire (1908, 1920, 1924) and Clare Dennis (1932). During the same period, international greats included Duke Paoa Kahanamoku (1912, 1920, 1924) from the United States, Johnny Weissmuller (1924, 1928) also from the United States and Arne Borg (1924, 1928) from Sweden. The year 1928 saw the birth of the iconic Australian swimwear label, Speedo. The company introduced an innovative design in 1929 called the racerback swimsuit, which reduced the suit's back width and centralized the straps to ensure they did not slide off the shoulder—essential for the serious swimmer. The design was developed for the Australian Olympic team; it was also adopted by teams from other nations. Arne Borg's endorsement of the racerback (Figure 5.1) declared that it had 'the maximum comfort and the minimum of resistance' (Hellmrich 1929: 8), design features that contributed to swimmers producing a number of world records and early international recognition for Speedo. Clare Dennis, who won Australia's only gold medal for swimming at the 1932 Olympics, won the 200-metre breaststroke event, although not without controversy. Dennis's regulation Speedo silk swimsuit nearly caused her disqualification for showing 'too much shoulder blade' (Raszeja 1993). It did ensure a public profile and notoriety as the swimsuit of champions and created the foundation that would in future decades secure for the company a reputation for producing performance swimwear that could shave seconds off swimmers' times.

It was not until the 1950s that Australian swimmers again surfaced as winners in the pool, with the interim years dominated by the Americans, Europeans and, in the 1930s, the Japanese. At the 1956 Melbourne Olympics, Australia was the swimming nation to watch: John Henricks, John Devitt and Gary Chapman placed first, second and third, respectively, in the 100-metre freestyle event, and Murray Rose won gold in the 400-metre and 1,500-metre freestyle events. Australian women Dawn Fraser, Lorraine Crapp and Faith Leech blitzed the 100-metre freestyle event. By this time, the Speedo swimsuit was established as the Aussie Cossie of choice for the Australian Olympic team and represented the 'real swimmer's uniform' (Wells 1982). Initially, the swimsuits were either silk

Figure 5.1 Speedo Racerback worn by Arne Borg. Photographed by Sidney Riley, Brisbane. Collection: Powerhouse Museum, Sydney.

or cotton as opposed to wool, as those materials were lighter and produced less water drag. By the 1960 Rome Olympics, Speedo had developed an advanced alternative to natural fibres—nylon tricot, which was knitted exclusively for the Australian racing team. Tricot refers to the type of weave, a plain warp knit that can be manufactured in natural, synthetic and blended fibers. A lightweight, strong fabric, nylon tricot absorbs minimal water; it has the added advantage of taking dyes and prints, often a problem for synthetic fibres at this time. The swimsuits supposedly gave the Australian team an advantage over their competitors, a selling point Speedo successfully used over the ensuing decades to position their products as performance-enhancing, whether true or not; this decade also marked the beginning of the company's expansion into the global market.

In 1963, Prestige Fabrics Limited in Melbourne developed for Speedo a vertical stripe fabric constructed of bri-nylon and terylene polyester yarns that was cross-dyed after knitting. Sixteen of the eventual eighteen gold medals for swimming were won by competitors wearing Speedos made of this fabric, reinforcing the company's position as the leader in performance swimwear. The 1964 Tokyo Olympics was another first when the Australian team wore gold-and-green striped swimsuits, as opposed to the traditional block colours. Speedo also modified the men's swim trunk, removing the skirt-front to produce less water drag; this also resulted in a more revealing style that filtered quickly into fashion swimwear. Female swimmers were not so fortunate with competitive swimsuits remaining skirted to protect their modesty for another twelve years, until the 1976 Olympics, when they were permitted to wear a skirtless, streamlined maillot. Gold medallist Dawn Fraser is remembered for scandals surrounding her swimsuit, as she was determined to have the skirt removed for competition events. At the 1964 Tokyo Olympics, Fraser incurred the wrath of officials when she chose to wear her own home-made swimsuit which she believed to be superior in fit and performance to the official swimsuit. It led to a ten-year ban, and Fraser was branded a larrikin who would not conform to rules and regulations (Smith 2001), although it was her single-minded focus and ambitious determination to win that were key ingredients in her success. Fraser's sporting achievements were recognized in 1999 at the World Sports Awards in Vienna where she was named World Athlete of the Century (Fraser 2007), retrospectively celebrating her individuality and sporting prowess.

By the 1976 Montreal Olympics, Speedo was appointed as an official swimwear licensee for the Games, with a number of nations choosing the company's products for their swim teams. Levine reports that the new Speedo swimsuits could shave seconds off of race times due to their briefer styling and lightweight textiles; additionally, swimmers wore suits two sizes smaller than their actual size (1976). The Australian team wore a distinct all-over print of green maps of Australia on a gold background created by Gloria Smythe (Speedo designer 1962–1990). The design caused heated debate with local fashion experts declaring it 'bastardised and gimmicky'. Former fashion model and commentator Maggie Tabberer declared, 'Australia is now a more sophisticated country, so surely we can have a sophisticated look about us'. But the president of the Amateur Swimming Union of Australia, Arch Stainback, explained that, 'it was aimed at making spectators and television viewers aware of the Australian competitors' (Robbins 1976).

While not particularly stylish, Smythe's graphic print created an association between the nation and its athletes, branding them for global consumption, although at this Olympic Games none of Australia's swimmers won gold.

In 1991, the British company the Pentland Group purchased a controlling interest in Speedo licensees in America and Europe and officially took over Speedo Australia, renaming it Speedo International. A core component of the company's design focus was continued research and development into creating performance swimwear that would beat their competitors' products as well as improve swimmers times. As a global company, designers now had broader access to textiles and technology which led to a number of innovations. In 1992, the S2000 one-piece cat-suit was launched at the Barcelona Olympics by the Australian team. The new style featured a high collar, no straps, and a zip up the back. The S2000 was produced in a polyester elastane that decreased drag, and swimmers wearing this design won 53 per cent of all medals. Speedo followed this innovation with the Aquablade in 1996 and the Fastskin in 2000. The design team initiated research into the flow-efficiency of sharkskin, aided by computer programmes such as Computational Fluid Dynamics (CFD), which is used for aerospace and naval engineering to solve complex air and water flow problems. The outcome was a fabric that mimicked the rough and smooth surfaces of a shark's skin that decreased drag and increased the speed of water flow over the body. According to Speedo, the fabric proved 3 per cent faster than all other fabrics tested. The Fastskin was produced in a number of styles, including full bodyskins with or without sleeves, knee skin and leg skin options, and was worn by 83 per cent of the swimmers who earned medals at the Sydney Olympics. The Fastskin FS11 followed and was launched at the Athens Olympics in 2004.

The ongoing design focus is obsessive; there is secretive research into performance textiles and styling that can claim the title of the world's fastest and the sales this can generate. Speedo has not been without its rivals including Arena, Adidas, Nike and Tyr; however, Speedo has consistently proved the most successful at promoting its endeavours to produce the next and best. The inset of Grant Hackett (Figure 5.2), 'inspired by the X-Men movies' (*The Sydney Morning Herald* 2004), illustrates a futuristic pursuit of perfection where sport is itself a form of entertainment mediated by national and global advertising campaigns and sponsored by commercial enterprises focused on cornering the market in performance swimwear.

Continuing the pursuit of space-age swimsuits, Speedo launched the performance-enhancing LZR Racer on 12 February 2008; this suit allegedly contributed to swimmers breaking a number of world records. The bodysuit is so tight it has been likened to a corset, with panels to stabilize the abdominal core to minimize fatigue during the race and to give the swimmer a better body position in the water. The worldwide launch took place in Sydney with Australia's leading swimmers modelling the polyurethane-coated design alongside a hologram appearance by American Olympic swimmer Michael Phelps—illustrating how contemporary sport merges entertainment and spectacle with a new breed of celebrity athlete. Over the next twenty-four hours, with similar launches in London, New York and Tokyo, a network of information about the product created an excitement

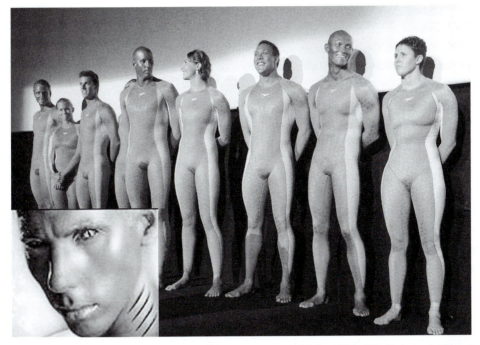

Figure 5.2 Swim stars including Petria Thomas, Geoff Huegill, Michael Kilm, Elka Graham and Massi Rosolino, Leisel Jones, Grant Hackett and Libby Lenton. Inset: Grant Hackett with 'fish eyes' in a new Speedo ad. Photo: AFP.

and interest from nations eager to provide their Olympic athletes with a possible advantage in the pool. The LZR Racer ('laser') is described as 'the world's first fully bonded, ultrasonically welded suit' (Hanson Sports Media 2008), with 10 per cent less drag than Speedo's Fastskin FS11. The Australian Olympic swim team is depicted in images promoting the LZR Racer, standing in rows android-like and expressionless, paving the way for performance swimwear where the body and swimsuit are one.

The suit's introduction was plagued by controversy, with commentators, sport spectators and FINA (Fédération Internationale de Natation), the international governing body of swimming, diving, water polo, synchronized swimming and open water swimming, questioning the value of the records achieved. The inference that the suit could represent a form of 'tech-doping', and as such render the swimmers who wear it as cheats. If a garment is deemed performance enhancing, thereby providing a swimmer with an advantage over competitors, FINA is obligated to rule against its use. Similar debates surfaced with the introduction of the Fastskin and the FS11, with FINA choosing to approve the swimsuits with nominal testing. Not all swimsuits are given the green light and FINA did rule against an Australian neoprene bodysuit developed by Brian Lowdon in 1986 for the Australian team and intended for the 1988 Olympics. On examination, FINA 'decided [it] provided buoyancy, thus contravening a FINA rule [6]' (Rushall 2008). This also brings into question the athlete's performance, with Australian Olympic swimming coach Forbes Carlile arguing that all bodysuits should be banned, commenting that 'they detract from the hard work and technique needed to be a champion' (Parnell 2008). Moreover, the LZR Racer suit highlights the divide between nations, institutes and families—between those who can afford to purchase the swimsuit and those who cannot.

Perhaps a more interesting aspect of the debate, touched on by Parnell, is the importance of establishing if a swimsuit like the LZR Racer and the new technological advances to performance textiles are impacting on the times achieved by elite swimmers, to some extent, 'if only to stop manufacturers acting like snake-oil salesmen as they spruik the hidden powers of their suits' (ibid.). Rushall's comprehensive analysis of the new generation of bodysuits suggests that claims made by manufacturers are overinflated, and regarding the LZR Racer suit, 'contain exaggeration, speculative statements, and largely are unsupported by evidence' (2008). Grant Hackett's performance at the Beijing Olympics is a case in point. Wearing the LZR Racer, neither Hackett nor another swimmer beat Hackett's 2001 1,500-metre freestyle world record. Rushall notes that there are a number of factors that contribute to new world records:

- Olympic Games stimulus—an increase in the number of world records is usually greatest in an Olympic year;
- technique improvements—an evolutionary process that involves the implementation of changes in technique; and
- training improvements—the Principle of Specificity and race-specific training and a greater proportion of pool practice.

In addition, the pool has a part to play. The Beijing Water Cube, designed by Australian company PTW Architects, may have contributed to the dozen world and Olympic records. The pool has ten lanes as opposed to eight, resulting in less wave bounce-back, and at three metres deep it is approximately 0.9 metres deeper than other pools, thereby contributing to making 'the water as flat and clear as possible' (Berkes 2008).

FINA made a decision to ban the full-body swimsuits in January 2010, revoking the organization's 2007 approval for the LZR Racer suit. Swimmers have supported the decision, aware that their achievements at the 2008 Olympics were eclipsed by the possibility that their performances could be attributed to the suit and not their ability. Speedo has continued research and development into textiles and as a result released a range of FINA-approved LZR products, which were available for the 2012 London Olympics, alongside products from competitors such as Tyr and Arena. Speedo has also proved resourceful and eco-friendly, collaborating with British sustainable fashion label From Somewhere to create an innovative collection from the surplus LZR Racers. Students from the London College of Fashion, University College Falmouth and University of Huddersfield also had the opportunity to reconstruct the suits into green fashions, creating a selection of inventive and original designs. This fusion of sport and technology with fashion is underpinned by a body-conscious aesthetic, and part of an ongoing conversation that stretches designers to rethink the relationship between form and function—performance sportswear and fashion.

Importantly, Speedo has proved resilient; like fashion companies and other sportswear manufacturers, branding and product placement is motivated by economic imperatives. As Breward notes, 'No manufacturer would develop a range of sports goods simply so they can be worn by a few dozen' (2008: 31). For sportswear brands, products are marketed and available to elite athletes and the average sportsperson, with the latter increasingly sourcing garments created for performance and fit. The message is that all sporting participants have potential, and if actively engaged in self-development and wearing the right performance enhancing clothes, may achieve seemingly impossible goals (see Adidas 2007; Speedo 2011). The bodysuits developed for Olympic swimmers over the last ten years illustrate how fashions in sportswear change yet stay the same. Kellerman wore a similarly streamlined unitard style of swimsuit in the early 1900s for competitive swimming and diving events. It was not heavily constructed or panelled to create a corset-like effect, and it was produced in a woollen knit, so Kellerman's bodysuit had none of the benefits of contemporary racer suits, resulting in a drag that most modern swimmers would have difficulty imagining. Part of Kellerman's fitness philosophy was to develop a strong abdominal core so the corsets women wore at that time could be discarded—at least when wearing swimsuits. In the 2000s, the underlying principle of the corset re-emerged to enhance performance and control the natural body, bringing the swimsuit full circle.

NATIONAL HEROES AND CELEBRITY ATHLETES

The Pioneers

Sport was and is important in fashioning the modern athletic body aesthetic, one that requires clothing that works with the body, ideally enhancing performance. Lipovetsky suggests that 'sports lent dignity to the natural body', freeing it from the constraints of 'excessive armature and trappings of dress' (1994: 62), although bodysuits such as the LZR Racer once again entrap the body. According to Warner, the swimsuit 'forced thinking—and clothing—in new directions' (2006: 61). Hence tracking the swimsuit's evolution through sport leads to the role of the athlete and the increasing fusion of spectacle and celebrity, and the transition for some from national hero in the sporting arena to careers in the entertainment, fashion and beauty industries.

In the early 1900s, Australia was home to a number of great swimmers. Fanny Durack was one of Australia's fastest women in the pool and was described in the *Bulletin* as 'the first Australian petticoat to represent this continent (officially) in great sporting events in the old world' (cited by Raszeja 1992: 85). Durack was an exceptional athlete and in Figure 5.3a is seated confidently in a relaxed pose on a sturdy rock with the waves gently lapping behind her. There is no false modesty and rather than coquettish,

Figure 5.3a   Portrait: Fanny Durack, 1912. Exchange Studios. Record ID 89140. National Library of Australia's Pictures Collection.

MISS FANNY DURACK
CHAMPION Amateur Lady Swimmer of the **WORLD.**

she has a natural quality with a warm and friendly gaze. There is nothing salacious about this image that could connect her with the raunchier postcard bathing beauty popular in the early 1900s. Durack demonstrates that, like a man, a woman 'had equally functional legs and feet' and 'active motion' (Hollander 1994: 147), and fits the caption describing her as a 'lady champion swimmer'. In Figure 5.3b a postcard bathing beauty enticingly peeps at the viewer through raised arms that frame her face and décolletage. Her bathing costume is sculpted and restrained by a corset and festooned with flowers and bows, and strategically draws the eye to erogenous body zones. Accessorized with hat, stockings and shoes, she is more suited to the boudoir than the painterly seascape background. Kellerman, to some degree, is a hybridized blend of the bathing beauty and the swimmer. In Figure 5.3c she wears a functional swimsuit similar to Durack's, but her pose and gaze are at odds with her drab swimsuit. With her hair coiffed and arms clasped behind her head, she invites the viewer to gaze on her bodily assets. Kellerman may have been a champion lady swimmer and diver but her sights were set on a larger pool.

Kellerman capitalized on her career as an entertainer and the fairy tale romance of a self-styled mermaid to collaborate with New York knitting manufacturer Ashbury Mills

Figure 5.3b   Bathing Beauty Postcard c. 1900.

to design and endorse a collection of swimsuits inspired by her performance swimsuits. According to fashion and textile curators at the National Art Gallery of Victoria,
Kellerman's two-in-one swimsuit (c. 1920) is 'practical, austere, yet revolutionary' and
'launched a brave new fashion which eventually gained acceptance' (Healy et al. 2003:
63). These swimsuit designs prefigure sporting/entertainer celebrity collaborations with
manufacturers to produce fashion collections for the mass market, adding to her credentials as the original celebrity athlete.

In the 1920s, Andrew 'Boy' Charlton (aged 15), described as 'Australia's first modern
swimming hero' (*Fair Sport* 2006), set a world freestyle record at the New South Wales
state swimming championships and was dubbed the 'Manly Flying Fish'. He represented
Australia at the Paris Olympic Games in 1924, winning gold in the 1,500-metre freestyle
event—the third Australian to win Olympic gold. Charlton successfully competed against
renowned Swedish swimmer Arne Borg and 'American Sensation' Johnny Weissmuller.
Shy and retiring, Charlton avoided publicity, refusing to turn professional on the grounds
that the Australian public would never forgive him for pursuing his sport for monetary
gains (Walsh 1979). Weissmuller was an Austro-Hungarian émigré who was a member of

MISS ANNETTE KELLERMANN.
Champion Lady Swimmer and Diver of the World.   SEARS, Melbourne
Copyright.

Figure 5.3c Annette Kellerman. Mitchell Library State Library of NSW Call No: PXE: 1028.

the US Olympic team in 1924 and 1928, winning five gold medals and setting a number of world records. Unlike Charlton, Weissmuller did not shun publicity and profited from his swimming career signing with US swimsuit manufacturer B.V.D. as a swimsuit and underwear model in the late 1920s. In 1932, contracted to MGM by Louis B. Mayer, he transformed into the legendary Tarzan and later Jungle Jim. While Charlton was consistently captured in photos in a sporty stance that revealed little personality, Weissmuller was immortalized in Hoyningen-Heuné's 'famous beefcake shot' (Bright 1998: 63), in which Weissmuller draws the viewer in with an intimate gaze. Provocatively framed by the changing-room doors, there is an aesthetic purity to the image with Weissmuller exuding a star quality that Lipovetsky refers to as 'the unique charm of their appearance . . . their bewitching seductiveness' (1994: 182).

Kellerman and Weissmuller radiated charisma and a unique style that successfully translated to the big screen and Hollywood star status. Both created an erotic layer to the swimsuit and became international identities associated with active glamour and a physical beauty embedded in athleticism. They were 'superindividuals'—part of a new modern world hierarchy populated by 'great actresses and great couturiers, sports figures and popular singers, movie stars and shoe-business idols' (ibid. 77). For Kellerman (and any aspiring Australian), her career trajectory involved travelling abroad to cosmopolitan and entertainment hubs in London and Hollywood to achieve her goals. Similarly, Weissmuller's move to the United States contributed to his career beyond the pool. In later years, his celebrity and name were lent to a number of business ventures with limited success, but he is remembered as the original and best Tarzan. By comparison, Durack and Charlton were elite athletes and national heroes knitted to Australia's cultural and sporting identity. Crombie explains that 'athletes, like soldiers, have an individual character but it is unusual to conceive of them operating independently of national origin and their successes are inextricably linked to national pride and progress' (Crombie 2004: 76).

Moving forward to the 1940s and 1950s, sport and film continued to shape swimsuit design. Esther Williams poised to dive or rising from a pool surrounded by equally glittering amphibious chorus girls embodied a grace and energy that glamorized the swimsuit and the athletic body. When Williams was at the peak of her career as an actress, a new Australian Olympian female swimmer was waiting in the wings. Aged nineteen at the 1956 Melbourne Olympic games, Dawn Fraser set a new world record in the 100-metre freestyle event. Sport would not be for her a launching pad for a film career, and due to her amateur status, Fraser was prevented from earning an income from her success in the pool. In an interview with Amanda Smith on *The Sports Factor*, Fraser discussed an absurd incident when, at age twelve, she was stood down as an amateur swimmer for two years by the Australian Swimming Union for accepting a two-shilling Christmas gift from the football club to which her family belonged to, deeming this classed her as a professional (Smith 2001). Although she did not substantially benefit financially from her sporting prowess, as a national sporting hero, her status as one of Australia's greatest swimmers resulted in the Sydney Balmain harbour side pool being named the Dawn Fraser Baths and earned her the adulation of the public for contributing to the nation's Olympic gold medal tally. Labelled a larrikin from early in her career, and as someone who does not conform to the rules, Fraser is unaffected and athletic rather than glamorous—attributes associated with Australianness. In recent years, she has benefited from her local popularity, penning an autobiography, *Dawn: One Hell of a Life*, and appearing as a contestant on Network Seven's *Dancing With the Stars*, and she maintains a comprehensive Web site for fans. Fraser is an elite athlete who has created ongoing public interest through new media and reality television programmes.

These images of Fraser and Williams (Figures 5.4a and 5.4b) illustrate the marked contrast between the Hollywood glamour swimsuit and the sporty swimsuit (preperformance swimwear); the professional and amateur swimmer; the MGM and Olympic pools. Williams's performances centred on spectacular aquatic routines, blending glamour and sport, which led to her inclusion in the Hollywood star system, elevating her to 'superpersonality' status. Her dazzling reinvention as a modern Hollywood mermaid follows a trend Kellerman had initiated fifty years earlier which can be described

Figure 5.4a Dawn Fraser, March 1956. Melbourne. VIC. Pic. Photo File Published: *Sunday Herald Sun*—20 July 2003, Page 36. Newspix.

as 'a modern individualist ideology' materializing as 'nonconformism, fantasy, uniqueness of the individual personality, eccentricity, comfort, and bodily display' (Lipovetsky 1994: 86). Athletes such as Fraser exhibited a number of these qualities; however, it would take a few decades before they would acquire the celebrity status of movie stars.

Williams, like Kellerman, was a pioneer who extended and mediated an entrepreneurial career beyond the pool and screen. While still at the height of her popularity as an actor, she negotiated an agreement with swimsuit manufacturer Cole of California to endorse the company's swimsuits. This was managed independently of her MGM contract and unheard of at that time. Her post-movie career led to licensing arrangements with a swimming pool company; part ownership in a gas station, metal parts factory and restaurant; followed at the age of sixty-seven by a collaboration with Misty Swimwear designing a swimwear collection (Chadakoff 1989). Williams has been nicknamed the 'mermaid tycoon' (Starr 2005), and in 2012, with a vibrant Web site, fans can access information and memorabilia and visit the online swimwear store that stocks swimsuits with a touch of Hollywood glamour. Williams has proved to be an enduring and media-savvy celebrity athlete/actor/entrepreneur.

Figure 5.4b   Esther Williams. Esther Williams.

The Beneficiaries

In the 1980s, a new breed of Australian swimmers surfaced, including Olympian Lisa Curry. A striking blonde, glowing with sporty health, she benefited from the softening of constraints that had prevented Fraser from earning an income through sponsorship deals and endorsements in the 1950s and 1960s. Curry competed in the Moscow (1980), Los Angeles (1984) and Barcelona (1992) Olympic Games but did not win a medal, despite winning fifteen gold, seven silver and eight bronze medals at the Commonwealth Games and holding Australian records in all strokes other than backstroke. It did not prevent her from a long association with Uncle Toby's, promoting the company's food products together with the value of physical fitness, and in recent years acting as a spokesperson for the all-female Fernwood Fitness Centres. In the 1990s, her career extended to work as a presenter on Channel Nine's *Wide World of Sports* and guest appearances on popular television programmes such as *Full Frontal* and *Home and Away*. In 1992, Curry launched a swimwear label, Hot Curry, with swimsuit designs she described as 'something groovy—not daggy or boring' (Rymer 1996), and made her mark with swimwear that was 'a unique blend of glamour wear for the physically fit' (Maynard 2000: 141). Kellerman and Williams drew on their fame as aquatic stars to collaborate with swimwear manufacturers to create their own signature collections; then in a decade when sport and fashion are fused, an elite athlete added another layer to the mix.

Sportswomen did not have exclusive rights to sponsorship and product endorsements; swimmer Mark Spitz led the way a decade earlier in the United States. In Australia, Olympic canoeist and ironman Grant Kenny raised public awareness and interest in surf athletes when he won four consecutive Australian Ironman titles. Blonde, bronzed and in the peak of physical condition, his advertisements for Kellogg's Nutri-Grain cereal, in which he is shown kayaking through rapids can still be viewed on YouTube. According to Booth, ironmen are 'the embodiment of Australian health and masculinity' (2001: 153), qualities that along with endurance are tested in ironman events such as the Coolangatta Gold held at Surfers Paradise in Queensland. Contestants are challenged by a 23 kilometre surf ski leg, 0.65 kilometre beach run, 3.5 kilometre surf swim, 4 kilometre beach run and a 5.5 kilometre board paddle, and finally a 10 kilometre beach run. The inaugural event, held in 1984, coincided with the production of a film of the same name (Auzin 1984). Starring Colin Friels as a contender for the title, he competes against Grant Kenny, the race favourite, playing himself. (Guy Leech won the actual event.) Kenny acted in and co-produced the television series spin-off from the movie, and 'Ironman became one of the most watched sports on Australian Television' (Meares 2003: 127). Since then, Kenny has developed a successful career as a property developer on the Sunshine Coast. He married Lisa Curry in 1986, and together they were part of a new generation of elite athletes and national heroes who used their sporting prowess and achievements as stepping-stones to careers in the fashion and entertainment industries. A bonus for Australia is their contribution to nation branding underpinned by sport, fashion (closely connected to the swimsuit) and active glamour.

At the end of 2007, Stella McCartney's collection statement for Adidas was 'Sport as an integral part of everyday life!' (Trendletter by Fashionoffice 2007). As McCartney brings an edge to sports clothes, celebrity athletes add sporty glamour to advertising campaigns. Sport is big business, and Australians are positioned to benefit as Australia punches above its weight in a number of sports, swimming in particular ('Sporting Pulse International 2007). Ian Thorpe, dubbed the Thorpedo, was one of Australia's most successful male swimmers in the 1990s and early 2000s. Thorpe did not follow the trend of most Australian swimmers and wear Speedos, choosing instead to sign a sponsorship deal with Adidas. The decision caused some problems, as Speedo was the official sponsor of the Australian swim team at the Sydney Olympics in 2000. Acceptance of an individual aligning with an alternative brand foregrounded the power elite athletes now claim to financial and commercial rewards from their sporting abilities.

In an interview with Thorpe, fashion journalist Marion Hume refers to 'the power of his own celebrity' which has led to a friendship with Giorgio Armani, a sponsorship deal with Emporio Armani, jewellery design for Broome pearl producers Autore, a signature fragrance and an underwear collection called IT (Hume 2002). In addition, Thorpe hosted a charity-based reality show called *Undercover Angels* (2002), which proved a huge ratings success coming in just behind *Big Brother* with 1.74 million viewers. It entailed 'dispatching three "angels" to do good deeds for the needy'; an article in *The Age* suggested it 'bodes well for a television career in Thorpe's swimming after-life' (*The Age* 2002). Although Thorpe has been a guest judge on *Australia's Next Top Model*, an ongoing television presence has yet to materialize. His name does continue to be associated with fashion brands including a partnership with international Dutch watch brand TW Steel (WatchPaper.com 2010) and, significantly, he represents the rise of a new generation of fashion-conscious men 'with interests outside the domain of the traditional, Aussie macho male' (Gotting 2003), a new target market for the fashion industry.

In the 2000s, Libby Trickett (nee Lenton), lauded as an Australian Swim Queen, won gold at the Athens 2004 and Beijing 2008 Olympics. As a result, Trickett earned a number of lucrative sponsorship deals that included Speedo, Uncle Toby's, Fuji, Lenovo and Audi. According to an article in the *Herald Sun*, Trickett together with fellow Olympians are 'marketing gold'; they ranked highly with sponsors and the public. Marketing expert Con Stavros suggests the qualities that contribute to an athlete attaining a high poll ranking are connected to being 'good-looking, humble, down-to-earth and successful—values that are seemingly distinctly Australian'. In comparison, athletes from nations such as the United States with ostentatious lifestyles are 'incredibly rich and incredibly distant with their palatial mansions and bodyguards' (Cogdon 2008). The Australian characteristics lend an authenticity and integrity to sponsors' products, and the athletes move beyond the world of sport to enter the realm of personality (Walshaw 2007).

Hartley's analysis of the integration of sport into consumer culture, in part through the cross-fertilization with fashion, sees sporting icons donning glamorous red-carpet creations and fashion photographers and stylists transforming elite athletes 'where all trace of "sport" seems to have been erased' (Hartley 2006: 418). This reinvention is mediated by magazines—'glossy illustrated monthlies and weeklies'—that produce 'narratives of transformation that connect[ed] the ordinary and extraordinary, the unlikely and the possible' (Gundle 2008: 379). For Trickett, the transformation was for *Alpha*, a sports magazine, as opposed to fashion bible *Vogue*, as part of 'a unique portfolio of photography, capturing Australia's female athletes as they've never been seen before . . . we wanted sexy, sassy and strong' (Pegley 2007: 52). This may be seen as a cynical and conventional method of feminizing and glamorizing successful female athletes thereby detracting from their alpha sporting status, or evidence of the integration of sport and fashion with a common toolbox for makeovers to create conventional beauty shots. Similar images of men such as Ian Thorpe and Britain's high-profile footballer David Beckham suggest it is more a method of fashioning the celebrity athlete and illustrates how they are groomed and repackaged for mass consumption through popular media. In the twenty-first century fashion and sport find common ground in performance and spectacle, a space where elite athletes continue to be heralded as national heroes and, for some, promoted as celebrities for national and global markets by media and advertising industries—airbrushed to perfection.

–6–

Shaping Up: The History and Development of the Swimsuit's Integration into the Fashion Industry

Swimmers and performers closely tied to entertainment, leisure and sport—at the beach, in the pool and theatre—together with early swimwear producers (underwear and stocking manufacturers), drove early design innovations in swimsuits. This chapter traces the story of swimwear to include a summary of the swimsuit's evolution decade by decade and its integration into the fashion industry, contextualizing local and global contributions from Australia, Europe, the United States and South America. Production methods and textile technology are included to provide an insight into the material side of the fashion industry. Historical information was sourced from trade journals such as *The Draper of Australasia* (1901–63) and mail-order catalogues—David Jones (Australia's oldest department store, established in 1838) and Sears, Roebuck & Co (1896) (see reference list for sources) in the United States. Over time, catalogues began to include less detailed information, and fashion magazines increasingly included swimsuits, so from the 1960s, American, British and Australian *Vogue* (and to a lesser degree *Harper's Bazaar*) are used to track swimwear trends. The choice to focus primarily on this syndicated publication is influenced by its early recognition as 'the definitive style bible' (Watson 2008) and because 'Vogue qualifies as a classic example for the worldwide marketing of a successful magazine brand . . . it represents one of the earliest globalized media outlets' (Roessler 2006: 43). Internet sources such as trend analysis and research Web site WGSN and online newspaper articles were also accessed to provide a broader perspective. The information has been collated chronologically to provide a broad historical brushstroke of how the swimsuit has developed stylistically over time, with a focus on Australia as a case study, in order to highlight an aspect of the swimsuit's evolution that has been overlooked or almost completely omitted from publications to date. Moreover, this focus on Australia reveals patterns of production from the periphery to the centre that contribute to the shaping of the constantly evolving global fashion industry.

The earliest swimsuit entries I found were in the Sears, Roebuck & Co catalogue between 1902 and 1905, and *The Draper of Australasia* beginning with the 1909 issues. Detailed images of the Sargent brand (Figure 6.1) manufactured by the Metropolitan Knitting & Hosiery Company in Sydney feature streamlined swimsuits, styles that 'by the end of the war (WW1), almost all Australian women were wearing' (Joel 1998: 67). By contrast, the bathing suits available to women in the American catalogues were modest

Figure 6.1 The Metropolitan Knitting & Hosiery Company Sydney, 1913. *The Draper of Australasia*. Collection: Powerhouse Museum Research Library, Sydney.

skirted tunics that 'continued to be worn well into the 1920s' (Warner 2006: 79). The 1916–17 David Jones catalogue illustrates the choices available to wearers, from the sleek Canadian swimsuit to the less daring skirted bathing costumes. Many are shown accessorized with a waterproof bathing cap or sun hat (far left Figure 6.2). The majority of swimsuits were produced in wool, a yarn that, although elastic, is prone to shrinkage and felting. Manufacturers had already applied shrink-proof processes to men's underwear and socks and recognized this treatment was essential for swimsuits. David Jones was confident that the all-wool knitted bathing costumes were unshrinkable through a 'special process' (far right Figure 6.2), and accordingly offered a money-back guarantee.

Probert observes, 'The swimmer was not part of the fashionable set until 1910' (1981: 7); elegance as opposed to fitness was the ideal look, and the swimsuit received little coverage in *Vogue* magazines prior to 1914. With the social upheaval caused by World War I, the swimsuit was accepted into the ranks of fashionable clothing; however, 'it took a certain amount of courage for the bathing-girl to appear in this daring

BATHING COSTUMES AND CAPS

Figure 6.2   David Jones Catalogue Spring/Summer 1916/17. David Jones Limited.

costume, and she really deserves the credit for firing the first shot in the Battle of Modern Dress' (*Vogue* 1914 cited by Probert 1981: 8). Australians, including Kellerman, did indeed fire the first shot. From 1905, when she travelled to the United Kingdom, Europe and the United States, she promoted the one-piece swimsuit, encouraging women to fashion their bodies through a focus on physical exercise and a healthy diet. The popularity of the swimsuit in Australia prior to its inclusion as fashionable foregrounds that it was neither a Parisian nor even a French innovation. Coco Chanel is attributed with creating sportswear for women, and at a time when pale skin was still considered fashionable, was recorded as sunbaking and inventing the tan (Charles-Roux 2004). By comparison, Australians had adopted the suntan with Melbourne's *Punch* magazine reporting in 1908, 'The browner the better' (Booth 2001: 20). Chanel would contribute to the popularization of the suntan in the 1920s, yet on the periphery, sunbaking and swimming were already a popular pastime. In 1914, a photo shows Chanel posing in a demure albeit stylish tunic bathing suit complete with white stockings, reflecting a conservatism that supports the opinion that the French did not initially influence or lead the swimsuit revolution.

According to Steele (1985: 223), 'The vogue for physical culture, however, (which was much less noticeable in France) had little direct or immediate effect on the design of fashion.' Integral to this new interest in the body was the swimsuit, a garment that acted as a second skin revealing the body's perfections and imperfections, and was consequently suited to the young and physically fit. Crane's research into the social significance of dress examines the style of clothing Frenchwomen wore in the early twentieth century, noting, 'The mature woman was the fashion leader for whom fashions were created' (Crane 2000: 107). By comparison, women in the United States and England were athletic and inclined to wear sporty clothing, expressing a greater freedom and independence than 'their French counterparts' (Crane 2000: 8). Similarly, Australian women epitomized the modern outdoor woman (Woollacott 2001: 157, 188–91), and this included female entertainers and Olympians who appeared publicly in one-piece swimsuits from the early 1900s, locally and internationally. Thus, it is realistic to sur-mise that the French fashion industry and designers did not drive the design develop-ment of the swimsuit at this time, and Australia played a significant role.

By the 1920s, Parisian-based designers Jean Patou, Jeanne Lanvin, Elsa Schiaparelli and Sonia Delaunay were designing innovative and glamorous beachwear for the rich and famous who frequented the beach resorts of Deauville and Biarritz. In particular, Patou, like Chanel, worked in jersey fabrics (a machine-made knit), and is remembered for his contribution to sportswear and swimsuits—'clothes for the modern woman' (Cal-lan 1998: 179–80)—on the condition she was wealthy. A visionary, Patou recognized the emerging sports-fashion trend and was the first to brand his designs with a signature

Figure 6.3a   The Dolly Sisters at Deauville. *The Home* 1 January 1927. Collection: Fryer Library, University of Queensland.

Figure 6.3b   Miss Vera Viner, Manly Surf Queen. *The Home* 1 December 1926. Collection: Fryer Library, University of Queensland.

logo, embellishing swimsuits and beach pyjamas with decoratively embroidered initials. Moreover, Patou's boutiques named Sports Corner offered an elite clientele fashionable garments for tennis, swimming and golf in dedicated sections (Kennedy 2007: 50).

Australians were kept abreast of European trends through print media such as the popular magazine *The Home*. The 1 January 1927 editorial 'Where Paris Wets Her Feet' offered a snapshot of the Deauville beach set. Included were the famous Dolly Sisters—identical twins, entertainers, gamblers and femmes fatales (Figure 6.3a). Readers were informed that they 'are protected from the sun by something new in the way of ostrich feather parasols' (*The Home* 1927). Their swimsuits are fashionably high-waisted, emphasized by contrast belts and embellished with placement embroideries. The 1 December 1926 issue featured 'A Place in the "Sun"' which highlighted entrants in the Surf Queen competitions. Miss Viner of Manly (Figure 6.3b) is described as an 'expert surfer and swimmer, as well as a tennis player and yachtswoman', while Miss Cauldwell of Bondi (Figure 6.3c) as the winner of 'a score of swimming championships' (*The Home* 1926). Miss Viner is fashionably attired, although her parasol is not decorated with

Figure 6.3c Miss Claire Cauldwell, Bondi Surf Queen. *The Home* 1 December 1926. Collection: Fryer Library, University of Queensland.

exotic feathers, and Miss Cauldwell's swimsuit is branded by place—Bondi—rather than a designer's initials. These women are distinctly Australian, and represent an athletic aesthetic and reflect a different type of beach culture than that experienced by the Dolly Sisters, a culture stitched to water sports and beaches accessible to ordinary citizens, rather than celebrity entertainers and the wealthy elite.

In 1927, British *Vogue* reported a trend for swimwear that was 'more and more skin on display: the body on show at the smartest beaches clad in the newest knitted, clinging fabrics'. Probert suggests, 'Haute couture began to take a leading role in designing new styles for all beachwear: a role played earlier in the 20th century by personal dressmakers and large stores' (1981: 27). Rather than new styles, it was a stylistic approach mediated and interpreted by the media. An illustration of a Patou swimsuit by Lee Erickson for French *Vogue* and an advertisement for an Australian swimsuit manufacturer (Figure 6.4) in 1927 reveal few differences in the swimsuit designs, and since the transmission of fashion information in the 1920s was not immediate, this demonstrates that Australian manufacturers were not directly imitating French designers. However, the differences in the mass market swimsuit and the designer swimsuit are clearly defined. The Patou is worn with confidence and elegance by a chic model striding out, accessorized

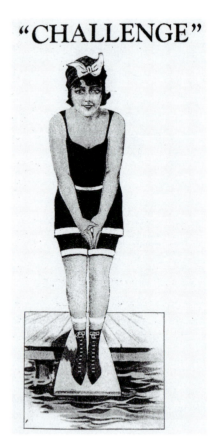

"CHALLENGE"

Figure 6.4 D & W Murray, Sydney 1927, Challenge Swimsuit. *The Draper of Australasia*. Collection: Powerhouse Museum, Research Library Sydney.

with an equally elegant canine. It is possible that the wearer may never actually engage in aquatic pursuits but just retire to a sun chair or the shade of a decorative parasol to sip champagne. By contrast, the Australian girl is modest yet cheeky, and posed on the diving board suggests she is an active outdoor girl at a local beach or public bath. It reveals a stylistic approach influenced at a national level, for the French (fashion) and for Australia (sport and beach), and as the Parisian correspondent for *The Draper of Australasia* reported in 1924, there are 'two classes of people who go to the seaside . . . those who go for the sake of sea pleasures and those on a snob expedition . . . the elegant bather who wants to show off her clothes much more than her feats in the waves'.

Of course, while French designers were creating glamour beachwear, and the Australians, swimsuits for local surf kings and queens, the American knitting mills were producing 'affordable fashions for millions of bathers' (Lenček and Bosker 1989: 44). At the forefront of these companies was Jantzen which, in the late teens, developed an elastic rib knit for bathing suits on the advice of a rower who wanted swimming trunks that would stay up without a drawstring. The rib knit, similar to that produced on jumper and cardigan cuffs, with noticeable lengthwise ribs, had more elasticity and durability than plain knits. The company proved to be astute advertisers and promoters of their products, launching the red diving girl logo in 1920. She was 'the consummate embodiment of intangible American ideals: youth, grace, sex appeal, and athletic prowess' (Lenček and Bosker 1989: 48). Jantzen tapped into the modern girl zeitgeist that was sweeping the world and became leaders in the swimsuit market, selling their products as 'the suit that changed bathing into swimming', and saturating the market with 'competitions and department store tie-ins' and instigating 'coast-to-coast "Learn-to-Swim-Week" ' (ibid.). The American swimsuit moved onto the fashion radar, in tune with a democratized fashion for all, filtering through mass media sources, countering the centralized French control of what could be fashionable. Jantzen was ahead of its competitors accounting for 75 per cent of swimsuit advertising in the United States, in magazines including the *Saturday Evening Post*, *Colliers*, *Cosmopolitan*, *Boy's Life*, *Photoplay*, *Shadowplay*, *Screenland*, *Silver Screen*, *Motion Picture* and *Movie Classic*—and 'practically all billboard advertising' (ibid.). In addition, recognizing the importance of a presence in fashion magazines, Jantzen was the first swimwear company to advertise in *Vogue* and *Harper's Bazaar* (Zehntbauer 1955). The sheer size of the US market combined with saturation advertising ensured that Jantzen made its mark as a powerhouse of the swimwear industry.

In 1955, the president of Jantzen, J. A. Zehntbauer, wrote a report outlining the company's move into global licensing. Due to high import duties aimed at protecting local textile and manufacturing industries, Jantzen developed a number of licensee deals in the late 1920s, initially with Australia, Britain and Canada (ibid.). Australia was of particular interest to Jantzen after a 1927 report highlighted its potential as a significant market. Although it was noted that the population was small, around six million people, Australians live close to 'beautiful beaches' and due to 'summers . . . long and hot . . . the people take to the water like no other people on earth do'. Boasting that there was no company 'equipped for making a suit like a Jantzen suit', Zehntbauer commented that the population, 'with their swimming facilities . . . would be equal to one of 18 million people in any other country'. He did concede that Australia had a number of great knitting mills, but they were turning out poorer quality and outmoded styles, creating a niche for the Jantzen products (Zehntbauer 1927). Subsequently, Jantzen opened a Sydney factory in Parramatta Road, Lidcombe, to cater to this demand.

Although Jantzen was confident about its market position and product, advertisements and articles in *The Draper of Australasia* in the 1920s indicate that Australian swimwear design was innovative and of comparable standard and style. A 1931 advertisement for David Jones Surf Suit Department (Figure 6.5) illustrates that Jantzen entered a healthy market, and Jantzen did not receive special treatment as an import, nor is there evidence that the company's products were considered of a superior quality. Indeed, the Jantzen swimsuits are the most conservative and plain swimsuits on the page. David Jones was also manufacturing swimsuits in the company's Sydney factories and they were featured in the central section of this advertisement. For the Australian brands, the fit and smart modern cuts that allowed for more tanning were important

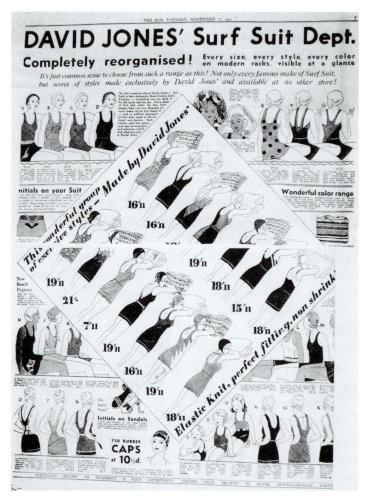

Figure 6.5 David Jones Surf Suit Advertisement. *The Sun*, Tuesday, 17 November 1931. David Jones Limited.

marketing angles, and David Jones merchandised 'every size, every style, every colour on modern racks, visible at a glance' (David Jones Surf Suit Department Advertisement 1931). There was no shortage of styles or design details, including individualized monogrammed initials. And manufacturers promised wearers that the swimsuit 'can be worn to advantage by every figure type'. Additionally, treatments such as Flex-O-Knit and salt-water shrunk ensured Australian swimmers were well catered for. It was the decade when the sunbather, surfer and serious swimmer in surf suits by companies such as Sunspeed, Sprinter, Sunkist, Seagull and Speedo came to represent the dominant image of what it was to be Australian.

Textiles played an important role in the development of the swimsuit for both performance and fashion swimwear. Early one-piece swimsuits were primarily produced in woollen knits, in part for opacity (modesty) and to attain stretch and control with minimal drag and sag when wet. The woolly swimsuits were heavy and ugly once immersed in water and required lengthy periods to dry and retained a musty odour. Australia is renowned for producing some of the finest merino wool globally, and although not noted for a strong textile industry, had a number of well-established knitting mills from the early decades of the twentieth century producing high-quality wool swimsuits. The 1930s was the decade that saw technological advances in textiles for the swimsuit with the introduction of Lastex, a yarn that had an extruded rubber core encased with wool, rayon, silk or cotton threads. Initially manufactured and patented by the Adamson Brothers Company, a subsidiary of the US Rubber Company, it was a rubber yarn that, unlike its predecessors, had considerably more stretch and control, giving designers the flexibility to create more figure-hugging and daring swimsuits. Australian manufacturers did not delay in adopting Lastex with distributors Dunlop Perdriau Rubber Company importing the 'Miracle Yarn' beginning in 1934 (*The Draper of Australasia* 1934b).

Lastex contributed to the development of the sleek, glamour swimsuit of the 1930s and 1940s stitched to Hollywood and the bathing-suited starlet. The lifestyle promoted was that of lounging by the poolside perfectly groomed and dry; this significantly influenced the direction of luxury fashion swimsuits in the decades to come. In Australia, the swimsuit industry was also thriving and Botany Knitting Mills Melbourne manufactured Black Lance and Seagull Water Fashions. Peter O'Sullivan (1904–1977) introduced designs for the company that were 'sparingly short and daringly smart' with in-built trunks for greater freedom in the hips and legs, and that incorporated imaginative design details such as decorative buttons, polka dot patterns and contrast trims. 'O'Sullivan was the first Australian to successfully design and manufacture swimwear for export to the United States' (Cuthbert 2009), a coup particularly as the United States dominated the swimwear mass market. Figure 6.6 illustrates a Black Lance design, the essential backless halter for strap-free sun tanning. Advertisements in *The Draper of Australasia* throughout this period highlight the vibrancy of the local swimwear industry. Elastic knit swimsuits were cleverly cut for sunbaking with attention to styles that ensured minimal sag, and there was an 'originality of design expressed in the form of appliquéd motifs, diagonal contrasts, woven insets, stripe effects as well as contrast bindings and straps' (*The Draper of Australasia* 1933). Lace, sponge, cord, honeycomb and novelty knits added texture, and the use of vivid shades complete a picture of swimwear that is 'exceptionally striking' (*The Draper of Australasia* 1934a). For 1937, the swimsuit revelation is a farewell 'to all dull shades' and a welcoming of 'Jubilee blues, Sicilian Greens, Imperial Golds, Flamingo Pinks'—and 'they are perfect fitting' (*The Draper of Australasia* 1936).

Not all swimsuits were mass produced, and a number of advertisements for Patons Crocus knitting wool in *The Home* promoted the idea that 'seaside fashion' could be 'hand worked', and as the 'products of busy fingers, will be your pride during the season at the beaches' (*The Home* 1930). A knitted bathing-suit pattern described as 'with suntan back for maximum tanning' together with other vintage patterns I have collected suggest a number of beach-goers knitted their swimsuits in the 1920s through to the 1940s (Figure 6.7). Whether hand-crafted for creative reasons or more likely financial

Figure 6.6   Black Lance 'Brigadier'-style swimsuit, designed by Peter O'Sullivan: gelatin silver print. Australian National Maritime Museum Collection.

reasons, this reinforces that accessible beach attire could be made or purchased by a large percentage of the population. However, talking to women who recall the hand-knit variety, even with additional crocheting to strengthen the necklines, it's evident that the sag factor was considerable.

In the United States, textiles produced from synthetic yarns such as Lastex, nylon (a synthetic polyamide commercialized by Du Pont in 1939), and the man-made fibre rayon, were increasingly replacing wool for swimsuit production. As World War II loomed and swimwear entries in catalogues lessened, the swimsuits showcased illustrate an American influence and Hollywood glamour. A Stirling Henry (Australia) swimsuit incorporated Lastex yarn and printed satin textiles and styling that reflected the company's main business of producing 'high grade lingerie' for the local market (*The Draper of Australasia* 1939). Swimsuits now shared similarities in production techniques with lingerie and, 'because of their shared proximity to the body' (Craik 1994: 136), the focus for designers and manufacturers became to produce styles that would provide support and control with foundation garments concealed by a beach aesthetic for public display.

Figure 6.7 Knitted Bathing Suit Pattern. *Australian Home Journal*, 1 October 1932. Collection: Powerhouse Museum Research Library, Sydney.

The 1940s began with a 'make do and mend' mentality towards fashion, with an emphasis on functional, utility clothing. The Nazis occupied Paris in June 1940, disconnecting the world from the influential Parisian couturiers and their seasonal collections, and as a result, designers in other countries 'were able to develop their own indigenous styles of dress' (Steele 1997: 6). British *Vogue*'s June 1940 cover does not pay homage to French fashion or the war effort, but to the swimsuit and the athletic body.[1] Photographer Horst P. Horst captured Swedish model Lisa Fonssagrives in a series of gymnastic poses to animate and spell out the letters of vogue, at the same time displaying her faultless, disciplined dancer's body to perfection. She was ideally suited to add another narrative layer to the swimsuit, stitching elegance and poise into the concept of physical fitness. This is an athleticism rather than Hollywood glamour that is also seen in the first photographic cover produced for British *Vogue* in July 1932 by Edward Steichen.[2] It features a model wearing a streamlined swimsuit as opposed to day or eveningwear, and rather than depicting a beach belle in an elegant pose, the model is tanned, athletic and sitting cross-legged—beach ball poised to create an edgy realism dramatized by the intense blue background starkly contrasted with the geometric balance of red and white. The result is a natural, relaxed elegance and, like Horst's 1940 athletic modern woman, signposts a new era that captured models in dynamic shots rejoicing in their athletic sensuality wearing body-baring swimsuits. It is a symbol of the modern woman, in a modern garment, captured by a modern medium.

The American style was underpinned by accessible, functional fashion associated with Claire McCardell designs, such as shirtwaist dresses, rompers, playsuits and innovative wool jersey swimsuits, which are recognized by fashion historians as the foundation blocks of American sportswear and a radical shift away from Parisian couture. However, McCardell's swimsuit designs did little to influence the large West Coast swimsuit manufacturers, which continued to produce garments that were created by Hollywood costume designers now working in fashion (Lenček and Bosker 1989: 93). The Hollywood-inspired swimsuit lacked the simplicity or utilitarian sensibilities of a McCardell's design, with stiff structuring similar to lingerie in shiny fabrics that were probably extremely uncomfortable.

From 1939 until the end of World War II, swimsuit entries in the David Jones catalogues were predominantly wool, in part due to a lack of imported synthetic yarns at this time. In 1939–40, Jantzen advertised 'new low prices', and in 1942–43, 'a smart continental style' and uplifting brassiere, styles that were conservative, modest and revealed less than those of the previous decade. It wasn't until 1946 that *The Draper of Australasia* again contained reports from its European and American correspondents and local manufacturers returned to advertising their products. Domestic textile mills and clothing manufacturers had channelled their energies into the war effort with 90 per cent of Speedo's production concentrated on items for military purposes. The Turner Parachute Company was a newcomer to the local swimsuit market in 1945 and 'placed the "Scamp" on the market' with 'brief, gay, and youthful designs'. It was the 'post-war fruits of a company' (*The Draper of Australasia* 1946); that produced swimsuits in plain and floral cottons 'all tailored with parachute precision to permit the maximum of tanning'. The styles and fabrication set them apart from American designs which were retreating from the minimalist suit to the new cover-up look (*The Draper of Australasia* 1947). Designer Ben Turner developed flexible details such as adjustable bandeau bras and laced-sided trunks, which could be reduced in width, and by 1947, with the increase in imported textiles, was manufacturing a percentage of the seasonal collection in Lastex and water-repellent nylon. Figure 6.8 illustrates how the Sydney Scamp label brought 'fashion to the beaches' (ibid.), as did Paula Stafford on the Gold Coast in Queensland.

SPLASH MAKERS

By the 1950s, American swimsuits were considered 'the world's classic suit, exported everywhere and imitated around the globe' (Lenček and Bosker 1989: 100). According to Joel and Wells, the big American swimsuit manufacturers Jantzen, Cole of California and Rose Marie Reid dominated the Australian market in this decade (Joel 1998: 164; Wells 1982: 104). These companies had a huge impact on the style of swimsuits

Figure 6.8   Scamp by Turner Parachute Company. *The Draper of Australasia*, 30 September 1946. Collection: Powerhouse Museum Research Library, Sydney.

available in department stores and boutiques nationally, and, importantly, both Jantzen and Cole of California had factories in Australia. David Jones was fittingly producing swimsuits locally under the Colony label (Figure 6.9), supporting the idea that Australians were following the American lead.

A 1952 review of the Jantzen collection in *The Draper of Australasia* reported that, while the company's designers and stylists looked to key trends on the continent and in America, 'the Australian beach girl has her own decided preferences. She looks for practical glamour or fashions that are swimmable.' The review continued, 'It [a swimsuit] needs more than glamour . . . the ability to "take it" is an essential so that at the end of a long, active season, the garment will still retain its sparkle' (*The Draper of Australasia* 1952). The combination of fashionable swimsuits with durability and practicality is a marker of Australian swimsuit design and continues to influence its design direction in the twenty-first century. Similarly, Fred Cole, president and founder of Cole of California, visited Australia in 1953 to inspect the operation of the local subsidiary California Productions Limited (factories in Sydney and Bathurst, New South Wales), and observed that the local standard of manufacture 'equaled, if not exceeded, that of the main factory in the U.S.A.'. He also noted that Australian girls 'looked healthier and use less make-up than American girls', and the beaches surpassed any in the world (*The Draper of Australasia* 1953). The rhetoric targets the colonists but is underpinned by both Jantzen's and Cole's recognition of the viability of the Australian market. The companies' expansion through production in local factories catered to a nation of swimmers connected to beach culture.

Figure 6.9   Cole of California and Colony by David Jones swim-suits. Spring/Summer Catalogue 1951. David Jones Limited.

It seemed only natural that Australian designers would feel best equipped to sup-ply the local market as well as export the Antipodean beach vision to the rest of the world. In 1952, David Waters worked in a knitting factory by day and cut out garments for his mother's stall at Melbourne's Queen Victoria Markets at night. Waters decided to experiment with a small swimwear line, and in 1953 registered the name Watersun (Wells 1982: 104). Initially there were no Melbourne retailers prepared to buy the label as 'they were all committed to the big-name American firms' (Joel 1998: 164). Travelling to Sydney and using his sister as a model, Waters successfully sold 200 units of a blue swimsuit design with convenient pockets. Subsequently, the label gained a reputation for printing 'gay designs' on imported cottons (*The Draper of Australasia* 1956), and by 1959, Watersun was exporting to Singapore and Hong Kong. Watersun, like the Paula Stafford label (discussed in Chapter 7), represents a distinctly Australian approach to swimwear design at this time, through businesses started at kitchen tables, by mums and home sewers, to create innovative youthful swimsuits that would compete with more traditional, international brands.

Comparing a 1955 Jantzen fussy two-piece swimsuit that modestly covers the navel featured in *The Draper of Australasia* with Stafford's napkin wrap bikini created five years earlier (Figure 6.10), it is evident the former is catering to a wearer who may not even go to the beach or go swimming. The designs are feminine and frilly but impractical, whereas the Stafford bikini is an innovative cut, but above all is practical for swimming at a beach. Moreover, Stafford's design moves beyond the structured cut associated with lingerie construction to produce a natural shape, foregrounding the less structured bikinis of later decades.

On the other side of the world, in another country also not traditionally associated with fashion, Lea and Armin Gottlieb founded the Gottex label in Israel in 1956. Unlike the Australian approach to swimwear design which was driven by a beach culture and a need for functional, hardwearing swimsuits, Gottex targeted the luxury market and 'staged shows based on the haute couture format' (Schoumann 2006: 9). Continuing the trend in luxury resort collections that started with beach pajamas in the 1920s, and extended by Jacques Heim who pioneered the pareo and sarong styles in complementary fabrics to the label's swimsuit designs from the early 1930s, Gottex created elegant

Figure 6.10 Paula Stafford Napkin Wrap Bikini, 1950. State Library of Queensland.

swimwear and ensembles that were not for the average beachgoer, and from the 1950s they were worn by style icons such as Grace Kelly and Jackie Kennedy. These women were not usually snapped by photographers dressed only in swimsuits, and continued a growing trend for resort wear pieces that could move from the pool/beach to the lounge. Significantly, the client base now included former film stars and presidents' wives, signposting the focus on a democratic pool of beauties chosen from a new aristocracy.

It was the decade when 'swimwear now expressed geography as well as the clothing and model and the added attribution of site' and 'confirmed that travel was an intrinsic part of the post-war adventure with the sea and swimming' (Martin and Koda 1990: 105). Fashion photographers including Norman Parkinson and Louise Dahl-Wolfe travelled to exotic locations capturing the swimsuit in its perfect habitat—tropical beaches. Australia was one of these destinations with its - its stunning beaches and local inhabitants such as surf lifesavers and surfers—ideal accessories for a fashion shoot. In 1959, *Vogue* Australia was launched, and 'no longer tied to English *Vogue* as a double number'. Rosemary Cooper, the first editor reported, 'From this issue onwards it is an edition of *Vogue* in its own right', proudly noting, 'There are now four *Vogues*. American *Vogue*, English *Vogue*, French *Vogue* and *Vogue* Australia' (Cooper 1959). In a special issue about *Vogue* in *Fashion Theory: The Journal of Dress, Body & Culture* in 2006, *Vogue* Australia was omitted from the *Vogue* timelines, just as the Australian swimsuit is often overlooked or barely mentioned in histories of swimwear. Although not recognized or part of the central fashion hubs, the introduction of *Vogue* Australia preceded Italian *Vogue* (1964), and this title existed decades before the launch of other national publications, reinforcing the drive Australians have to interpret concepts gleaned from Europe and the United States, and an ambition to transmit ideas from the periphery to centre.

In the first issue, one of the fashion spreads was swimwear photographed by Helmut Newton titled 'Early Beach Appearances', a reference to the first beach experience of the season. It marks a time when there was a conservatism in fashion photography and models were modestly captured in lady-like poses (Goatly 1999: 129). As a result, photos were elegant and suitably demure. The feature image (Figure 6.11) has the model immersed to the knee in an expanse of water with delicate ripples circling her lithe frame. There is a sense of space and no specific geographic location. Unlike photographers who travelled to Australia to infuse fashion shoots with beach backdrops, Newton captures Janice Wakeley surrounded by water, suggesting Australia's island status and distance from the rest of the world.

By the late 1950s and 1960s, swimsuit textiles were dominated by nylon and polyester yarns. These synthetic yarns are produced from chemicals obtained from petroleum and branded under various trade names such as bri-nylon, Celon, Perlon (nylon), and Terylene and Dacron (polyester) to name a few. In common, all these fabrics are strong, easy to wash and quick drying. The popular Helanca (Swiss) was produced in either nylon or polyester yarn and bulked to breathe and handle like a natural fibre, plus it could be successfully dyed and printed. Another advantage was Helanca fabrics stretched with the body, then 'returned permanently to shape due to the inbuilt nature

Figure 6.11 *Vogue* Australia—'Beach Appearances', Spring/Summer 1959. The Newton Estate.

of the stretch', and could be 'combined with natural fibres or different synthetics to produce a better texture and performance'. Helanca was manufactured in Australia under license by B.L.B. Corporation in Bendigo Victoria, and one of its best applications was in swimsuits (*The Draper of Australasia* 1960). Thus, local production ensured labels including Watersun and Scamp could compete with big American companies that had access to an extensive range of textiles.

The Youthquake movement in the 1960s pushed traditional boundaries, and the entire structure of the fashion system was challenged from the high street. The influence of Parisian couturiers was weakened by the vibrant boutique businesses on London's Carnaby Street and Kings Road. The new styles were youthful and exciting, and popularized by Mary Quant, whose aim was to produce 'clothes for ordinary girls like herself' (Steele 1997: 50). Targeting young, working-class girls as opposed to the social elite, Quant's ready-to-wear collections which included miniskirts for leggy, boyish London girls were the antithesis of haute couture. The mini, with its emphasis on the body itself, challenged the fashion aesthetic that favoured the elegant, sophisticated woman and a rigidly structured silhouette engineered with complex undergarments. The result was similar to the impact of the 1920s swimsuit, in that women were freed and enslaved simultaneously by the stark exposure of their bodies. It heralded a new social order in which physical beauty outranked the blueblood, and models such as Twiggy and Jean Shrimpton were representative of a new breed who influenced what clothes and body type were fashionable. The swimsuit had set the scene at the beach—now the mini was taking it to the streets.

Americans finally adopted the bikini and one-piece swimsuits became less structured, although still had built-up cups and modestly cut leglines. Watersun developed its own version, the 'Unquestionable Bra' which moulded to give a more natural bustline than its offshore competitors. However, Rudi Gernreich led the deconstruction of the swimsuit from 1952 when he designed the first bra-free swimsuit and continued over the ensuing years to produce fashion-forward swimsuit designs for Westwood Knitting Mills. Gernreich devoted 'much of his time freeing women from re-straining clothes' (Moffitt, Claxton, and Luther 1999: 15), and created innovative and clever swimsuit collections which embodied a challenging aesthetic underpinned by a lack of formality, stiffness or extravagance (Felderer 2001: 14). Unfortunately, he is most remembered for the scandalous Monokini (1964) rather than his innovation firsts which include the soft transparent bra marketed as the 'no-Bra' bra, designer jeans, the unisex look and men's underwear designed for women (Moffitt, Claxton, and Luther 1999: 9).

Gernreich understood the importance of media representation—'get the editorial first and the stores and customers will follow' (ibid. 15). It was an edict Paula Stafford adopted using beautiful girls, Gold Coast beaches and daring innovative bikinis to promote her label. In the 1960s, Stafford staged a number of fashion shows both locally and internationally, participated in Australia's trade promotions in Asia, the United States and Europe, and exported her products to Hong Kong, the United Kingdom and the United States. At home, her popular Bikini Bar on Cavill Avenue was a drawcard and hotspot for international celebrities, and included among her clients were Ann Margaret, the princess of Thailand and Sammy Davis Jr. Likewise, Watersun established a strong presence, promoting its swimwear through ingenious public relations exercises such as presenting entertainer Eartha Kitt with a signature bri-nylon animal print swimsuit that 'Miss Kitt was so delighted by . . . she could not wait to try it on' (The Draper of Australasia 1963). The swimsuit and celebrity entertainer moved into a new and equally successful stage in this decade, continuing the fusion between fashion and the entertainment industries.

At this time, the swimsuit was closely associated with the beach movie and teenage stars such as Sandra Dee, who played a wholesome Californian girl named Gidget. Her summer adventures with surfer-boy love interests saw the casts attired almost entirely in beachwear and acquainted conservative moviegoers with the bikini. Teenage beach blanket movies were not the only genre Hollywood used to expose and naturalize actors' bodies and the swimsuit on the big screen. The Bond girl appeared in a swimsuit in the 1962 James Bond 007 film Dr No, with Ursula Andress as Honeychile 'Honey' Ryder, complete with a hunting knife reminiscent of Kellerman as a swashbuckling heroine fifty years earlier. The Australian beach and bikini girls also made it to cinemas in *They're a Weird Mob* (1966) (Chiari and Powell 2003). 'A time capsule of the period', the movie 'successfully represents Aussie workers—or at least . . . a very appealing facsimile, a bunch of builders who come across as pretty good blokes' (Hourigan 2008). The story explores the experience of newly-arrived European immigrants and the perceived role of women in Australian society. Along with notable tourism icon Sydney Harbour Bridge are scenes of Bondi Beach which provide an interesting snapshot of beach fashion. One of the characters, Judith Arthy, wears an unstructured bikini that is 'possibly the briefest seen in mainstream cinema at this time' (Cockington 2004: 12), and, together with other shots showing a number of girls in similar styles, builds a picture of the Australian beach as home to a relaxed informality and less conservative swimsuit styles. Notably, Arthy's beach bag is a Qantas airline travel bag featuring the iconic flying kangaroo logo, marking a new era when not just the wealthy travelled overseas. While the swimsuits featured in this movie are brief and appear to be made in the natural cottons favoured by Paula Stafford, Maglia, a Melbourne-based swimwear company, was creating designs in bri-nylon and tapped into an international trend for geometrics influenced by Op Art. *Vogue* Australia readers are encouraged to 'escape to adventure in Maglia' (Maglia 1966).

Brian Rochford was one of the new breed of Australian designers catering to the youth market of the 1960s with swimwear label Splash Out and ready-to-wear label Dolly Gear. Rochford acknowledged the influence of Carnaby Street on his early collections, and, like Gernreich, was eager to deconstruct the swimsuit, removing its constraining inner construction. While Speedo worked with DuPont in this decade to create technologically advanced, performance-enhancing textiles for competition swimwear, Rochford went further, closely collaborating with DuPont and Heathcote Textiles in Melbourne to create lightweight Lycra fabrics for fashion swimwear. Lycra is the brand name, once owned by DuPont, that is now Invista, and generically known as elastane or spandex, and is part of the elastomeric family of stretch fibres. It is always blended with other fibres and recognized for its strength and ability to contour and shape to the body. Although invented in 1958, issues with stabilizing fabrics containing Lycra were not resolved until the early 1970s. Rochford recalls laying out a length of fabric and leaving it overnight, only to find that it had shrunk back by 50 per cent in the morning; part of his collaboration with DuPont entailed solving this problem. It took years to find a way to lay the fabric by machine, one that had to be created especially for Lycra in the company's cutting room. 'Tables were widened and cutting was a whole new ballgame' (Rochford 2009). Moreover, Lycra fabrics require a special machine foot to feed the fabric through the sewing machine without dragging or stretching the fabric, and working with his production manager, Rochford developed a foot for this purpose.

Rochford's vision was to thread form to function to create youthful, edgy swimsuits, which were fashion garments with the added ability to withstand high usage, an ethos adopted by a number of enduring Australian swimwear companies established at this time. Warren and Vicky McKinney started Sunseeker, a Western Australian-based company, in

1970 after returning from a sailing holiday in the Caribbean. The swimsuit designs were patterned on the idea of a beach lifestyle and having fun, a philosophy Paula Stafford stitched into the bikini from the 1940s. Starting with crocheted bikini designs, the label evolved to produce distinctively clean, sharp designs primarily manufactured in imported Italian textiles developed exclusively for the company. Sunseeker became a dominant brand nationally over the next twenty years and continues in the 2000s as part of the Skye Group. Seafolly, currently one of Australia's largest swimwear companies with a major export market, was launched in 1975. Similarly, its designs focus on the beach lifestyle, practical separates and bold prints. Seafolly, Sunseeker and Rochford built on a tradition started by knitting mills in the 1920s and 1930s, continued by Paula Stafford, Watersun and Maglia, to name a few, from the 1940s and 1950s, and all reflect a uniquely Australian approach to swimwear fused to the beach and a holiday lifestyle.

By the early 1970s, there was a diversity of styles available in both prints and plains for the one-piece and the bikini. The lean, leggy body aesthetic with swimsuits now stripped of internal structuring reduced the potential to create an illusion of well-proportioned body dimensions. This new minimalism led to more intensive exercise and dieting regimes than seen in previous decades: 'Suddenly, discipline and artistry were no longer bad words when it came to preparing the body for public display' (Lenček and Bosker 1989: 131). These athletic women regularly participated in sports such as swimming and gymnastics, clothed in swimsuits that provided a freedom of movement that men had benefited from since the 1930s. Martin and Koda (1990: 131) suggest that in the 1970s 'women too expressed themselves as the jocks men had long been'. Figure 6.12, Maglia's 'Seeing is Believing' advertisement in *Vogue* Australia, illustrates the choice of styles that included bandeau and triangle bikini tops, bikini bottoms with different treatments and widths, sleek maillots and a 'clever swimdress'. In this graphic scene, the models are indeed enjoying the activities associated with blokes—fishing, drinking beer and reading the newspaper; the photographer capturing the posing models is also female, cementing the idea of an egalitarian society suited to the swimsuit, a quintessentially democratic garment.

Prue Acton, one of Australia's new generation of designers, developed a reputation for creating 'smart outfits, in simple styles, for the average working girl' (Maynard 2000: 56). Known for her sense of fun and lack of Parisian formality, Acton created resort wear that captured the holiday spirit associated with an Australianness already built in to local swimwear designers' collections. Similarly, she followed the well-established design approach to resort dressing which included matching cover-ups and dramatic, bold prints. Textiles included Filamel jersey, a fine antistatic tricot often used for lingerie such as slips, and added a new accent to an already flourishing swimwear industry. Acton is recognized as the first 'Australian designer to export internationally on a regular basis' (Mackay 1984: 68; Maynard 2000); however, this claim reveals a lack of recognition for Australian swimwear designers and companies including Stafford, Watersun and Speedo that had successfully exported their products for decades, and highlights how swimwear was treated as a bit player in the fashion industry.

Figure 6.12 *Vogue* Australia—'Maglia', October 1972.

One of Australia's fashion forward swimsuit designers in the 1970s was Robin Garland, a former international model, who created minimalist swimsuit designs for those with well-proportioned bodies. Joel describes her designs as 'racy', and although David Jones buyers had reservations due to their miniscule size, they 'sold like hot cakes' (Joel 1998: 207). 'Vogue *Australia: 50 years of Australian Style*' (2009) features Garland's iconic bikinis with the word *Bondi* tantalizingly positioned as a placement print on the bottoms to mark the 1970s fashion plates in the book. No other words are needed. The toned models, branded by Australia's iconic beach, ensure everyone knows the place to be seen and what to wear. The original exposure in *Vogue* Australia (1974) was accompanied by text that suggested the potency of this bikini design (on the right body): 'Time for sun, for baring the body in a blissful new bikini, shaping up that body, making it lithe and slender . . . You'll find inspiration right here. Robin Garland's chauvinistic silk cotton knit bikinis' (*Vogue* Australia 1974: 19).

Garland received regular editorial in *Vogue*, as well as a special citation for swimwear in the David Jones Awards for Fashion Excellence. By mid-decade the company was exporting to 'Europe and mini-Europe—Nouméa and the New Hebrides' (*Vogue* Australia, August 1976), joining a growing number of Australian swimwear companies selling internationally. Innovations such as the nappy bikini, a simplified version of the style popularized by Paula Stafford in the 1950s, and a reputation for using Italian fabrics and unique prints made Garland an important contributor to the Australian swimwear industry at this time. Figure 6.13 illustrates how itsy bitsy a Garland bikini could be, and, shadowed by a male clown with ruffled collar and full-body black second-skin costume, the spectacle and theatricality of the barely dressed body are emphasized.

Although Speedo was principally focused on performance swimwear, the company also ventured into fashion swimwear, creating the Minimates line from 1966–1980. Originally, the co-coordinated garments, one-piece swimsuits, bikinis, suncovers, patio pants, shifts and caftans were produced in nylon tricot, the fabric used for Speedo's performance swimwear, with later collections produced in bri-nylon. Advertisements stated, 'First came the sun, then Speedo and you' (David Jones Catalogue 1972), and although the styling was conservative compared to Garland's designs, the cuts were flattering and well-suited to the mature wearer and mass market. The Speedo racer maillot did make an appearance in fashion spreads in the United States and Australia due to the fitness craze and growing popularity of sportswear-inspired styling, and 'the Speedo hat for competition swimming moved fleetingly into high fashion' (Probert 1981: 57). In May 1978, *Vogue* reported the Speedo swim cap 'the snuggest, sleekest' and 'a real find . . .

Figure 6.13 Robin Garland bikini, *Vogue* Australia, August 1976. David Jones Limited.

racers wear them', and in *Vogue* Australia (September 1974), the Speedo racer-style one-piece maillot was fashioned as 'swim-skins with sophisticated styling'.

Vogue Australia (December 1978) tells its readers, 'Legs on show. Longer because maillots, sliced high extend to the thigh', and encourages them to firm flabby thighs with tennis, dancing, swimming or 'bare your feet and walk off thickening ankles'. Consequently, athleticism and the fitness craze reached a fever pitch. Women endeavoured to comply and tone notoriously difficult body parts—the upper thighs, buttocks and high hip—and 'for those who could wear it, the thigh-high swimsuit of the 1970s became an instant badge of superiority, telegramming the victory of machine over flesh' (Lenček and Bosker 1989: 131). Sport, the swimsuit and fashion became inextricably interwoven and the swimsuit could double as a leotard. *Vogue* Australia (August 1979) featured a Rochford strapless maillot with 'lots of shoulder . . . newsy ruffle trim around the top and high-cut on the legs' and, combined with tennis shoes and socks, accompanied by a male model wearing tennis clothes, reinforced the flexibility of the swimsuit to move beyond the beach to other recreational spaces.

At the cinema, the Australian beach movie *Puberty Blues* made its debut in 1981 (Kelly et al. 2003). With none of the glamour of the glossy Californian Malibu set, this gritty drama showed an aspect of Australian surf culture—a male chauvinism that valued girls merely as spectators to their surfing pursuits or for sex in the back of a panel van. Girls who wanted to surf were jeered at and discouraged, not dissimilar to the treatment of female surfers in the real world at this time. The main characters, Debbie and Sue, are keen to join the local Greenhill Gang at Cronulla Beach on Sydney's south side. From their journey as losers to popularity as beach babes to Debbie's transition to a competent surfer, the audience experiences a raw insight into a less mythic Australian masculinity and the drive of some Australian women to challenge the status quo. Classic scenes such as that shown in Figure 6.14 reveal a sizzling relationship with the

Figure 6.14   Film still from *Puberty Blues*, 1981. Bruce Beresford.

sun, as the girls, oiled up, expose as much as possible in minimalist bikinis to ensure a premium suntan, and in relation to the Greenhill Gang, a chance to attract the local surfer boys.

The swimsuit was now regularly featured in glossy fashion spreads. London-based American designer Liza Bruce created streamlined maillots in new improved Lycra and nylon synthetics that hugged the body. Bruce's swimsuit collections focused on ' "the body" as the basis of the emancipated wardrobe of the eighties', and Bruce was determined to portray 'women . . . as strong, athletic, emancipated and sensual' (Liza Bruce Biography). Bodybuilder Lisa Lyon embodied this strength and, photographed by Robert Mapplethorpe (who, together with Bruce Weber, was known for creating erotic images of men) in Liza Bruce swimsuits, marked an increasing obsession with fitness and muscularity for women. Weber captured a model wearing a Bruce asymmetric maillot for British *Vogue* in 1980, and, flanked by bronzed Bondi surf lifesavers, fashioned a link between physical fitness, Australian beach culture and the swimsuit for international readers. In New York, Norma Kamali was also making her mark with 'sports-swimwear . . . her vision of gym fanatic, boxer and swimming pool attendant chic . . . set the pace for swimwear design' (Kennedy 2007: 240).

The 1980s saw a marked increase in the number of luxury brands creating swimwear and resort wear collections, and Killoren Bensimon reports that 'it was possible to sunbathe in Dior, Chanel, Versace or Geoffrey Beene' (Killoren Bensimon 2006: 186). An advertisement for Dior swimwear in 1980 shows a model diving into a darkened space scattered with floating money, disconnecting her from typical tropical or watery associations. It does, however, explicitly locate the swimsuit as expensive and a luxury item that may or may not be worn at the beach. She wears a diamond bracelet and earrings; her hair is sleek and coiffed. The wearer is asked to 'profit from the perfect fit of the swimwear from the Christian Dior collection' (*Vogue* 1980)—at a price of course—with the company hoping to profit from the investment in a luxury product that, when stripped of its accessories, was essentially a simple maillot design.

Patrick Russell, *Vogue* Australia's creative director, recalls that on his return to Australia from Paris he found the light harsh and the cityscapes drab. Russell realized that 'the real truth of Australia—the beach, the Speedos, the minimalism, that's what they all understand . . . I can talk to them via the beach . . . from then on I could help unfold a landscape' (Clements and Tulloch 2009: 92). In the fashion spread *Ripper Looks*, Russell continues a tradition of using local surfers as extras in fashion shoots, and notes that, 'it was easy and fun. It wasn't dark and forbidden and hidden. There was never anything sinister about those boys. They were like a glass of cold water on a hot day' (ibid.). Flanked by surfers, the model wears a body-conscious maillot with T-shirt under which reflects the swimsuit's versatility. It could be worn when the wearer 'uses the beach as an outdoor gym to hop, run, play beach ball or walk along the sand' (*Vogue* Australia 1983). Australia made the cover of British *Vogue* in July 1980 in the 'Inside Australia: Fashion for the GREAT OUTDOORS and Travellers' Guide'. The fresh-faced cover model in mosquito-netting hat and summery, white blouse encapsulates 'Vogue's

Eye View' which includes the outback and the beach when the team travels 'upside down to the sun in Australia' (A Month of Sundays 1980). It would seem British *Vogue* shared Russell's vision with *Coastal Stripping* and *Beauty and the Beach Boys—Bondi* (British *Vogue* 1980).

Swimsuit fashion-spreads split into two distinct narratives: inventive fantasies, often located on island paradises, and a continued emphasis on the sporty energetic angle. And just as the Speedo swim cap was a popular fashion accessory in the 1970s, so too the Speedo maillot was splashed onto the fashion pages of *Vogue* Australia with the accompanying caption, 'Swimwear patterned for the all-Australian girl' (*Vogue* Australia 1986). The model, caught mid air in an athletic jump with exotic palm trees as a backdrop, exudes health and agility. Other swimsuits in this spread foreground the swimsuit's functional athletic qualities with captions such as 'muscle-back', 'the understatement' and the bikini makes the cut—'but the attitude is sporty'. In the September 1989 issue, this trend continues with 'Swim'—'If you have one outfit this summer, what would it be? Swimwear! You wouldn't be an Aussie without a Cossie' (*Vogue* Australia 1989: 221). Russell's vision of Australia as a land of sun, sand and water regularly filters into the magazine's fashion aesthetic and features locally produced swimsuits designed by established and emergent companies such as Seafolly, Sunseeker and Jets.

By the 1980s, Rochford was renowned as 'Mr Swimsuit' and the 'King of Swim' and had won a number of awards for fashion excellence. He was recognized for introducing the soft bra top and the concept of bikini separates, ideal as few women fit the standard bust/waist/hip proportions used in clothing manufacture. This purchasing flexibility ensured a broad cross-section of girls and women, from size 8 to size 16, could wear a Rochford swimsuit. Additionally, the collections were in line with general fashion trends, offering a plethora of styles in both one- and two-piece designs. According to Rochford, a core influence was the styles selected by buyers and consumers, ensuring his designs had a commercial edge. Promotional campaigns were fresh and fun, and the personalized messages from Brian became a trademark and highly successful method of branding the company's products (Figure 6.15). Rochford believes Australians are leaders in swimsuit design because it is a form of fashion where everything was experimental and new—so there was nothing to copy. There is a belief that Australian swimwear is competitive because it is shaped by a beach culture, and equally this lifestyle has been a tool to sell Australian swimwear around the globe.

Australian fashion designers now carved a niche internationally (from kitsch to couture), with designs regularly adorned with Australian motifs including icons such as the Sydney Harbour Bridge and Bondi Beach (Ken Done), as well as flora and fauna. Particularly memorable was Jenny Kee's koala knit jumper worn by Princess Diana in 1982. According to Craik, the use of Australiana 'takes art and design out of the rarefied environment of the cultural elite and gives it circulation among a wider public', thus the wearer 'dons a striking symbol of national identity and cultural difference' (Craik 2009: 432). Olivia Newton-John sold this national identity, exposing the American market to

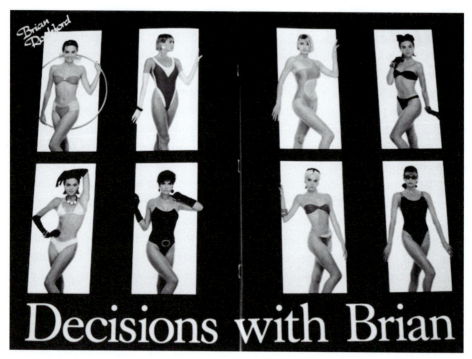

Figure 6.15   Brian Rochford Advertisement, 'Hero', September 1986. Brian Rochford. Photograph of magazine by Karri Hartley.

designs that were boldly Australian in Koala Blue Boutiques in Beverley Hills and Florida. In Sydney, creative partners Jenny Kee and Linda Jackson (later Bush Couture) founded an innovative boutique, Flamingo Park, creating colourful prints and knits that celebrated indigenous culture and the Australian landscape. Kee and Jackson travelled to Europe in 1977 to showcase their collection with Australian native flower themes. Anna Piaggi (Italian *Vogue*) described their designs as 'one of the most inventive "free" collections of fashion we have seen in recent times' (Joel 1998: 214). Significantly it is Kee's Opal prints that Karl Lagerfeld used for his first prêt-à-porter collection (spring/ summer 1983) for Chanel (Kee and Trenowith 2006: 226). In 1989, Kee collaborated with Speedo to create a swimwear range drawing on 'the colours and forms of Australian native plants and animals, the landscape, brilliant opals and the art of Aboriginal people' (*Vogue* Australia 1989), and demonstrated 'a new level of Australian confidence and pride' (Craik 2009: 434). Kee developed three-print stories including Barrier Reef, Waratah and Black Boys (the latter now known as Grass Trees). Local swimsuit designers did not follow this trend and the use of Australiana or Indigenous designs was not a regular feature, with Hawaiian flowers and African-inspired patterns a more likely choice for print designs (Figure 6.16). However, whether imprinted with Australian flora and fauna, or motifs from other cultures, in Australia, the swimsuit itself was communicating a sense of national identity and style.

Figure 6.16   Jenny Kee for Speedo: Waratah and Black Boys.
Vogue Australia, September 1989. Jenny Kee.

FASHION CASTS ITS NET

This chapter has so far traced the swimsuit through the twentieth century initially through trade journals, newspapers and fashion and women's magazines to describe how swimsuit styling, the designers, the photographers, editorial and advertisements contributed to narratives knitted to physical fitness, beach culture and the modern body. Significantly, the 1960s marked 'the growing autonomy of the fashion press and the dissolution of a singular Parisian fashion lead', a shift most closely associated with *Vogue* publications (Breward 2003: 122). These changes are pertinent to the tracking of the swimsuit and its independent development away from the traditional fashion hubs. *Vogue* (America 1892) had extended its reach through the introduction of national editions in Britain (1916) and France (1920), which was followed extraordinarily by Australia (1959) 'on the other side of the world' (Clements and Tulloch 2009: vi). This geographic reach illustrates 'the modern idea of fashion as a global phenomenon' (Breward 2003: 122), and presents an opportunity to investigate the role Australia has played in transmitting fashion ideas from the periphery to the centre.

In its first thirty years, *Vogue* Australia (1959) provided limited editorial for the swim-suit, and in Australia, early publications favoured American swimwear brands and more conservative Australian labels. Paula Stafford, for all her business success and publicity in popular media such as newspapers, is not featured. The first bikinis, included in the summer 1960 issue entitled titled, 'The Young Idea' and photographed by Helmut Newton, are modest 'daisy-splashed . . . rose-strewn' and produced by Ada of California. Newton captures an important aspect of the bikini, with one of the models shading her face from the sun with a book entitled titled *The Art of Spying*. Continuing the trend for less daring swimsuits, the late summer issue of the same year features designs by Rose Marie Reed (California) and Kay Hilvert (Sydney) that are technically closer to a two-piece (although just below the navel). Again, the swimsuits are 'beach flowerings . . . glorious blossom-ing . . . prettily frilled' (*Vogue* Australia 1960), diminishing any sense of youthful rebellion initially associated with the bikini. As the decade progressed, Maglia and Watersun were often featured, and by the 1970s, Robin Garland's designs were regular inclusions, in addition to occasional Jantzen and Speedo swimsuits. Spreads are aligned to summer, physical fitness, the beach and resort holidays. With headlines such as 'Sea Secrets', 'Summer Shadows', 'Making a Splash' and 'Built for Action', there is a simplicity to the underlying narrative. The 1980s continued these themes with 'Ripper Looks', 'Bold Lines', 'Freestyle Dressing', and 'Swim'. European brands made an appearance includ-ing Charles Jourdan, Gucci and Versace, alongside local labels Robin Garland, Seafolly, Brian Rochford and Jets. However, according to Rochford, his designs received regular editorial in popular rather than fashion publications, in particular, *Dolly*, *Cosmopolitan* and *Cleo*. Similarly, Paula Stafford and other contemporaries such as Sunseeker, who were successfully exporting Australian swimwear to international markets, were off the radar of magazines such as *Vogue* Australia.

International publications (*Vogue*, *Harper's Bazaar*) included iconic images of the swimsuit captured by photographers Norman Parkinson, Bruce Weber and Herb Ritts in particular. According to Martin and Koda (1990: 105), 'Exoticism inflected the settings of swimwear, with the airplane making Hawaii, Mexico, and the Caribbean accessible and thereby advancing a new geography of American swimwear', and to Australia, although not mentioned. The 1980s swimsuit embodied a freedom and raw energy expressed most visibly in Parkinson's 1982 photograph on a Barbados beach of a model in a sleek black-and-white zebra stripe maillot (Norma Kamali OMO), rolling blissfully in the sand beside an equally exuberant racehorse. Swimwear photography 'splashed with real-life wetness and youthful joie de vivre' (ibid. 116) encapsulated an aspect of modern life and an ever-important fashion niche connected to resort wear and leisure.

Grace Coddington, the creative director at *Vogue*, now immortalized in *The September Issue* (2009) documentary, is attributed with creating the 'Style Essay', a fashion nar-rative 'that is designed to generate a sense of surprise and glamour . . . framed as an epic visual fantasy . . . to captivate the reader by means of a story' (Angeletti and Oliva 2006: 263). By the 1990s, it was 'refined and perfected . . . influenced by the vision of each photographer' (ibid. 265), and the swimsuit rated inclusion. In a swimsuit spread titled 'Beyond the Beach,' readers are told: 'Designers have stretched the concept of the bathing suit so far that it now included pieces as sophisticated as evening dresses' (*Vogue* 1991). With references to the golden years of Hollywood, the styling is described as 'more refined than traditional maillots', and the voluptuous models attributed with 'star-level presence'. Urban landscapes and a distinctly American sensibility reinforce cultural associations with pin-up style glamour and poolside beauties, just as Kee's Australiana-print Speedo maillot set against white sands and blue sky evokes imaginings of Australia. Featuring designs by Norma Kamali OMO (On My Own), Karl Lagerfeld for Chanel and Moschino Mare, the swimsuits are sophisticated and have stretched the swimsuit to fit each brand's recognizable aesthetic and handwriting. For example, the Chanel swimsuit references the 1920s with a simple boy-leg styling and signature buttons and placement with a classic Chanel jacket. The accompanying text suggests Lagerfeld has crossed 'another boundary—with a great "little black dress" that's really a swimsuit' (ibid.).

Brian Rochford's black streamlined maillot and a Speedo performance swimsuit are given fashion status in *Vogue* beyond the beach and the Olympic pool. A British *Vogue* fashion spread photographed by Patrick Demarchelier and entitled 'Blue Belles' includes a Speedo swimsuit described as 'an intense turquoise' combined with an extravagant 'Esther Williams-style swimming cap . . . topped with silk rose, sequins and raffia' created by haute couture milliner Stephen Jones. The racer-style maillot's value is further enhanced by a glamorous description as 'Cascades of scintillating watercolour caught in a Hollywood heat wave' (British *Vogue* 1990). Similarly, Brian Rochford's sleek black maillot, shot at Quay West apartments Sydney, is accessorized with a Chanel belt (price on application), and the model is stretched to create a columnar shape that mimics the glossy architectural background, transmuting the meaning of an Australian swimsuit, reshaped to fit glossy fashion magazine glamour (*Vogue* Australia 1992).

Fashion designers played with the swimsuit in the 1990s, and it was 'used by haute couture as a less serious exercise' (Alac 2002: 191). In 1996, Chanel created retro one- and two-piece swimsuits with pearl necklace prints, an ironic postmodern reference to Coco Chanel's early faux jewellery, and an eyepatch bikini that made no attempt to be a classic Chanel garment. The novel product placement of the distinctive interlocking C logo on two eye-catching discs that barely cover the nipples parodies the swimsuit's function and distances it from a sporty aesthetic, repositioning it as whimsical. Similarly, an Yves Saint Laurent 1999 wedding bikini festooned with flowers mocks traditional bridal attire, symbolically sexualizing the bride stripped bare. And Grace Coddington (photographed by Herb Ritts) sets the bikini adrift in 1996 with a model atop a raft in a pale pink bikini clasping a pink poodle, accompanied by Louis Vuitton luggage with a ragged 'Help' flag raised (*Vogue* 1996). Designers such as Versace, Gucci and Hermès featured exotic swimwear and resort wear collections that focused on luxury, glittering details and sequined excess destined for poolside glamour and targeting an elite clientele.

Alongside the European luxe swimsuit and resort wear collections, fitness and sport continued to influence how the swimsuit was styled in fashion magazines. In a 1991 fitness special, readers are informed, 'Fitness wear was made for honed bodies of the overexercised generation. Now there's only one catch: in order to wear her wardrobe, a woman can't stop exercising' (*Vogue* 1991: 276). The article tracks the fashionable swimsuit's evolution from weighty wool to high-tech second skin, its cross-breeding with sportswear, underwear and exercise wear, resulting in the interchangeable fashions of the 1990s. The prediction is, 'It may be that the sports enthusiast will emerge as fashion's true avant-garde' (ibid.). In Australia, 'the strength and endurance (not to mention the bodies) of sporting heroes such as the Iron Men and surf lifesavers' frame the swimsuit feature and the way Australians 'look at fitness'. Titled 'Out in Front' (*Vogue* Australia 1993), it depicts an energetic slice of beach life interspersed with Nippers (junior lifesavers who begin training from as young as four years old) and fashion models wearing one- and two-piece swimsuits designed by Speedo and Brian Rochford. 'Swimsuits with stamina' clearly defines an essential ingredient for the Australian surf and for a nation culturally knitted to the beach.

US *Vogue* featured Speedo's streamlined athletic maillots in May 1995. The catsuit styles are similar to the Speedo S2000 worn by racers at the 1992 Olympics, and the caption, 'Built for Speed', whether intentionally or not, is reminiscent of the original 1929 Speedo design and motto: Speed on your Speedos. The editorial highlights the significance of performance swimwear to the elite athlete as well as wearers intent on fashioning a sporty physique. The emphasis is athleticism 'that can also be sexy', something Australians had long realized. These new-to-fashion swimsuits, in quick drying textiles that sculpted to the body, could be worn under skirts, shorts or pants and were now seen thanks to fashion's gatekeepers as a stylish fusion of performance swimwear and fashion.

While established Australian swimwear brands Brian Rochford, Sunseeker and Seafolly continued to expand their market share in the 1990s, newcomer Zimmermann combined fashion-forward swimwear and resort wear in striking colours and prints for local and international markets. The Zimmermann philosophy was affordable fast fashion with Nicky Zimmermann commenting, 'We don't create garments for you to have for ten years' (Coffey 1996), a sensible edict for swimsuits, considering their short life spans. Anthea Loucas reported that its designs were 'sassy and stylish' featuring 'graphic prints and risqué cut-away designs . . . illustrating that a swimsuit could be more than a pair of Speedos'. For Zimmermann, 'We just never understood why swimsuits and fashion had to be exclusive' (Loucas 2003), and in this decade, the swimsuit was in tune with seasonal trends, colours, patterns and prints with styling not restricted to one cut. Bikinis, one-pieces, thongs and boy-legs were all fashionable, inspired by anything from Hollywood glamour to grunge and retro-hippie. Fashion cast its net and the swimsuit in all its forms, from simple Speedos to an intricately pieced and printed Zimmermann, meshed and cross-fertilized. And, when the swimsuit returned to the 'bare essentials' (*Vogue* Australia 1996), it is a Zimmermann bikini that embodies an Australian luxe tied to a simplicity and purity of line and fittingly worn by Sarah O'Hare, an iconic Australian fashion and swimsuit model.

The year 1995 marks the inaugural Mercedes Australian Fashion Week (MAFW) in Sydney and a fresh approach to promoting Australian designers locally and internationally. Although a young event, it has proved successful. According to fashion journalist for *The Times* Lisa Armstrong, Australian fashion weeks are 'sexy and commercial' attracting a number of international buyers (2004). Together with a number of designers who have successfully grown their businesses and achieved international recognition (Collette Dinnigan, Easton Pearson, Akira Isogawa), Zimmermann has showcased its collections at MAFW since its inception and as a result has been picked up by Harvey Nichols department stores in the United Kingdom (Loucas 2003). By 2000, the company's collections were bought by all major US department stores including Saks Fifth Avenue, Bergdorf Goodman and Bloomingdales, and also included in the Victoria's Secret catalogue. Moreover, the label not only made significant inroads into international high-end and popular retail markets, but it also gained exposure in fashion magazines such as British and US *Vogue* and *Elle*. 'Australian Fashion Week proved a defining moment for Zimmermann', providing a platform to establish credibility and access to international buyers and to establish a strong foothold in the fashion industry [Austrade (Australian Trade Commission) 2003]. What set Zimmermann apart from a number of already successful swimwear companies at this time was the label's ability to blend the concept of Australian swimwear as a lifestyle product with a more European approach to swimwear that positions it as a luxe fashion product and the sharp American sportswear aesthetic popularized by Norma Kamali's OMO label from the late 1970s. As a result of Zimmermann's newsworthy shows, inclusion in international fashion magazines and a successful contemporary business model, swimwear collections have come to play a significant role in Australian fashion weeks.

Brazil added a new voice to swimsuit design in this decade and, like Australia, has built a reputation on a sunny, relaxed lifestyle and beaches teeming with beautiful women, presumably with large buttocks and small pert breasts, wearing daring Tangas teamed with skimpy triangle bikini tops. (This contrasts with the sporty, athletic the sporty, athletic girls on Australian beaches, who wear slightly less revealing bikinis.) Similarly, São Paulo's first fashion week took place in 1996. According to Newbery (2007: 73), ' "lifestyle" of the country sells', and both Brazil and Australia have used this as a tool to increase global exposure as homes to competitive swimwear designers and manufacturers. Moreover, both countries have a reputation for producing highly successful fashion and swimwear models (Brazil: Giselle Bündchen, Mariana Weickert, Isabeli Fontana; Australia: Elle Macpherson, Sarah O'Hare, Miranda Kerr) who transitioned to successful international careers, reinforcing the concept of a geographic pooling of genetically beautiful women. However, unlike Australia, the Brazilian textile industry is substantial, 'with the world's sixth-largest textile plant capacity . . . second place in the global ranking of denim producers . . . third in knitted fabrics' (Da Silva 2006: 122), thus it represents a different model of production.

Australian swimwear designers have consistently worked towards producing swim-suits that blend function and innovative design to create fashion swimwear for the beach and pool. Kennedy (2007: 276) notes that Australian designers 'have to keep it fresh and new for Australian women, who wear and buy swimwear far more than their Eu-ropean counterparts', adding that the 'Australian edge' is less fussy. Brazilian swimwear companies include Rosa Chá, Poco Pana, Água de Coco and Cia. Marítima represent an alternative view with more extreme cuts, ruffles and skirted briefs, as well as a 'trend for jewellery trinkets' such as 'good-luck charms and friendship ribbons attached to the side of Tanga briefs or between the breasts on a triangle bra' (ibid. 274). What this illus-trates is how fashion is shaped by national markets and then sold on to global wearers.

Australia and Brazil, remote from the fashion hubs of Europe and the United States, have built national identities and fashion narratives underpinned by beautiful women and men in swimsuits enjoying a lifestyle that is tropical, exotic and always on holiday. This story has played a part in Australian and Brazilian designers establishing a foot-hold in an increasingly saturated market. Zimmermann built its reputation as born and bred in Sydney at Bondi Beach and similarly, brands such as Rosa Chá are associated with Rio de Janeiro and Copacabana Beach. Amir Slama, (designer/owner of Rosa Chá) stated in an interview with WGSN (the trend analysis and news service for the fashion in-dustry) that the main competitors were likely to come from Australia due to a similar cli-mate and lifestyle, and mentioned Zimmermann as a significant threat (Hudson 2003). Marketing their collections globally, and being stocked in local and international holiday hotspots, have given these companies a competitive advantage connected to place and ideas such as, 'If Sydney was personified, she'd be bronzed, brazen and almost certainly wearing a Zimmermann bikini' (Loucas 2003). Claims such as 'Ipanema beach is the bikini's Promised Land . . . Today if you think of Brazilian women you think of the bikini' (Knechtel 2010) have added to the mythology. Australian swimsuits represent an atti-tude and lifestyle, and Nicole Zimmermann explains, 'In Australia there's not such a dif-ferentiation between swimwear and clothing. You're in your costume all the time'; she continues, 'The swimsuit can be worn either under a dress or sarong at restaurants and bars' (WGSN 2000). Similarly, Brazilian fashion and swimwear model Lays da Silva re-ports she has over 100 bikinis, and the bikini is an important garment in her everyday wardrobe. The swimsuit is a specialized product and international buyers look to these countries for future trends.

A core difference is that Australia has been designing and manufacturing swimwear since the modern swimsuit's inception in the early twentieth century. Companies such as Speedo, Quiksilver, Billabong, Seafolly and Zimmermann foreground a diversity of ap-proaches to swimwear design, target markets, business size and manufacturing that is underpinned by an ability to embed design innovation and creativity together with sport and lifestyle products closely associated with Australia. Brazil is a textile industry pow-erhouse and has in recent times tapped into the swimwear industry successfully, and, like China and India, cannot be discounted as purely a source of mass-produced goods and textiles. According to the president of the Brazilian Textile and Apparel Industry

Association (ABIT), the local industry 'is selling style with a national brand included'. Moreover, Brazilian swimwear and lingerie has a 'sensuousness built-in' that has proved popular globally (Da Silva 2006: 126) and reflects Brazil's drive to be recognised as a country full of innovators as well as producers. Just as high street designers in the 1960s challenged the supremacy of Parisian fashion, countries on the periphery (such as Australia and Brazil) are now making a significant contribution to a globalized fashion industry, competing with European and US counterparts.

DESIGNED IN AUSTRALIA—MADE HERE AND THERE

The 1990s was a watershed decade for the Australian fashion industry. The last quotas restricting imports were dismantled in 1993, thereby removing protection for locally produced fashion. As a result, a number of manufacturing companies either moved manufacturing offshore, closed down or merged (Kellock 2010: 246). Historically, the development of the Australian fashion industry has been hindered by 'a lack of sufficient capital to produce high-quality, competitively priced fashion textiles' and attempts to 'convince the world that its garments are of a high enough quality' (Maynard 2000: 86). This is illustrated by Australia's global reputation for producing the finest merino wool that has traditionally been exported with minimal processing to China (50 per cent) and to high-end textile companies in Europe, in particular Italy (Gattorna and Ellis 2008). Moreover, Australian fashion has had 'a low profile on the international scene' (van Acker and Craik 1996: 23), and Maynard (2000: 88) reports that 1996 was 'one of the worst clothing retail sales years on record'. The swimwear and surfwear industries offer an alternative and successful business model. Initially, knitting mills were able to produce high-quality wool swimsuits and by the 1960s and 1970s, local designers and companies actively contributed to developing specialized swimwear/surfwear fabrics (Speedo, Brian Rochford, Rip Curl). In addition, Australian companies sourced unique textiles from Europe, Italy in particular (Sunseeker, Robin Garland). Unlike other textile, clothing and footwear (TCF) sectors, locally and internationally produced fabrics did not prove as problematic for the swimwear and surfwear sectors. Manufacture has not been straightforward, and the unit cost for production (for all TCF sectors) is substantially higher in Australia than Asia. However, the patterns and construction of swimsuits and boardshorts are relatively simple, and as a result swimsuit designers encountered fewer technical issues than designers endeavouring to produce tailored high-end fashion.

From the late 1980s, sales figures for swimwear were buoyant and both Sunseeker and Brian Rochford had an estimated turnover of $15 million with exports to Europe and Asia. Rochford strongly supported the local fashion industry, manufacturing the bulk of his collections in the company's Chippendale factory in Sydney, and by the late 1990s had twenty-nine stores Australia-wide. Unfortunately, his determination to manufacture in Australia contributed to the business's demise in 1998. A decade later, Australian swimwear companies had developed a flexible and realistic approach to manufacture.

Established labels manufacture in China—for instance, Zimmermann has 60 per cent of its garments made in China, with plans to increase this percentage, while for Watersun, 99 per cent of swimwear production is offshore. Seafolly maintains 50 per cent of its production locally to supply a stock service in separates (bikini tops and bottoms), a mix that fluctuates and requires a fast turnaround. It is primarily 'smaller labels that typically don't have the volumes required to manufacture in China where minimum orders are higher' (Wells 2009) that are manufacturing locally. However, whether Australian-made or not, Australian swimwear and resort wear continues to go from strength to strength and is 'seen from Paris to Peru' and, significantly, is 'one of the few examples of where a product can affect Australia's "Country Brand"' (Harcourt 2009). According to Seafolly's managing director, Anthony Halas, unlike other fashion industry sectors, swimwear has proved 'recession proof' (ibid.). Reviewing the success of Australian swimwear from the early twentieth century, economic downturns and textile and manufacturing challenges have not deterred swimwear and surfwear designers and manufacturers from influencing and shaping the swimsuit to create a distinctly Australian niche in global fashion.

RIDING THE WAVE OF POPULARITY INTO THE TWENTY-FIRST CENTURY

The 2000s mark the swimsuit's full integration into the fashion system. The *Vogue Australia* November 2001 issue includes a cross-section of 'hot styles', covering all bases with both international and national swimwear designs—fashion, swimwear and surfwear brands. Laid out flat without the benefit of a model, atmospheric background or narrative layers, it is difficult to see any significant difference between the individual designs other than the obvious branding on the Versace bikini. (The company's Medusa head logo is recognizable to those in the fashion loop.) The bikinis present a range of styles with prices that range from AUD$60 for the Mambo design to AUD$685 for the Louis Vuitton, starkly delineating between the luxury and lifestyle products by retail price point. However, it is different to the clash 'between the worlds of elite couture and mass casual wear', exemplified by the 'competition from the US-driven leisure and sportswear markets such as Levis, Adidas, Nike, Reebok, Nautica, Guess Gap, Hilfiger and many others' that has led to a number of designers 'attaching their elite names to very ordinary clothing' (Taylor 2000: 131). When designers such as Rei Kawakubo of Comme des Garçons (CDG) collaborated with Speedo to create maillots with distinctive CDG graphic prints, it resulted in 'statement swimwear . . . that pleased the fashion world' (Cook 2007). Swimwear and resort fashion represent a specialized niche market that has long been shared by European fashion ateliers and specialist swimsuit designers in a number of countries including Australia. Moreover, 'resort is no longer a type of clothing . . . it's an aesthetic, or even a mood' (Milbank 2009: 40), one that transmutes the label of ordinary clothing, whether pinned out flat or as a second skin on a beautiful model.

Over the life of the swimsuit in the twentieth century, virtually all variations to the cut have been explored. Innumerable trick and trim design details and prints have been applied to one- and two-piece styles. There are now established patterns of design and manufacture catering to all market segments from couture to the high street, from performance sportswear to attitude (surf) swimwear. Viewing the market globally, swimsuit design is fractured by national spheres and specific categories of production. A cross-section of current brands that are exported and sold globally include the following:

Fashion Swimwear Brands

Europe	Eres, Huit, Liza Bruce, Gottex, La Perla, Princess Tam Tam
United States	Catalina, Tara Grinna, Miraclesuit Swimwear, Red Carter
Australia	Zimmermann, Seafolly, Jets, Tigerlily
South America	Rosa Cha, Cia. Marítima, Poco Pana

Fashion Brands that Added Swimwear to their Product Mix

Europe	Dior, Chanel, Dolce & Gabbana, Hermès, Pucci, Missoni, Versace, Louis Vuitton, Burberry, Diesel
United States	Norma Kamali, DKNY, Ralph Lauren, Michael Kors, Calvin Klein
Australia	Collette Dinnigan, Lisa Ho, Camilla and Marc

Surfwear Brands

Australia	Rip Curl, Mambo
United States	O'Neill, Body Glove
International	Quiksilver, Billabong (originally Australian)

Performance swimwear

Europe	Arena
United States	Tyr
International	Speedo (originally Australian)

Celebrity swimwear

United Kingdom	Elizabeth Hurley Beach
United States	Jessica Simpson Swimwear
Australia	Cozi by Jennifer

In a review of the global swimwear market, Newbery (2005: 50–54) suggests that 'brands matter to the swimwear market', and although the market is segmented into categories that define the swimwear as glamorous, sporty, beachy or purely functional, the ingredients are the same:

- fibres that stretch and control
- fabrics body shaping and aerodynamics
- style and cut
- the advertising offer, feel good, perform well

Newbury points out that it is a product group not dominated by a few multinationals and details three main approaches to the market:

1. Large companies with a stable of brands designed to appeal to different segments of the consumer market;
2. Companies driven by a single product and lifestyle ethic usually recent start-ups in the performance swimwear, surf, and water sports segments;
3. Smaller niche players (Newbery 2005: 58).

Examples of well-known large companies include LVMH (Moët Hennessy—Louis Vuitton) and the Gucci Group, which owns a large swag of luxury brands that include swimwear in their collections. Australia cannot claim any high-profile fashion conglomerates, rather companies such as The Apparel Group and The Just Group, which own a number of chainstore brands such as Peter Alexander (sleepwear) and Witchery, and swimwear is not a significant part of the mix. However, lifestyle companies have proved highly successful and include Quiksilver and Billabong (global leaders), creating surfwear that has leaked into the young urban market. Australia has also made its mark on performance swimwear with Speedo. In addition, a number of niche players such as Zimmermann and Seafolly continue to expand exports and dominate the local market. What the lists reveal is the designer fashion swimwear market is crowded. European and American designers and manufacturers still represent a powerful fashion industry force, with Australian and Brazilian companies edging into the market through sport and/or selling the nation's beach lifestyle. In effect, it is a snapshot of how globalization plays out in one sector of the fashion industry.

Swimsuit editorial in fashion magazines such as *Vogue* and *Harper's Bazaar* provide readers with snapshots of the season's best and insights into individual designers' inspirations, together with holiday destination hotspots and forecasts for current and future trends. Style essays draw the reader into a fantasy world; for example, Helmut Newton's 'Bound for Glory' where 'you can't keep a bad girl down. Especially when she's spiked, strapped, and ready to do battle in one of the season's killer swimsuits' (*Vogue* 2001). Newton's vision was to create 'radical new ways of melding sex and desire with the glamour of fashion' (Angeletti and Oliva 2006: 290), an aspiration achieved in this shoot with a visual narrative pinned to erotic models wearing sleek black swimsuits and skyscraper heels engaged in mortal combat. Mario Testino captures the luxe swimsuit on location in a Rio de Janeiro penthouse in the same year with 'She's so money'. The 'pampered princess holds court' in designs by Chanel, Sonia Rykiel and Louis Vuitton and, surrounded by suave, tuxedoed 'men about town', enjoys the high life. In addition, location shots with sandy beaches and lush tropical backgrounds or a solitary model against neutral backdrops compel the reader to investigate the swimsuit's pedigree in the accompanying text if it is not obviously branded.

The majority of Australian swimwear companies have not, historically or currently, chosen to advertise in fashion publications such as *Vogue*. Because they are lifestyle products, rather than high fashion, alternative methods have been employed. Seafolly, Australia's largest privately owned swimwear business with thirty-five years experience, has focused on developing more direct lines of communication with potential wearers. The brand's aesthetic is underpinned by swimwear and beachwear for 'the girl next door', and the company works closely with retailers at point of sale. Products are also tested on staff to ensure designs and the fit measure up to customer preferences; this has contributed to Seafolly's ongoing success. Similar to Rochford's approach in the 1980s, the company's business model is highly commercial and focused on the mass market. In recent years a well-designed Web presence has included a seasonal catalogue and an online shop; these are essential tools for sales and marketing and, unlike fashion advertisements for elite fashion brands that jostle for attention page after page in fashion magazines, provide an increasingly sophisticated platform for product branding. Moreover, they illustrate that contemporary wearers have adopted a knowledgeable and confident approach to consumption and adapted to e-commerce even for a garment such as the swimsuit which in the early years of the Internet would have seemed improbable.

Seafolly catalogues feature models closely identified with the Australian 'look' including Miranda Kerr, Catherine McNeil and Jessica Hart (Figure 6.17), strengthening the concept of Australia as home to a beach culture with the best swimsuit models and swimwear. Genelle Walkom, Seafolly's designer for twenty-five years, refers to the company catalogue as 'the bible', and clearly there is no need to rely on fashion magazines to build the brand's credibility, reflecting an autonomy that has always set the swimsuit apart from other fashion garments. Moreover, advertising campaigns include imaging on the side of bus shelters, a populist rather than elitist approach to product promotion, which has proved highly successful. In line with inclusiveness, Seafolly has extended the size range to include D and DD cups and up to a size 16, and the online shop ships goods to North America, Europe, Africa, Middle East Asia and the Pacific. Jessica Hart, in a vibrantly printed bikini with surf behind her and the wind in her sarong, is the epitome of the Australian beach girl in her natural environment.

Jets is an example of a company with a chequered history (not unusual in the fashion industry); it has changed hands twice over the label's lifetime. Initially launched in the 1980s as fashion-forward swimwear by Suzy Middleton, the company struggled financially

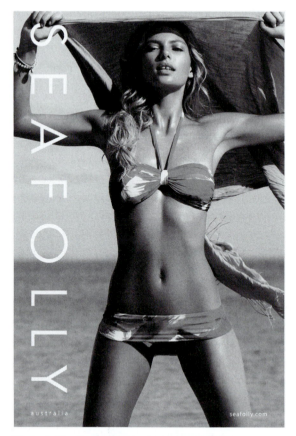

Figure 6.17   Photography by David Gubert for Seafolly, Summer 2009. Model: Jessica Hart. Seafolly.

and was bought out by Seafolly in the early 1990s. It was a sign that it would be another decade before the market was ready for an edgier design approach which was popularized by Zimmermann. Designer Jodie Boffa replaced Middleton; however, it was not until Jessika Allen took the helm in 2001 that the company expanded. She has since positioned Jets as a premium luxury swimwear brand. The aesthetic is feminine and elegant and in tune with European brands that focus on poolside glamour. A core marketing strategy to position Jets as an aspirational, premium brand has entailed concentrated advertising in high-end fashion magazines such as *Vogue* and *Harper's Bazaar*. However, like the majority of Australian swimwear companies, the swimsuits are fused to functional principles which ensure durability and the ability to perform in the surf for wearers who take the plunge.

A new generation of Australian swimwear designers continues to benefit from Australia's unique nation branding and the strong foundation created by existing swimwear brands including Seafolly and Jets. Both established and emerging designers continue to create new layers of innovation, individualizing the swimsuit to add a valuable and fresh dimension to swimwear design.

Jodhi Meares, a successful fashion model and entrepreneur, launched Tigerlily at MAFW in 2000. The label built early associations with glamour and luxury creating exotic and expensive bikinis encrusted with pearls and diamonds. MAFW 2001 is remembered for Tigerlily's diamond bikini worn by Kristy Hinze, complete with a live snake as an accessory. Meares noted that 'swimwear styling is becoming slick and stylized' (*The Age* 2005); this signposts the swimsuit's closer ties to seasonal fashion trends. Tigerlily made a splash in part due to Meares's success as a fashion model and her high profile marriage to media mogul Jamie Packer, who initially bankrolled the company. Although the label had the cache of a celebrity designer, former fashion editor for *The Australian*, Edwina McCann, included her as a designer with industry credibility because 'Jodhi uses quality fabrics and sells at a very good price point' (McCann 2007a). This highlights a key aspect of fashion, that no amount of hype or glamour can sustain a label if the product does not have the right ingredients.

Tigerlily built a following by creating memorable designs such as bikinis with strawberry appliqués on the bottoms, and has received regular editorial in *Vogue* and *Harper's Bazaar*. In 2007, Meares sold the label to Billabong for an undisclosed figure, remaining on as creative director. The financial benefits of this deal led to six stand-alone boutiques and a strong export growth to twenty overseas countries (Safe 2010). Senior designer Amelia Stanley believes the label's strength is 'staying true to our beach lifestyle and not getting caught up in what everyone else is doing internationally', and 'a relaxed, earthy aesthetic' (personal correspondence 2010). To date, the company has manufactured in Australia, and 'what got our business off the ground'; however, Stanley did voice concerns about continuing local manufacture as production numbers increase. Tigerlily regularly shoots campaigns in exotic locations, often beyond Australian shores, reflecting that Australian swimwear is at home in all tropical holiday destinations.

Melbourne-based Flamingo Sands (from 2004) has taken a different approach to its northern competitors with daringly brief cuts and jewellery embellishments more in line with a Brazilian swimwear aesthetic. Nicky Rowsell suggests that Australian women are more conservative, 'despite what we may think of ourselves', and accordingly the label has modified designs to tailor to the local market (personal correspondence 2010). Newbery reports that there is evidence that Brazilian women have body image issues with Brazil rated second only to the United States for plastic surgery procedures. According to a study by Unilever in 2006, over 800,000 breast enhancements were performed and, allegedly, 'before Carnival, it is common to hear on the news that the country has run out of silicone' (Newbery 2007: 71). These statistics suggest Flamingo Sands design tweaking for the local market is a positive as opposed to a negative, and has not dampened international interest in the label. Kate Moss wore the brand's bikinis for the September 2006 issue of *W Magazine*, adding celebrity gloss and glamour. Although Flamingo Sands is targeting 'the high-end international market niche' (Safe 2006), there is a distinctly Australian voice, with Rowsell commenting that 'the label is very tongue in cheek . . . we don't take ourselves too seriously . . . fashion is meant to be fun' (Rowsell

2010). Drawing inspiration from music, film, nature, photography, old magazines, vintage fabrics, architecture and people illustrates a design process that is in tune with contemporary culture. The 2010 collection, entitled 'L.A. Woman', references 'the song by The Doors, and the playgrounds of Los Angeles, Miami, and Las Vegas, cocktail parties, trouble and lots of fun' (ibid.). This foregrounds the concept that 'being from Australia these cities/holiday destinations always seem so wildly glamorous' (Roswell 2010), and that not all Australian swimsuit designs will end up seen at Bondi Beach. The state of fluctuation and volatility of the fashion industry, especially for smaller companies, is illustrated by Flamingo Sands ownership change in mid-2011 to Charlie Goldsmith, Melma Hammerfeld and Julie Milnes. Currently the label is not being produced due to tough retail market conditions and intended plans to relaunch in 2013–14 will be underpinned by a strong online presence and e-tail (Internet-based retail) approach to sales and marketing (Milnes 2012.)

Two *Vogue* fashion editors, Anna Hewitt and Lill Boyd, with no previous industry experience, launched Anna & Boy in 2005. It was their belief that they had a 'fashion headspace' which could be applied to swimsuit design. Working as stylists for *Vogue* Australia gave them exposure to a variety of local and overseas designs, and this inside knowledge enabled them to identify a gap in the market for a fresh stylistic approach (Huntington 2006). The label's launch received a high level of press coverage due to the designers' fashion connections, and no doubt contributed to early label recognition. However, like Tigerlily, without a quality product and a unique signature style, the company would not have survived or continue to grow and expand its market share. Anna & Boy focuses on prints and details such as bows, and playing with the cuts to give designs a quirky edge. In 2008, the summer collection, 'the couture of cossies' (Safe 2008), was shown at Miami Swim Week in Florida. This event is a huge investment for an emergent company but it has paid off: the label is now stocked in the United States, Europe and the Middle East. Most designers interviewed for this book commented that the financial outlay for this event was a deterrent and other than Zimmermann not an option for most. Anna & Boy also showed at Rosemount Australian Fashion Week (originally and from 2012 Mercedes-Benz Fashion Week, MAFW) and in 2009 added another level of publicity with *Australia's Next Top Model* entrant Cassie Van Den Dugen modelling in their show (Figure 6.18). Van Den Dugen gained a reputation as the TV programme's wild, cigarette-smoking bogan[3] rather than her credentials as an aspiring model, which is not necessarily bad press for a young Australian swimsuit label striving to make its mark.

Hotel Bondi Swim (HBS) also focuses on unique prints that are influenced by the local culture and geography of iconic Bondi Beach. Although many Australian swimwear labels draw on nostalgic memories of beach holidays and beach culture, HBS adds another layer, inspired by the 'crumbling peaches and cream façade of the Bondi Hotel and the colourful fish at north Bondi's boat ramp' (Hotel Bondi Swim 2008); it's an aesthetic that is determinedly local and 'real life' as opposed to poolside glamour. Focusing on a hand feel with watercolour illustrations and paper cut-outs that are then passed through the

Figure 6.18 Anna & Boy. Rosemount Australian Fashion Week 2009. Wendell Levi Teodoro @ ZEDUCE.ORG <http://ZEDUCE.ORG/>.

modern technology of digital or sublistatic (heat transfer) printing does not compromise the originality of the designs, a quality also maintained by retaining flaws and subtleties of the original artworks. Moreover, designers Fern Levack and Damion Fuller supported the local industry; they have invested in building a relationship with textile mills, printers and manufacturers in Australia—at a cost: it is expensive and increases the retail unit price of the brand's swimsuits. To date, this has not been a problem, with customers prepared to pay for quirky prints and styling such as HBS's ubiquitous Australian garden gnome print complete with letterboxes, dandelions and weeds reminiscent of a Bondi backpackers front yard, and imaged onto a fashion-forward high-waist two-piece. Interestingly, Levack and Fuller recently relocated to California and, while continuing to produce HBS collections, they are also designing for the innovative American specialty retail company Urban Outfitters, which seems at odds with HBS's strongly 'local' mission statement. It does highlight a contemporary aspect of the fashion industry and the complexity of a network where designers wear a number of design hats, move between brands, and collaborate with retailers, resulting in a fluid and flexible system of production and distribution. Moreover, as companies create online stores with stylish and personal profiles about the designers and their products to connect with interested consumers around the globe, retaining a sense of individuality and customer loyalty is increasingly difficult.

The new generation of Australian swimwear labels discussed represents only a percentage of a growing number of start-up swimwear businesses in the 2000s. Other notables receiving fashion and newspaper editorial include Seventh Wonderland, designing 'fashion-savvy swimsuits for the beach and music festivals', and We Are Handsome, a collaboration between Indhra Chagoury (Oscar and Elvis swimwear 2004) and Jeremy Somers (People Like Us, creators of unique iPod and iPhone covers) which produces limited edition swimsuits with artistic high-density ink placement prints. Although the majority of swimwear companies are concentrated in Sydney, established label Riot Swimwear and newcomers White Sands and 2 Chillies are reinventing the Gold Coast for a new wave of tourists. In common with competitors south of the border, these designers have well-crafted Web sites, some with online stores or at least links to online stores such as The Grand Social (a marketplace for Australian and New Zealand designers) and Shopbop (now part of the Amazon.com Inc. group of companies) that sell their products. And for established brands Zimmermann and Jets, together with new generation brand We are Handsome, their products are available from the prestigious online fashion retailer Net-a-Porter which sells luxury brands from around the globe. Western Australia, originally home to Sunseeker, is now the location for Kooey, a company that specializes in swimwear with distinctive Indigenous dot-art prints. As a result of this business and design diversity, there may be a greater chance of survival in this high-risk industry, and potentially larger market exposure, a continuing benefit of early exports brokered by Australia's strong reputation in swimwear design.

As Australia strengthens its position in the global swimwear market and expands resort wear collections (of particular note are Zimmermann and Tigerlily), an increasing number of fashion designers are following the lead of designers in Europe and the United States and including swimwear to their collections (Lisa Ho, Camilla and Marc). A high-profile case in point is internationally acclaimed Collette Dinnigan. Dinnigan launched her label in the early 1990s with a collection of luxury dry-clean-only lingerie. With a theatricality and entrepreneurial edge, her first show was held at the Alice Motel in Tamarama (beachside, in the eastern suburbs of Sydney); for the show, models wearing clear plastic dresses over the lingerie and carrying water pistols paraded up and down the restaurant (Thompson 2008). The collections evolved from lingerie into ready-to-wear which is shown in Paris; Dinnigan is the first Australian designer to be invited to show on the Chambre syndicale du prêt-à-porter des couturiers et createurs de mode schedule. Then followed a designer-for-chainstore collaboration with Target for which Dinnigan produced a lingerie collection called Wild Hearts. In 2007, a swimwear line was added to the cruise collections that included one- and two-piece swimsuits; these blended the luxury of 1930s glamour (peephole effect cut-away pieces and ruching) with Australiana fauna and flora. Dinnigan's career trajectory from Sydney to Paris, from luxury lingerie to glamorous eveningwear, to mass market lingerie, to cruise collections and swimwear, reflects a pathway now possible for aspiring fashion designers as the fashion system expands to include talented individuals from around the globe and distribute designer fashion to diverse target markets.

A further diversification is the collaboration or cobranding between high-fashion designers and major sportswear brands; examples include Comme des Garçons designer Rei Kawakubo and Speedo, Stella McCartney and Yohji Yamamoto designing collections for Adidas, and the late Alexander McQueen designing shoes for Puma. The fusion of fashion and sport is a marriage that can earn the parent company kudos and, for the designer, exposure to a new market. According to brand advisor Rob Mitchell, this doesn't necessarily translate into profits with 'returns ill-defined' (Mitchell 2005). However, in a new decade, Kawakubo continues her collaboration with Speedo, and strengthens and expands the product mix for a company closely aligned with performance swimwear. As designers fit the swimsuit into their ever-expanding repertoires, the swimsuit becomes layered with different stories that reflect the continuing globalization of fashion in which clearly defined aesthetics and consumer segments have blurred.

Adding to the mix, 'celebrities are making their presence felt within the industry, too' (Kennedy 2007: 292), and whereas in the United Kingdom, it is Elizabeth Hurley, and in the United States, Jennifer Lopez and Jessica Simpson, who have ventured into the fashion industry with swimwear collections, in Australia it is Miss Universe 2004 and sunny beach girl Jennifer Hawkins (Cozi), and fashion model Megan Gale (Isola). Hawkins launched and modelled the Cozi collection in 2008 at the Myer (department store) summer collection parades in Sydney, and continues to build on the label's early success. The *Harper's Bazaar* November 2009 cover illustrates the potent combination of an Australian beauty and the swimsuit, combined with a Christophe Decarnin 'IT' jacket for French atelier Balmain.[4] Editor Edwina McCann commented that the jacket was 'given an Aussie welcome at the beach' and that 'this image couldn't come from anywhere else on earth' (McCann 2009), as Australian models and swimsuits continue to assert an influence on global fashion. As the chief economist for the Australian Trade Commission, Tim Harcourt, notes, 'When everyone else is losing their pants in these times of global financial distress, it's good to know that Australians can at least be reassured that our world-renowned Aussie swimwear has got us covered' (Harcourt 2009).

SPEEDO AND AUSSIEBUM: IMPRINTING THE MALE BODY

Like most accounts of fashion, this history has predominantly focused on the evolution of the women's swimsuit, with the exception of an investigation into performance swimwear (Speedo) and surfwear (boardshorts) in other chapters. Similar to the one-piece maillot and the bikini for women, the Speedo brief and the swim short or boardshorts represent the core foundation for men's swimsuit design in the twentieth and twenty-first centuries and it merits further unpacking.

> Male dress was always essentially more advanced than female throughout fashion history, and tended to lead the way, to set the standard, to make esthetic propositions to which female fashion responded. (Hollander 1994: 6)

Women did follow and adopt the men's woolly one-piece swimsuit, although more quickly than other male garments, with only a twenty- to thirty-year gap for most wearers, and none for competitive female swimmers. Women's clothes were (and are) 'quite ancient and general sartorial costumes' that consist of 'elaborate headwear, difficult footwear, cosmetics, extraneous adornments and accessories, constriction and extension' (ibid. 9), and the swimsuit was indeed a modern garment that stripped away sartorial layers, exposing the body and removing the conventional social and cultural conversations between male and female fashion. The body once revealed has led to an ever-increasing obsession with a physical beauty that is athletic and finely tuned for both men and women. Hollander describes the tailored men's suit as a set of clothes that in its pure, classic form 'express[es] a confident adult masculinity . . . it is a modern look of carefully simplified dynamic abstraction that has its own strong sex appeal' (ibid. 113), a description that equally describes the classic Speedo briefs, albeit they are less forgiving and concealing, and only sexy when worn by a well-formed man. Where the tailored suit cleverly concealed bodily imperfections such as narrow shoulders, spindly legs or less-than-perfect chest-to-waist ratios in the same way the corset constrained and reshaped the female body to create desirable proportions, the swimsuit needs the body to play a leading role. Moreover, it is a garment associated with leisure and sport, less formality and a new set of values.

Once the men's one-piece swimsuit was reduced to a swim trunk, beginning in the late 1930s, two enduring design staples evolved over the next decade. The 1949/50 David Jones catalogue illustrates the style of swim trunks or swim shorts (boxer shorts) that were popular at this time. The swim trunks (Figure 6.19, on the right) were belted and had a full skirt-front for modesty, and were produced in conservative colour palettes of fawn, grey and blue. The swim shorts (Figure 6.19, on the left) had a full-knit inner support layer and elastic waistband, manufactured in sand, grey, blue or tan. Swim shorts also had a limited availability in floral and geometric prints, and *The Draper of Australasia* shows matching sets in a bright-figured cotton for men and women from the 1940s with a distinctly Hawaiian influence. The styling is functional and practical, suggesting that men's swimwear was continuing a tradition of sensible clothing devoid of the trick or trim associated with women's fashion. However, from the 1960s and 1970s, this would change with the introduction of seasonally updated bold and colourful skirtless swim trunks and boardshorts. Further, the evolution of the Speedo brief, initially developed for elite swimmers, streamed men into swimwear fashions that heightened a focus on the body, one that would need to shape up to a physical ideal.

Speedo, a recognized dictionary term for a pair of men's swimming trunks, is a testimony to how significantly the Australian style has influenced men's swimwear design. Peter Travis, Speedo's head designer from 1959 to 1962, was convinced that the real

Figure 6.19   Pure wool swim trunks. 'Casben' swim shorts. Pure wool swim trunks 1949–50. David Jones Limited.

breakthrough was to design briefer trunks that were more functional; the design intent was to create a garment 'you can swim in', focusing on the hip as the stable point of the male body as opposed to the waist. Travis experimented with the cut, optimizing performance qualities by shaping the pattern to account for leg movement, and contributed to the development of the classic Speedo brief. However, as can be seen by the Speedo design timeline (Figure 6.20), the Speedo brief or male bikini did not reach its contemporary minimalist form until 1972, and was not skirtless until the 1964 Olympic Games in Tokyo.

The Speedo brief has played a role in glorifying the male body, with early examples such as Mark Spitz wearing the briefest, most revealing cut at the Munich Olympic Games in 1972. Proving his superhuman sporting abilities with a seven gold medal tally cemented the connection between the sporty alpha male and Speedos in flashy style. An advertisement for Speedo in the early 1970s entitled 'The Sun People', and images in Sears, Roebuck & Co. and David Jones catalogues, provide an alternative snapshot of the Speedo brief at this time. Typically produced in fabrics such as stretch terry, in bold stripes and checks or block colours, the styling is less revealing, with a square boy-leg and waistline just below the navel. Daniel Craig popularized this style again in the 2000s

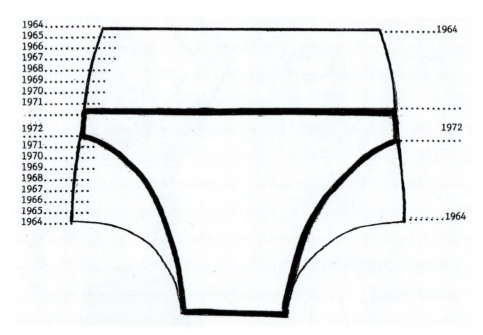

Figure 6.20 Timeline for Speedo brief design evolution, created by Gloria Smythe, Speedo designer 1962–90. Gloria Smythe.

when he emerged from the surf in *Casino Royale* wearing a pair of La Perla pale blue swimming trunks. According to celebrity and movie Web sites it was not a scene that had actually been written, but gained inclusion because 'when he came out of the water all the women gasped . . . he made a real impact' ('Craig's Swimwear Scene a Close Call' 2006). Craig's swimsuit scene has been likened to the Ursula Andress scene in *Dr No* (1962), and although a man in a swimsuit is not yet page three news, there has been a growing emphasis and dynamic focus on the male body in popular media since the 1970s.

Fashion trends in swimwear for men in the 2000s are now extending beyond 'a pair of racing briefs or baggy shorts', and Tim Hunter believes that, like women, men are now 'spoilt for choice'. There is 'a flood of styles, colours, fabrics and prints and it's all about bright, colourful and sexy' (Hunter 2007). As men embrace fashion-forward swimwear, Australia is well positioned as a global trendsetter in men's swimwear design (Speedo, Billabong, Quiksilver, Mambo), a mantle taken up by AussieBum which was launched in 2001 by Sean Ashby to international acclaim. Ashby is quick to admit that AussieBum has, in large part, 'derived success on the back of another brand that has long sold well internationally—Australia' (Petersen 2008), and of course the archetypal Speedos set the benchmark. AussieBum has taken the Speedo brief into the twenty-first century, tapping into seasonal trends and adding the innovative Wonderjock pouch technology (2006), a popular option for some customers. The design ensures a bulging crotch even in the coldest of weather and is a potent marketing tool. The all-Australian-made brand is stocked in the world's leading department stores and sold in seventy-five countries, although initially the label was rejected locally which only added to Ashby's determination to succeed. The company has taken advantage of e-commerce to build a business that is run chiefly via its Web site and sells over 1,000 units per day. Celebrities including David Beckham, Ewan McGregor and Daniel Radcliffe have been snapped wearing AussieBums, contributing to the brand's success and global renown. 'AussieBum has nailed the market both in underwear and swimwear (including boardshorts that "make your arse look good")' (O'Brien 2009). In an advertising campaign for the company's underwear, Ashby ironically reinterprets a renowned Tom Roberts painting entitled *Shearing* (1890), modernizing an aspect of Australia's national identity connected to the bush for contemporary audiences. According to Ashby, it is a reminder that 'more iconic businesses and traditions like shearing are either being sold overseas or dying off' (National Gallery of Victoria 2008). A bush scene in Figure 6.21, the men stripped to their colourful jocks, suggests a shift from bush to beach and towards popular culture. Significantly, AussieBum adds a male voice and perspective to a buoyant swimwear industry and in the process contributes positively to brand Australia.

The Debate

As to the Speedo versus boardies debate, it seems to have escalated rather than diminished since Tony Abbott's very public surf swim late in 2009. Fashion editor Georgina

Figure 6.21 AussieBum. Sean Ashby.

Safe cautions that 'they are only for six-pack posers or pollies in search of the paparazzi' while advising, 'Don't let your boardies be too baggy—opt for a slim fit' (Safe 2010). The AussieBum philosophy is more pragmatic, especially as the target market is 'any 18–80 males with a credit card'; however, the company does recommend, 'If you doubt your-self, wear something else', which is reinforced by the boardshort collections currently outperforming briefs in terms of sales (personal correspondence 2010). It illustrates that men are subject to body anxieties similar to those experienced by women, and, al-though many ignore the social pressures to conform and shape up or cover up, they are subject to public scrutiny and sensitive to criticism.

THE AUSSIE COSSIE AS REFERENCE POINT: WATER BABY

Australia has made its mark on the swimsuit. In September 2009, *Vogue* Australia in-vited some of the world's top designers including Karl Lagerfeld, Christopher Bailey for Burberry, Dolce & Gabbana and John Galliano for Christian Dior to draw on the Aus-sie Cossie for inspiration for a spread called 'Water Baby'.[5] The result is 'a collection of swimsuits that reflect our down-to-earth beauty and unique style' (*Vogue* Australia 2009). The individual comments from contributing fashion designers validated the con-cept that Australians channel an active glamour. Lagerfeld's design for Chanel cleverly merges a red bikini and sleek zip-front black wetsuit, referencing the two garments Aus-tralians have influenced and fine-tuned since their design inception. The ironic and play-ful fusion of styles reflects characteristics associated with Australian national identity, and we are invited to tap into a multilayered narrative that appliqués Chanel's witty and distinctly luxe aesthetic onto one of fashion's foundation blocks.

The caption accompanying the Dior swimsuit states that Australian swimmer Clare Dennis, who won the 200-metre breaststroke event at the 1932 Los Angeles Olympics, inspired Galliano. Similar in styling and colour to the 1980 Dior swimsuit advertise-ment discussed earlier, it is not significantly innovative; however, the design intent is de-scribed through the image and text and pinned into place as a Dior luxury product. The reader is invited to dip into a fairy tale narrative that has no foundation in facts: Clare Dennis turning heads on board a cruise liner on her way to the Olympics drenched in a Hollywood dream. The designers also reflected on Australia's 'magnificent weather', 'the chic simplicity of summertime', 'a gorgeous country . . . with unique sophisticated and beautiful women', adding allure to their creations. Nevertheless, the swimsuits express the aesthetic and signature styles of the individual designers and brands (e.g. Burb-erry's signature check pattern); this leaves a space open for Australian swimwear de-signers to continue designing world-class swimwear that are authentic Aussie Cossies.

Woollen Mermaids

Drawing the focus back to Australian fashion as international designers find inspira-tion in the Aussie Cossie, the Woollen Mermaids project looked to Australia's original mermaid, Annette Kellerman, as a muse, and to Parisian fashion and the little black dress, which is synonymous with Chanel. I developed this project as part of my role as fashion and concept consultant for the Australian National Maritime Museum's (ANMM) travelling exhibition *Exposed: The Story of Swimwear* in 2009, and as a platform to feature designs by Australia's foremost contemporary and new generation designers, including Zimmermann, Seafolly, Jets, Tigerlily, Anna & Boy, Flamingo Sands, Hotel Bondi Swim and AussieBum. The design brief was to reinterpret the one-piece swimsuit in classic black for the twenty-first century using a technologically advanced wool-Lycra (a reference to the Australian wool industry and the original swimsuit yarn) to emphasize fashion's energetic quest for invention and reinvention. Constrained by monochromatic black and the one-piece template, it presented an opportunity for designers to dazzle with their creativity and virtuosity, to craft swimsuits that reflected their signature styles and the design brief. The whimsy and beauty of the final designs, the diverse ideas, treatments and cuts, revealed why Australia has a global reputation for producing exceptional swimwear.

Figure 6.22 illustrates the different approaches of four of the designers. Tigerlily created a glamorous and theatrical effect. A dramatic contrast is achieved by cut-away side sections that draw the eye to the entwined body beneath glittering cascades of jet beads. Anna & Boy's swimsuit is reminiscent of a Victorian corset in styling with subtle textural details such as laser-cut trims creating a lacy, feminine effect. By contrast, the

Figure 6.22 Swimwear designs in response to the museum's 'Woollen Mermaids'. From left to right: Tigerlily, Anna & Boy, Zimmermann, Jets. Photographer: Michael Armstrong. Reproduced courtesy of Australian National Maritime Museum.

Zimmermann swimsuit is minimalist, devoid of trims—sharp, clean and geometric with the lattice-like cut-outs creating effective peepholes to the body. Jets makes a statement with a centre front feature panel and armbands both encrusted with antique black bugle beads. Seafolly created a full-length swimsuit with tendrils of fine, frilled chiffon that paid homage to Kellerman and fairy tale mermaids. The designers' response to the design brief—their personal vision and interpretation—demonstrated a high level of expertise in a highly specialized segment of the fashion industry, and embody a distinctly Australian style.

Branded Nation: A Place in the Sun

In the new millennium, nations around the globe pursue policies and strategies to position or reposition their countries and cities as fused to cultural production, fashion in particular. With the choice of over forty fashion weeks, there is intense competition from aspiring fashion capitals 'which expose local designers to a global audience and catapult some of them to bigger stages in New York and Paris Fashion Weeks' (Wilson 2008). This final chapter investigates the economic and cultural benefit of fashion to Australia, specifically in relation to swimwear and surfwear—with its uniquely Australian history—to show how a nation has captured a share of the global fashion market through place branding strategies.

Away from the urban cosmopolitanism of Europe on an island continent surrounded by magnificent beaches, major cities and towns grew close to the coastlines. Although beaches are a generic zone, Australians adopted beach culture as an inherent part of their national identity. J. S. McDonald, director of the Art Gallery of New South Wales (in 1931), idealized the utopian qualities of the Australian coast and the physical beauty of its dwellers, portraying a paradise inhabited by gods and goddesses (Crombie 2004: 188). By the 1920s, a society had evolved that was driven by the hedonism of sunbaking and surfing, inspired by a level of freedom and leisure pursuits unknown in previous centuries. An article in *The Home*, an Australian quarterly magazine (1920–42), expressed this aspect of Australia's cultural investment in the beach:

> Getting rich. Australians know exactly what they would do if, by dint of cutting out a surf and working one hour longer every day, they became rich. They would knock off working one hour earlier, put on a well-worn bathing suit and go for a surf. Why toil to get rich, in order to do exactly the same thing you are doing now, not-rich? Why get all hot and bothered over More Production when the thing you want is produced by the Pacific, cost-free? (Curlewis 1929: 31–32)

Australians embraced beach and surf culture with zest, and combined with a sporting history in competitive swimming, shaped Australia's national identity. Although *Lone Hand* magazine celebrated both bush and beach as integral to the national character (Woollacott 2001: 189), the modern Australian is typically depicted as a relaxed, beach-loving individual, comfortable in his or her own skin and perceived as an enduring emblem of Australianness.

As the beach was colonized and popularized, there was an increase in the number of drownings at unpatrolled beaches leading to the establishment of surf lifesaving clubs.

Australians were at the forefront of this movement globally, organizing clubs initially at Bondi and Bronte in Sydney in 1906–7; this spread to other beaches, states and territories over the next two decades (Lenček and Bosker 1998: 179). Lifesavers encapsulated the god-like physical beauty referred to by J. S. McDonald, and were model sportsmen whose activities were aligned to regimented, athletic endeavors as opposed to leisure and recreation. Surf lifesaving was an egalitarian movement with members drawn from all social classes and 'one of the last major national types to be added to the catalog of Australian icons' (Crombie 2004: 85). Women were not encouraged to join the ranks, as clearly demonstrated when Edie Kieft, the first woman to qualify for the Surf Bronze Medallion (1923), was not awarded a medal due to her sex; it was not until 1980 that women were eligible to enlist as active patrolling surf lifesavers (Surf Life Saving Australia Limited 2007). The early 'soldiers of the sea' or 'sons of Neptune' were a motley crew who wore V trunks over one-piece swimsuits similar to those worn by competitive swimmers. Over the next twenty years, surf lifesaving clubs developed their own unique costumes, with distinctive embroidered club motifs, and held regular carnivals that presented an opportunity for surf lifesavers to display their physical strength and skills in the surf and swimming events, and their Adonis-like bodies on the beach; teams in their club swimming costumes led by a flag-bearer marched to music and carried a surf reel, line and belt.

While the beaches were patrolled by surf lifesavers protecting swimmers from often-invisible riptides, surfers (a number of whom were also lifesavers) took to the waves in what has become known as a lifestyle sport, a category that also includes other extreme sports such as snowboarding, skateboarding and kite surfing. According to Wheaton (2004: 3) an aspect that defines these sports is that 'these activities are appropriately (or usefully) conceptualized as forms of play rather than sports, and have highlighted the importance of their artistic sensibility'. The playfulness and artistic nature of surfing was depicted in travel posters in the 1930s; it was also depicted as a fashionable pastime for women. And for Australia, it was a promotional/marketing tool to attract international tourists. Fashion magazines encouraged readers to invest time at the beach—'exercising (especially with the Michelin push-ball), swimming and diving' (Probert 1981: 30). US *Vogue*'s 1938 travel issue glamorized the nascent sport of surfing with a model in a floral two-piece swimsuit riding tandem through the crashing waves. These women surfers fitted more broadly into the beach girl mould, as opposed to the extreme sportswomen, and in Australia, 'joined the retinue of archetypal images' associated with Australianness and the healthy outdoors. The 'lady surfer in the foreground (Figure 7.1) . . . was added to the shot, [and] the superimposed image completed with the aid of an airbrush, which hid the edges of the two images' (Walding 2008: 154); this illustrates that artificial techniques used to create invented narratives are not exclusive to fashion media. According to Booth (2001: 5), in the 1930s and 1940s representations of women boardriders were rare, and female surfers did not appear in numbers until the 1950s and 1960s with the introduction of the 'lighter, more maneuverable Malibu boards'. While lady surfers added a fashionable and decorative edge to surfing,

Figure 7.1 Travel Poster, 1931. Artist Unknown. Published by the Australian National Travel Association. Photolithograph. Australian National Maritime Collection.

Australian Pub post targeted males, depicting athletic surfers and lifesavers to advertise locally-produced beers and ales, clearly demarcating between the sexes.

Alongside images of surfer girls, travel posters such as Percy Trompf's *Australia* glamorized iconic Bondi Beach, stitching the beach to dynamic urban symbols such as cars and densely packed dwellings on the headland, combined with views of a crowded beach with rippling waves. The boundaries between city and beach, work and leisure are blurred to create a resort city. Two women, one in a sun yellow swimsuit worn with a boldly printed skirt, matching hat and flamboyant two-toned shoes, and the other in elegant palazzo pants and a bright spotted blouse and chic sunhat, gaze out to sea, synthesizing beach and day fashion seamlessly. An equally stylish man in a boldly striped one-piece swimsuit is walking up the stairs beside them, emphasizing a natural relaxed approach to the body stripped to the bare essentials in this idyllic beachscape.

Travel posters were a popular form of tourism advertising around the globe including for popular French Riviera resorts such as Antibes. A destination for European and American socialites, its exclusivity was captured by Roger Broder's *Antibes* poster

Figure 7.2   Beachobatics: George Caddy. Paul Caddy.

c. 1930[1] which depicts a sparsely populated beach scene. The focus is two sophisticated women, elegantly attired in sleek swimsuits, languishing under a beach parasol;
two sailboats dot the calm blue sea in the distance and there are several discrete villas
on the water's edge. Henry George Gawthorn's 1933 Brighton poster[2] illustrates another
type of resort, this one by the English seaside, accessible by train from London; there is
no beach in sight. Moreover, the tourists are fully clothed, with men in suits and women
in fashionable day dresses; it is a scene reminiscent of the late nineteenth century, a
bygone era, before the advent of designer resort collections and acceptance of the one-
piece swimsuit for all beachgoers.

Kennedy reports that the European and American resorts were different, in that the
Côte d'Azur beaches were awash with beautiful, daringly underdressed bathing belles
and a sheer natural beauty that 'rendered anything else unnecessary', whereas, people on the northern Europe and East Coast US beaches, which featured less clement
weather, 'required spectacles and entertainments to take their minds off chilly breezes

and occasionally unfriendly seas' (Kennedy 2007: 37). Certainly entertainment destinations such as Atlantic City (where one could see beauty pageants and performances
by entertainers including Kellerman) were economically driven and targeted ordinary
citizens as opposed to the elite St Tropez set. Moreover, at this time vaudeville was extremely popular with US audiences and influenced the type of entertainment found in
seaside resorts. There was another destination that was a hybrid of both these models:
Bondi Beach, termed 'the playground of the Pacific'—a resort in a city where Australians
and international tourists were able to enjoy the best of both worlds. The accessible,
scenic beach, temperate climate and the Bondi Pavilion (built 1928), with a grand ball-
room, cabaret theatre, Turkish baths, gymnasium, café and shops, ensured Bondi Beach
made its mark.

A popular pastime in the 1930s and a unique aspect of Australian beach culture was
beachobatics. 'Muscle-bound men and agile young women' would gather at the south
end of Bondi Beach, 'strip off into the most daring costumes of the day' and create
gymnastic poses and human pyramids (Meacham 2009). In Figure 7.2, a young woman
displays her strength, suppleness and dexterity balancing her muscular partner on her
lower back while simultaneously knitting—an enchantingly, feminine contrast to her gym-
nast skills. Rather than professional entertainers and a formal stage, these amateurs
delighted crowds with their athleticism and spectacular, at times quirky, displays in Australia's natural theatre—the beach—articulating the 'narrative of the beautiful swimming and surfing Aussie body' (Craik 2009: 427).

GOLD (PLATED) COAST: GLITZ, GLAMOUR, SUNSHINE
AND THE LUXURY OF LEISURE

Sydney is not the only home to an iconic Australian beach. The Gold Coast in Queensland
stretches from the commercial centres of Southport and Surfers Paradise south to Coolangatta, and 'it became the place to be seen, and to invest' (Longhurst 1995: 5). From
the 1880s, Brisbane residents enjoyed the pleasure of bathing at Southport's Broad-
water, and with the introduction of bathing regulations in 1888, it was 'suitable [to be]
the Colony's "aristocratic watering-place"' (ibid. 4). The development of the region took
a different path from the Sydney beaches, in part because the Gold Coast was a holiday destination that entailed travelling from cities such as Brisbane, Sydney and Melbourne. Also, from the architectural style to the names of the beaches and local towns,
it was influenced by Californian's Santa Monica and Venice Beach. The Spanish American aesthetic was mimicked and 'the virtual hero-worship of the life saver . . . owed
much to Hollywood and a new wave of athleticism purveyed by the cinema' (ibid. 5).
'Surfers Paradise, together with Bondi [were] the beaches that most clearly [stood]
for the dominant myth of the Australian beach' [Fiske, Hodge & Turner (1987) cited in
Moore 2005: 189], even though they featured quite different cultural constructions. Arguably, Surfers Paradise is the least picturesque and idyllic beach on the Gold Coast;

however, through sustained promotion and advertising campaigns, and as the major centre of ongoing residential and commercial developments, it is a tourism Mecca for national and international holidaymakers.

Eddo Coiacetto suggests that the Gold Coast 'has been written as a history of individual actors rather than an abstract industry. Accounts tend to present the early developers as *small*, entrepreneurial, risk taking and even heroic businessmen' (2009: 10). Conversely, from the 1950s, with the development of canal estates, the Chevron Hotel (1958) to the Palazzo Versace (2000) and QI (2005) developments in the 2000s, 'it would seem the Coast is and never was the realm of small operators' (ibid. 12). The Gold Coast 'has attracted an array of players from both development and nondevelopment backgrounds including pop stars, fashion designers and [Japanese] plastic components manufacturer Nifsan' (ibid.), and it has become the locus for a number of swimsuit and surfwear designers. Australia has struggled for recognition as a design or fashion hub and 'the Gold Coast's main claim to fame—at least until Versace arrived on the scene—was the local surfwear company Billabong, a sporty and mildly nonestablishment product that has successfully penetrated the global youth market' (Griffin 2004: 75). And indeed, the company's achievements should not be underestimated. The Gold Coast's history, cast as populated by white-shoe brigade developers, gold bikini meter maids, and bottle-blonde, bejeweled, nouveau riche women, has led to a reputation as 'tawdry, vulgar and meretricious' (ibid.). Despite these stereotypical images, segments of the Gold Cost industry, in particular the fashion industry, embodies a distinctly Australian approach to product design and lifestyle promotion. In particular, pioneer bikini and beachwear designer Paula Stafford and innovative family company Fiesta were based in Cavill Avenue at Surfers Paradise from the late 1940s. The company expanded from its fast turnaround ensembles for beachgoers to include retailing and wholesaling to department stores and boutiques in Australia and high-end resort retailers internationally.

Stafford is attributed with designing the first bikinis in Australia. Beachgoers on the Gold Coast were exposed to the daring 'French two-piece swimsuit' popularized by Réard and Heim in France, and 'publicized in Australian newspapers and women's magazines' from the mid-1940s (Rainbird 1988). Stafford's early design career developed alongside a jointly owned beach-equipment-for-hire business she ran with her husband, Beverley Stafford. She had studied design in Melbourne prior to moving to the Gold Coast and understood the basic principles of pattern construction, which she applied to developing bikini and one-piece swimsuit patterns that could be adjusted to individual body measurements. Stafford commented, 'I just made them up as I went along, and I made blocks straight away for my best sellers' (Stafford 2005). She began cutting out modest two-piece styles on a flattened canvas secured in the sand at the beach. Clients could order their swimsuit in the morning; the pattern pieces were often cut from tea towels and tablecloths due to war rationing and shortages; these pieces would then be made up at home on Stafford's kitchen table, and the suit would be ready for pick-up in the afternoon. Stafford had 'an exceptional talent for size estimation (measurements were not usually taken) . . . strengthening her burgeoning reputation as a talented de-signer' (Rainbird 1988), and Figure 7.3 reinforces her hands-on approach to design. Articles in Australian newspapers and magazines in the 1950s credit Stafford with fine-tuning the bikini, reporting that this design reached its full potential in Surfers Paradise. An innovative design detail included a side-tie on the bikini bottoms which allowed the wearer to reduce the width and briefness, tailoring to varying degrees of modesty or daring. Before long, tourists could buy a Stafford bikini as part of their holiday experi-ence on the Gold Coast, where 'beach laws had long been elastic' (Wells 1982: 26).

As discussed in *Testing the Waters*, in 1952, a model wearing one of Stafford's swimsuits was ordered off the beach by a male beach inspector because the suit was deemed too brief. Stafford regrouped and, understanding the significance and value of media coverage in creating a demand for her designs, arranged for newspaper report-ers, the mayor and a priest to witness five girls on the beach the next day in similarly daring swimsuits. The Gold Coast's reputation as the bikini capital of Australia was ce-mented, and a Stafford bikini 'became a status symbol' indicating 'you had "travelled"

Figure 7.3 Paula Stafford—late 1940s—with model Dolores De Cruz. Collection: State Library of Queensland.

and done goodness knows what else' (ibid. 113). Stafford later introduced an innovative fully reversible bikini constructed with rust-free reversible zips, and subsequently organized the first Australian bikini parade at the Sydney Town Hall in 1956. Fiesta was a consumer-driven business managed by a visionary designer who saw a gap in the market. The designs, made on site, competed with swimsuits from conservative, international swimwear brands, synthesizing product and place.

In a personal interview in 2005, Stafford discussed the fabrics she used, and recalled meeting with representatives of Swiss textile companies that mainly produced cottons. At this time, she had only purchased their products at a retail level, because her production runs were small. As business expanded, these fabrics became staples for collections, and although woven textiles required specialized fitting, cottons and silks were part of her signature style. In the 1950s, her use of lightweight natural fibers contrasted with American swimsuit imports which were made of heavy synthetics. Reminiscing about a Cole of California two-piece swimsuit she had worn in the late 1930s, Stafford commented that it was very conservative and inspired her to create swimsuit styles that were briefer and fun to wear. Consequently, her swimsuit innovations included using textiles not used for conventional swimwear production by larger manufacturers in the United States and Europe; these textiles formed a foundation for creating styles that proved to be both durable in the surf and fashion-forward.

The bikini was the swimsuit of choice not only for young girls but also for a number of matrons on the Gold Coast, due to Stafford's refined made-to-measure skills. Bikinis were produced for women with body measurements such as a bust 42, waist 32, hips 44 (inches), but former Gold Coast mayor and property developer Bruce Small promoted the acceptance of all body types claiming, 'Here we accept the human form in the same way as we accept it when shown in a gallery' (Wells 1982: 106–9). Small's lofty sentiments are admirable, and no doubt underpinned by sound business principles to ensure an optimum number of tourists, whatever their size, on local beaches. And, Australia's adoption of briefer swimsuit styles was driven by a desire to optimize the beach and leisure experience, regardless of hip measurements. A Stafford bikini symbolized a bodily freedom all Australian women could access if they wanted to.

Stafford is remembered as the 'Bikini Queen', and when discussing her designs, local Brisbane women who had purchased her label in the 1950s and 1960s also recall her seasonal beachwear collections, which were ideal for permanent residents in the tropical north. In line with bikini designs, tops, shorts and dresses were often reversible, a feature that increased a garment's versatility and appeal, as well as producing a neat finish. Designs for leisure were not new, European designers from the 1920s (Patou, Lanvin) had included a luxury resort collection for places such as Deauville, and from the 1930s and 1940s American designers and manufacturers were producing playsuits and rompers for the mass market. However, in Australia, particularly in Queensland, a Stafford design reflected a lifestyle that did not have clearly defined boundaries between work and play, and for many Australians, it was part of their everyday wardrobe.

On the Gold Coast, the swimsuit was also taken out of its natural habitats—at the beach, pool or on the stage—and put on the street when meter maids were introduced in 1965 as a tourist attraction (Figure 7.4). Local businessman Bernie Elsie devised a plan to protect unsuspecting shoppers and business people from traffic infringements. It involved beautiful young women in Stafford-designed, coin-encrusted lamé bikinis, with sashes similar to those worn by beauty contestants, promenading the main boulevards in Surfers Paradise inserting coins in expired traffic meters. Needless to say, it was a success that attracted widespread media coverage, strengthening the Gold Coast's image as a glitzy Vegas-like destination, swimming with underdressed, beautiful women. It was a new accessible luxury, and Stafford led the way for Australian swimwear designers. The Fiesta label was underpinned by designs clothed in promotional material stitched to the Gold Coast, a breezy lifestyle bathed in sun, surf and, importantly, the luxury of leisure.

Figure 7.4   1960s Meter Maids—Gold Coast. Gold Coast Meter Maids.

BOMBORA: SURFING INTO FASHION

We put on our boardshorts and the girls put on their bikinis!

(Bernard 'Midget' Farrelly quoted in Rymer 1996)

Quiksilver CEO Bob McKnight commented that it wasn't until after World War II 'when the decades of prosperity began that the style of the surfer started to emerge' (McKnight 2006: 35). In Hawaii, home to the first surfers, local label Lyn's of Hawaii 'had cornered the Hawaiian tourist market with snug trunks with the trademark stripe down the leg'. McKnight continues that although the styles were popular, some surfers were 'looking for a more authentic (not to mention cheaper) look' (ibid.). This led to a number of small operations in back-of-the-store sewing rooms popping up to cater to a growing market. At the same time in California, 'some of the more outrageous surfers were making their own bold fashion statement . . . buying white sailor's pants at thrift shops and cutting legs off just below the knee to create prototype "Baggies" ' (ibid. 36).

While Sydney was home to Speedo and performance swimsuits for Olympic swimmers at home and abroad, Australian surfwear brands materialized in the late 1960s and early 1970s located close to Australia's best surf beaches—Bells Beach in Torquay Victoria (Rip Curl 1969, Quiksilver 1970) and the Gold Coast Queensland (Billabong 1973). It marks an era when 'surfers took a sport and transformed it into a way of life' (Polhemus 1994: 48), and Allan Green, co-founder of Quiksilver, recalls that 'it was the start of the last summer of the 1960s; the hippie movement was all over the mainstream news and, in our little world, the summer psyche was all-pervasive' (Green 2006: 22). Australians were not the first surfers, however, a lineage of champion surfers can be traced back to the winners of the first world championships held at Manly Beach (Sydney) in 1964—Bernard 'Midget' Farrelly won the men's title and the women's title was won by Phyllis O'Donnell. Subsequent world champions who have made their mark include Nat Young, Wayne 'Rabbit' Bartholomew, Mark Richards, Tom Carroll, Mark Occiluppo, Mick Fanning, Joel Parkinson, Pam Burridge, Layne Beechley, Stephanie Gilmore and Sally Fitzgibbons. And, although not the first to design and manufacture surfwear, Rip Curl, Quiksilver and Billabong, now known as the 'Big Three', all started 'by surfers and made for surfers', have grown to become global leaders who together with US companies O'Neill and Ocean Pacific account for 75 per cent of the total market supply (Stewart, Skinner, and Edwards 2008: 211).

The story of surfwear design is clothed in stories of young entrepreneurial enthusiasts—visionaries driven to produce garments for fellow surfers that were in tune with a surfing philosophy that was rebellious, countercultural and anything but mainstream. Surfers 'wanted to live within and according to the rhythms of nature—to go with the flow' (Polhemus 1994: 48), and the foundation of the surf wardrobe became T-shirts or short-sleeved oversized shirts and boardshorts worn with thongs or similar casual footwear. Boardshort design evolved in response to the surfer's need for a functional and durable garment that did not restrict movement while surfing; could withstand the constant rubbing on a waxy board; would not dig into the body; would stay on in rough surf; and would be quick drying. Boardshorts and T-shirts were also the background template for innovative print designs that evolved to reflect individual surf brand identities, and were worn on dry land by surfer and nonsurfer alike.

According to Craik, in an analysis of subcultures and uniforms that includes surfers, 'Visibility is one of the distinctive features of subcultures, hence members aim to create an instantly recognizable appearance so that both fellow travelers and nonmembers can identify who they are and are not' (Craik 2005: 193). Quiksilver's first print advertisement (1974) affirms the importance of communicating to these 'fellow travelers' with a pair of boardshorts superimposed onto a tubing wave with accompanying text 'Don't be OUT! When you drop IN!' (Jarratt 2006). In this case, boardshorts must have a level of quality and authenticity, and there is no need to include a surfer/wearer in the image, 'he' knows who he is. Surfwear companies did not follow conventional fashion industry methods of marketing and promoting their products, rather focusing on sponsorship of professional surfers and international surfing events. Moreover, advertising in surfing magazines such as *Tracks*—'The Surfer's Bible'—set their products apart from the mainstream and directly targeted members of this subcultural group. Unlike fashion brands with a singular, recognizable corporate identity that flows through all products and promotional material, a number of surfwear brands experimented with creating diverse and imaginative logos, swingtags and label designs that were constantly updated. The soul surfers of the 1970s could buy products that were produced and promoted by members of their tribe, creating a sense of belonging.

Australia was a home to surfing culture, and a number of key innovations can be traced to local surfwear producers. These innovations include Elastomax and Slickskin technologies for wetsuits (Rip Curl); the first technical boardshorts with snaps and Velcro closures; concept stores; first dedicated female surf brand—Roxy (Quiksilver); and multiple innovative logos (Billabong). And all three companies are major sponsors of the best surfers and surfing events globally. According to Stewart, Skinner and Edwards (2008), the success of these companies is the result of 'a highly competitive local climate [that] in turn created a culture of innovation where products were continually tested on local beaches, and sold in local retail outlets to discerning customers'. The big three represent brands, like Speedo, that have 'actively launched themselves into global markets' as opposed to national brands such as Vegemite that were taken over by global corporations (Sinclair 2008: 227). It is a uniquely Australian business model that sells lifestyle sports, athleticism and beach culture to extreme sportsmen and women around the globe. Conceptually stitching the nation's brand to surf culture has ensured a strong $23 million dollar global export market for these products (Rip Curl, Billabong) which 'spring to mind in the same way that Germany and BMW are linked, or Ikea and Sweden' (Harcourt 2008).

Although surfwear's origins are subcultural and stitched to an alternative lifestyle, there are a number of characteristics that are more generally associated with Australia and reflect Curlewis's 1929 impressions of the beachgoer who aspires to freedom, less work and a bracing surf. Likewise, the Australian style of dress has long been viewed as casual, less conservative—'a blend of ironic individualism, sometimes mixed with anarchic playfulness' (Maynard 2000: 5)—and that makes Australia and surfwear a natural fit. Another aspect is the timing which dovetailed with a new era of casual dressing globally in the 1970s, and whereas 'sportswear . . . is often seen as inherently American' (Salazar 2008: 11), surfwear with its transgressive underpinnings is decidedly Australian. Mambo, launched in Sydney in 1984, blended 'surf, art and humor', and was the first brand 'to move out of the surf specific market and into the more eclectic, surf and streetwear market where it continues to operate today' (Superbrands). Founder Dare Jennings's inspiration for the label name was not the dance but rather a tongue-in-cheek acronym: **M**eans of **A**cquiring **M**odels, **B**ucks & **O**piates, and was a response to existing surfwear brands that marketed surfing as a cult lifestyle. The Mambo manifesto reflected 'a new ironic currency' (Jennings 1998: 5), simultaneously mocking surf and mainstream culture, and religion. Drawing on the talents of a number of artists and designers including Reg Mombassa, Paul McNeil and Matthew Martin, the brand created products imprinted with satirical commentary that conflated surf culture with adages such as 'More a Pair of Shorts Than a Way of Life'. In the iconic 1997 McNeil print (Figure 7.5), the message is loud and clear that surf culture cannot be wholly claimed by the United States, and from the periphery, 'voices of 'Australian Islanders' can be heard around the globe selling an attitude fused to a bold, colourful aesthetic.

Surfing was predominantly a male sport until the mid-1990s with surfwear brands unashamedly catering to men. Quiksilver was the first to recognize a gap in the market and launched Roxy in 1990, and 'new independent labels quickly followed suit' (Booth 2001: 13), including Mambo Goddess and Billabong Girl. The introduction of boardshorts, designed and cut specifically for the female body, was a belated response to the surfer girl's need for a functional garment, and like men's boardshorts, a style that was also adopted by nonsurfers. According to *Surf, Dive and Ski*, the expansion into women's surfwear targeted the 20- to 25-year-old market, with a 'stronger youth focus' on a group of people who 'are very brand and lifestyle conscious'. Consequently, the 'womenswear ranges do tend to be more in tune with contemporary fashion trends and follow a fashion base' (cited in Vaughan 1998: 206–7). Booth suggests that although the inclusion of women consumers has economic benefits, 'They also pose a threat to the very cultural authenticity on which the industry depends' (2001: 16). And although women have a stronger presence in surfing competitions and now receive lucrative sponsorship deals, the approach to advertising products such as Roxy surfwear and surfboards communicates a fashion edge, cemented in 1996 when the brand moved closer to fashion and away from the fringe, debuting the collection Girl's Rule at New York Fashion Week. Similarly, advertisements evoke surfer girl imagery popularized in the 2002 film *Blue Crush*, and together with fashion collaborations (Cynthia Rowley 2010), reflect Roxy's commercial, mainstream branding (Ragtrader 2010).

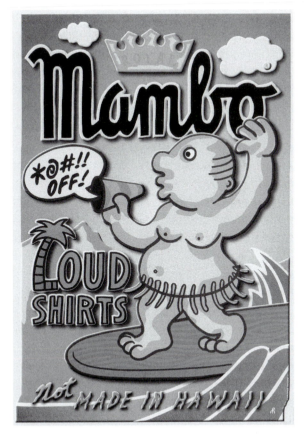

Figure 7.5 Paul McNeil for Mambo 1997. Mambo Licensing.

Surfer style is both a streetstyle (Polhemus 1994; Craik 2005) and, for Australia, part of its cultural identity, creating a complex web of meanings. Increasingly, surfwear brands have transformed into fashion apparel for young urban (often nonsurfer) individualists. Quiksilver has established flagship stores in London, Paris and New York; Billabong has a lifestyle concept store at The Camp in Costa Mesa, California; and Mambo a flagship store in London. For surfwear brands, authenticity is diminished by some being publicly listed companies, or in the hands of private equity groups, 'with principals whose names appear on annual lists of the country's richest individuals' (Sinclair 2008: 227), and as a result of extended target markets expanded store locations to include global fashion centres. Moreover, as surfwear brands leak into fashion hubs, fashion labels appropriate surfing motifs and themes creating an interactivity and circularity of ideas as opposed to a trickle-down or bubble-up process. [Trickle-down refers to 'the diffusion from high society to the mass market', whereas bubble up is the reverse with streetstyle innovations adopted by high fashion (Polhemus 1994: 9; see also Davis 1992).]

In 2007, Edwina McCann reported that 'Australiana is cool' and there is a 'uniquely Australian perspective connected to beach and surf culture' that European fashion designers are adopting. Nicolas Ghesquière for Balenciaga transformed wetsuit materials into sculpted dresses, and Lagerfeld featured surfboards with the distinctive interlocking C logo on the runway, making them instantly fashionable. McCann laments that it is not Australian designers leading the way claiming, 'Wetsuits, swimsuits, surfers . . . are for our designers to plunder' (McCann 2007a). It is evident Lagerfeld cherry-picked design ideas associated with performance swimwear and surfwear as early as the 1991 Chanel spring/summer collection when jammers (athletic fitted shorts) were teamed with an iridescent, mermaid blue jacket featuring classic Chanel details and accessorized with a surfboard. Hence, this intermittent plunder positions surf culture as part of a treasure chest of 'stylistic ideas from everywhere' that can be in one season and discarded the next by 'the ultimate empire of fashion' (Polhemus 2005: 89).

Australia contributed to this ongoing fashion conversation when *Australia's Next Top Model* (ANTM) winner from the fifth season (2009), Tahnee Atkinson, posed for *Harper's Bazaar* in an extravagant red carpet evening dress designed by Alex Perry, accessorized with a facsimile of a Tiffany necklace and casually shouldering a Chanel surfboard. High fashion is also open to ironic interpretation, and new values challenge the imperialism of a centralized fashion system. The message sent from the periphery declares that the surfboard may have been branded, but the object is only temporarily borrowed. Likewise, Australian designers not only have a talent for designing swimwear and surfwear, and although in Atkinson's case, post-ANTM she was deemed overweight in New York by modeling agencies and told to lose a few kilos (*Who Magazine* 2009), she expresses an elegance and glowing beauty worthy of gracing fashion magazines, at least in Australia. Wearers as global citizens are invited to tap into a multilayered narrative that playfully appliqués designers' and brands' signature styles onto fashion foundation blocks whether it is daywear, eveningwear, resort wear or a surfboard.

NATION BRANDING AND FASHION

As a nation clothed in the imagery of the beach, an island paradise with a unique identity associated with swimmers, surfers and beautiful women, the beach is centre stage, reflecting a modern landscape where individuals work and play, and the past is washed away by the tides. The beach offers people an opportunity to revitalize the body and soul in a state of delicious abandonment beneath the blazing sun. In September 2007, Bondi Beach was the site of the largest swimsuit shoot with 1,010 bikini-clad women gathering to set a Guinness World Record (Figure 7.6). *Cosmopolitan* magazine editor Sarah Wilson, who coordinated the event commented, 'We love a challenge, we're not afraid to show our bodies, we love the beach and we don't take ourselves too seriously' (Safe 2007). The women conveyed a casual informality that, according to BBC style

Figure 7.6   1010 Bikinis, September 2007. Reuters.

commentator Jeff Banks, has influenced Australians' approach to fashion. Banks, in Australia for the Melbourne Cup (November 6, 2007), was astounded at 'the amount of exposed female flesh', commenting, 'Australians do love to show some skin'. He at-tributed this relaxed attitude to bodily display to the amount of time spent outdoors particularly at the beach in bikinis. Banks wryly noted that it would be beneficial if the standard of dress at Flemington racecourse were more in tune with race-wear (ideally stylish and understated) than Bondi Beach (ibid.). However, it is doubtful his comments will influence future fashion at the races, as Australian women remain independent and individualistic in what they wear, even if international arbiters of style do not deem it to be in good taste.

Bondi Beach continues its high profile exposure through television programmes *Bondi Rescue* (2006–current) and *Bondi Vet* (2009–current). *Bondi Vet* transforms a familiar pets and vets format by its geographic location threaded with scenes of athletic vet Chris Brown surfing, swimming and running along the beach with his dog. *Bondi Rescue* focuses the spotlight on contemporary heroes, surf lifeguards. (Local councils employ lifeguards whereas lifesavers are trained volunteers.) The programmes are stitched to an iconic beach, a modern symbol of Australia's national identity, and it is unlikely if named *Manly Rescue* or *Chatswood Vet* they would have the same resonance with ei-ther local or international audiences. These programmes embroidered to Bondi Beach a national emblem of Australianness foregrounding the significance of place. Unlike the American television series *Baywatch*, which was bereft of a storyline, instead focusing on beach babes with pneumatic breasts and muscled actors impersonating lifeguards, *Bondi Rescue* tracks the very real drama of saving hapless swimmers from drowning in the treacherous riptides. The rescue attempts are not always successful. Audiences experience a slice of Australian life, and a new form of celebrity in the form of contemporary working heroes. 'The lifeguards whom we have come to know as individuals over the long weeks of summer . . . are skylarking elite athletes . . . who work together as a finely tuned machine to keep beachgoers safe' (Australian Screen 2007), and, like the *H2O: Just add water* mermaids, they are successfully sold to global audiences.

Before television's fascination with the surf lifesaver, these 'Australian native[s] . . . [were] used to decorative effect in fashion spreads' (Clements and Tulloch 2009: 34). As early as 1961, *Vogue* 'made the journey to our shores . . . chose our beaches as the backdrops for their fashion shoots' and enhanced already 'superb beach shots' with bronzed lifesavers (Sproat 2007). Australia's 'sons of Neptune' moved onto the fashion page; they were exemplary male specimens suitable for carrying refined and regal models in modest and sensible swimsuits on wooden surfboards towards the lapping waves (*Vogue* 1961). Helmut Newton's 1964 photograph for *Vogue* shot on location at Wanda Beach (New South Wales), humorously and wittily evokes an Australia that does not take itself too seriously, and there is an incongruity in the caption, 'The Special Look of American Sports Clothes', when the subject is the swimsuit and the location, an Australian beach. The swimsuit by Cabana is innovatively cut and the model, groomed, sleek and sophisticated, imperiously soaks up the sun with her exotic pet kangaroo named Ethel leashed and passive beside her. There is a sense that the beach is one environment that may not be totally conquered or colonized as a backdrop for another nation's designer fashion, as an Australian flavor may filter through with or without the kangaroo.

The March 2010 issue of *Vogue* Australia continued the transmission of Australian beach culture to the global fashion community, featuring Bondi Beach as the location for shooting the European spring/summer 2010 ready-to-wear collections. Clements reports, 'One of the biggest trends emerging was a kind of scuba/swim sexiness. How Australian can you get?' (2010). World top-ten Australian fashion model Abbey Lee Kershaw, with wild hair, bright lipstick and nails, continued a recurring trend accessorized with both surfers and surfboards in a spread titled 'The Life Aquatic'. Electric bold colours and body-baring fashion interspersed with black-and-white images of young local boys enjoying the beach sends a message that is reinforced with captions 'a fresh wave' and 'really modern feel' which suggest this will not be the last time Australia is mined for its fashion models, beach culture or idyllic locations.

Countries are brands . . . however unrealistic, stereotyped and fantastic (there are presumably women in Brazil who do not wear tiny g-strings, men in Argentina who are not macho cowboys, football players or tango dancers, people in Holland who do not smoke marijuana, Russians who so not drink vast quantities of vodka, Australians who don't surf, Italians who are not great lovers, etc.), and such national brands have enormous power in the world today, with profound political and economic effect. Other than tourism, however, no industry is as interlinked with national branding as fashion is. (Polhemus 2005: 85)

Polhemus identifies the significance of national image and identities (whether cli-chés or not) to branding, economic wealth and the impact on others' perceptions and response to a nation's products, fashion in particular. Brand Australia is 'fashioned by geography' (Martyn 1976: 11), influenced by sea, sand and sun—a concept swim-wear and surfwear designers have benefited from and used to optimize global expo-sure. Moreover, Australia's isolation forced thinking in different directions and created an edge to building international recognition for this specialized fashion industry niche from the margins. As a result, there is a consistent and longstanding image of Austra-lians who, if not in their Speedos or bikinis, are dressed in resort wear clothing, and in the 2000s, a new generation of swimwear designers are positioned to profit from this imaginary Australia.

This narrative demonstrates how a country that has quite rightly not rated inclu-sion in histories that investigate designer fashion centred in Paris, New York, London and Milan, has played a significant role in the development of a new order that has led to countries around the world positioning their nations and fashion via place branding strategies. Austrade chief economist Tim Harcourt reported in 2006 that 'Australia reg-istered as the number one country-brand in the world', a position that was strengthened by Sydney's inclusion in the top ten fashion cities in the world, and Melbourne placing number eleven (2010), by the Global Language Monitor (GLM). Moreover, this reputation is strongly connected to swimwear and surfwear, garments for a modern world that is obsessed with leisure and pleasure, and reflects a global fashion industry that is con-stantly changing and open to new influences and regional players.

It shows how creative innovation across different domains (fashion, sport, media, personal wellbeing, tourism) can be harnessed to develop a powerful component of national branding for both export and cultural development, thereby contributing to national competitiveness underpinned by an increasing focus on the growing impor-tance of consumer culture and service industries to the global economy (Craik 1997; McKercher and Du Cros, 2002). Revisioning the swimsuit through this narrative creates a real-world understanding of how individuals, designers, companies and teams partici-pating in fashion, sport and entertainment have contributed to public understanding of this vital economic sector. It is a sector that has been important to Australia's history, and in a contemporary context, to its national branding for international trade and tour-ism. This social, cultural, historical and contemporary story creates a community of meaning that celebrates inventiveness, innovation and bare-faced ambition, beautiful bodies, athleticism and a garment that is a second skin.

Notes

CHAPTER 2 TESTING THE WATERS: MORALITY AND UNDRESSING THE BODY

1. View the Sicilian murals at http://en.wikipedia.org/wiki/File:Casale_Bikini_modified.jpg.

CHAPTER 3 SHOW AND TELL: POPULARIZING THE SWIMSUIT

1. Kellerman's surname is spelt with two 'n's on her birth certificate; however, searches in publications such as the *Daily Mirror* and in promotional posters vary with either one 'n' or two 'n's; I have kept to the former throughout.
2. Although usually on pages nine to thirteen, Kellerman did make page one on 23 July 1928 wearing a full-length unitard at Deauville; she was also featured on page five 4 October 1952 (archival image) alongside Esther Williams as part of a story promoting the Williams movie about Kellerman's life. Interestingly, by this time a full-length swimsuit would have been unusual, with most beachgoers wearing a short one-piece swimsuit.
3. Cooee is an Australian term. It is a call particularly used in the bush to attract attention and/or locate another person.
4. The legend of Annette Kellerman and her popularization of the one-piece swimsuit is often linked to her arrest for indecency at Revere Beach in Boston in 1907 or 1909, depending on the source. However, Barbara Firth (co-author of Kellerman's biography with Emily Gibson), in personal correspondence (16 September 2007), was only able to provide a list of newspaper articles dated 1935, 1961, 1980 and 2006 that report this as an actual incident, and it is often recounted by Kellerman herself. Firth suggested I contact American children's book author Shana Corey, who was also researching Kellerman and published *Mermaid Queen: The Spectacular True Story of Annette Kellerman, Who Swam Her Way to Fame, Fortune & Swimsuit History!* (2009). On 4 October 2007, Corey replied to my inquiry stating she had been unable to find proof and wondered 'if the arrest story came about as a way to add conflict to the movie plot.' I then gained access to the Kellerman collection held at the Mitchell Library (State Library of New South Wales), and no supporting documents were discovered, other than the aforementioned articles all published many years after the event. In the Gibson and Firth biography, there is a detailed account of the incident. Firth interviewed Kellerman not long before her death in 1975. Apparently there was a court case and Kellerman's arrest received extensive reportage both in Boston and further afield. I contacted the reference archivist at the Massachusetts Archives, Jennifer Fauxsmith, who checked for information in relation to the arrest in the Metropolitan Park Commission and also checked the Revere

Beach Reservation records. Again, there was no evidence that Kellerman was arrested. In addition, Fauxsmith checked the Suffolk County Sheriff's Calendar which lists arrests, and there was no mention of Kellerman. At this juncture, I contacted the Boston Public Library. If Kellerman was arrested, I assumed it would have made the local papers. I received a reply from Anne Fahey-Flynn, the micro-text reference librarian, on 6 October 2007. The only mention she was able to locate was in an article in the Boston *Sunday Globe* (11 October 1958). Fahey-Flynn also checked the *Revere Journal* to see if there was any mention of the arrest and found no articles. Whether she was arrested or not is really not an issue; however, it adds to the mythology of Kellerman and the swimsuit in the early twentieth century. Kellerman was a highly skilled self-promoter, which is an essential ingredient of successful individuals. Coco Chanel is a high-profile example, whom fashion historian Valerie Steele observes, 'Lived to tell generations of journalists that she alone was responsible for putting women in skirts and sweaters' (Steele 1992: 120), although a number of her contemporaries, including Jean Patou, Jeanne Lanvin and Vionnet, were influential contributors alongside Chanel. However, these designers often do not receive due recognition as they are outperformed by the media-savvy Chanel. This does not diminish Chanel's contribution, but rather highlights the importance of the media in creating a fashion narrative. Similarly, Kellerman successfully used the media as a promotional tool, and the arrest angle added a newsworthy layer and notoriety that ensured ongoing interest from the public.

5. Hans Christian Andersen's fairy tale of *The Little Mermaid* begins in the land of the sea people, who live far out in the depths of the ocean where a sea king, a widower, lives with his six daughters and his mother, who acts as guardian to the young mermaids. The six sisters create their own underwater gardens with sea flowers and treasures they have found on sunken ships. The youngest princess chooses only flowers coloured like the sun and a statue of a beautiful young boy for her garden design and, combined with the stories about the human world told to her by her grandmother, she longs for the time when she will turn 15 and be allowed to swim to the surface to see the forest and cities of the land folk for herself. Time passes and on her fifteenth birthday she 'rose as light and clear as a bubble up through the water' to gaze upon the surface of the ocean, drenched in the warm colours of the setting sun and the sound of boisterous sailors singeing on a large ship where a party was in progress for the young and handsome prince. She watches them, mesmerized by their frivolity and gaiety, unaware that the storm brewing is more than additional fun for all. The ship is destroyed and the prince thrown into the waves, where the little mermaid saves him from sure death, depositing him safely on land before returning to her underwater world to pine for both the handsome prince and the human world. Her grandmother compounds her unhappiness by explaining that, unlike humans who have an immortal soul, merfolk live for 300 years, only to dissolve into the sea foam as though they never existed. In addition, the only way to gain an eternal soul is through the faithful love of a human being. The little mermaid determines to leave her underwater paradise and fish tail behind and seeks out a sea witch to transform her to human form. There is, of course, a costly price to pay—her tail will be replaced by beautiful legs, however, the sea witch warns, it will be 'as though sharp swords are slicing through you'. Further, she demands that the little mermaid relinquish her voice, to which the little mermaid exclaims, 'What shall I have left?' The sea witch replies, 'Your beautiful figure, your graceful poise and your expressive eyes'. The deal is struck and her tongue is cut out. The little mermaid faints and floats to the surface and is washed up

near the palace. She is discovered by the prince with her new and painful legs and taken to the palace where they dress her in 'costly garments of silk and muslin'. Although mute, she enchants everyone with her graceful dancing, especially the prince, who keeps her at his side as a constant companion. He has boy's clothing made especially for the little mermaid so she can go horse riding with him. Alas, his love for her is that of an adult for a child, and when the time comes for him to marry, he travels to a neighbouring kingdom to seek a bride. The little mermaid's chances of an immortal soul fade, and she knows her sacrifice has been in vain and that the sea will claim her and her body dissolve into foam. Her sisters attempt to save her, offering their beautiful long hair to the sea witch in exchange for the little mermaid's life. Again, the sea witch's bargain is cruel and tortuous. The little mermaid will have to kill the prince with a magic knife and have his blood splash on her feet for her legs to transform once again into a tail. The little mermaid loves the prince and, as there is no chance of an immortal soul, sees no point in killing him, choosing instead to accept her fate, throwing herself into the sea. She does not die, however, her spirit rising to the Daughter of the Air who grants her the opportunity to earn an immortal soul by performing 300 years of good deeds. The little mermaid's suffering has been rewarded with the potential to create an immortal soul for herself, and she floats away on a rose-coloured cloud. (This synopsis is an abridged version of the translation by Ash and Higton 1992.)

CHAPTER 6 SHAPING UP: THE HISTORY AND DEVELOPMENT OF THE SWIMSUIT'S INTEGRATION INTO THE FASHION INDUSTRY

1. Lisa Fonssagrives, British *Vogue* cover 1940. View at http://www.vogue.co.uk/magazine/archive/issue/default.aspx/Month, August/Year, 1940.
2. Edward Steichen, British *Vogue* cover 1932. View at http://www.vogue.co.uk/magazine/archive/issue/default.aspx/Month, July/Year, 1932.
3. *Bogan* is an Australian colloquial term that represents a stereotypical image of a person from a working-class demographic who lacks cultural or aesthetic values; exhibits a pronounced lack of dress sense in social situations; and has a distinct vocabulary. See http://www.bogan.com.au/definition/index.php.
4. Jennifer Hawkins, *Harper's Bazaar*, November 2009. View at http://www.harpersbazaar.com.au/jennifer-hawkins-nov-2009.htm?index=2.
5. 'Water Baby', *Vogue* Australia. View at http://fashiongonerogue.com/water-baby-karlie-kloss-suits-up-for-vogue-australia-september/.

CHAPTER 7 BRANDED NATION: A PLACE IN THE SUN

1. Antibes poster; view at http://www.art.com/products/p14566306-sa-i2995205/antibes-vintage-poster-europe.htm?sorig=cat&sorigid=175692&dimvals=175692–1837&ui=299375629d6241dda60617aa70ce73a3.
2. Brighton poster; view at http://www.flickr.com/photos/iposters/3546317627/photos/iposters/3546317627/.

References

AUDIOVISUAL MATERIAL

Auzin, Igor. 1984. *The Coolangatta Gold*. Magna Pacific [Movie].

Bacon, Lloyd, Busby Berkeley, Manuel Seff, James Seymour, George Barnes, and James Cagney. 1933. *Footlight Parade*. Warner Brothers. [Videorecording].

Buzzell, Edward, and Jack Cummings. 1989. *Neptune's Daughter*. Culver City: MGM/UA Home Video. [Viderecording].

Kelly, M., Nell Schofield, Jadranka Capelja, Joan Long, Geoff Rhoe, Bruce Beresford, Gabrielle Carey, Kathy Lette, Umbrella Entertainment., and AV Channel. 2003. *Puberty blues*. Australia: Umbrella Entertainment. [Videorecording].

Knechtel, Albert. 2010. *Bikini revolution*. Neutral Bay, N.S.W.: EnhanceTV Distributor. [Videorecording].

LeRoy, Mervyn, Arthur Hornblow, Everett Freeman, Busby Berkeley, Esther Williams, Victor Mature, Walter Pidgeon, and David Brian. 1989. *Million Dollar Mermaid*. Turner Entertainment/ MGM/UA Home Video. [Videorecording].

Morice, Tara, Michael Cordell, Ian Collie, Special Broadcasting Service (Australia), AVRO Holland, and Film Finance Corporation Australia. 2002. *The Original Mermaid*. Australia: Netherlands: Film Finance Corporation Australia. AVRO. [Videorecording].

Newton-John, Olivia. 1981. 'Physical'. Universal City: MCA. [Music Video].

Pichel, Irving. 1948. *Mr. Peabody and the Mermaid*. Los Angeles: Republic Entertainment. [Videorecording].

Powell, Michael, and Walter Chiari. 2005. *They're a Weird Mob*. Australia: Roadshow Entertainment. [DVD].

Rymer, Judy. 1996. *Nothing to Hide*. Learning Essentials (distributor). [Videorecording].

Shiff, Jonathan M., Colin Budds, and Jeffrey Walker. 2007. *H2O: Just Add Water*. Gold Coast: ZDF Enterprises. [Television].

Sullivan, James. 1924. *Venus of the South Seas*. Grapevine Video. [Videorecording].

Thompson, Peter. 2008. Collette Dinnigan. In *Talking Heads*. ABC TV. [Television].

Walters, Charles, George Wells, Johnny Mercer, Arthur Schwartz, and Dorothy Kingsley. 1953. *Dangerous When Wet*. Turner Entertainment/MGM/UA Home Video. [Videorecording].

BOOK AND BOOK CHAPTERS

Alac, Patrik. 2002. *The Bikini: A Cultural History*. New York: Parkstone Press.

Angeletti, Norberto, and Alberto Oliva. 2006. *In Vogue: The Illustrated History of the World's Most Famous Fashion Magazine*. New York: Rizzoli.

Anholt, Simon. 2007. *Competitive Identity : The New Brand Management for Nations, Cities and Regions*. Basingstoke and New York: Palgrave Macmillan.

Ash, Russell, and Bernard Higton. 1992. *Fairy Tales from Hans Andersen*. London: Pavilion Books.

Batterberry, M., and A. Batterberry. 1977. *Mirror, Mirror: A Social History of Fashion*. 1st ed. New York: Holt Rinehart and Winston.

Becker, Sue. 1971. *Boomph with Becker*. London: BBC Publications.

Bell, Quentin. 1976. *On Human Finery*. 2nd ed. New York: Shocken Books.

Booth, Douglas. 2001. *Australian Beach Cultures: The History of Sun, Sand, and Surf*, *Sport in the Global Society*. London and Portland, OR: F. Cass.

Breward, Christopher. 2003. *Fashion*, *Oxford History of Art*. Oxford and New York: Oxford University Press.

Breward, Christopher. 2005. 'Ambiguous Role Models: Fashion, Modernity and the Victorian Actress'. In *Fashion and Modernity*, edited by C. E. Breward. Oxford: Berg.

Breward, Christopher. 2008. 'Pure Gesture: Reflections on the Histories of Sport and Fashion'. In *Fashion V Sport*, edited by L. Salazar. London: V & A Publishing.

Bright, Deborah. 1998. *The Passionate Camera: Photography and Bodies of Desire*. New York: Routledge.

Callan, Georgina O'Hara. 1998. *The Thames and Hudson Dictionary of Fashion and Fashion Designers*. New York: Thames and Hudson.

Callaway, Anita. 2000. *Visual Ephemera: Theatrical Art in Nineteenth-century Australia*. Sydney: UNSW Press.

Charles-Roux, Edmonde. 2004. *The World of Coco Chanel: Friends, Fashion, Fame*. 1st ed. London: Thames & Hudson.

Clements, Kirstie, and Lee Tulloch. 2009. *In Vogue: 50 Years of Australian Style*. Pymble, N.S.W.: HarperCollins.

Cockington, James. 2004. *Itsy Bitsy*. Sydney: Manly Art Gallery & Museum.

Cockington, James. 2005. *Banned: Tales from the Bizarre History of Australian Obscenity*. Sydney: ABC Books for the Australian Broadcasting Corporation.

Colmer, Michael. 1977. *Bathing Beauties The Amazing History of Female Swimwear*. London: Sphere Books.

Craik, Jennifer. 1997. 'The Culture of Tourism'. In *Touring Cultures: Transformations of Travel and Theory*, edited by C. Rojek and J. Urry. London and New York: Routledge.

Craik, Jennifer. 1994. *The Face of Fashion: Cultural Studies in Fashion*. London and New York: Routledge.

Craik, Jennifer. 2005. *Uniforms Exposed: From Conformity to Transgression*. Oxford: Berg.

Crane, Diana. 2000. *Fashion and Its Social Agendas: Class, Gender, and Identity in Clothing*. Chicago: University of Chicago Press.

Crombie, Isobel. 2004. *Body Culture: Max Dupain, Photography and Australian Culture, 1919–1939*. Melbourne: Images Publishing Group in association with National Gallery of Victoria.

Cumes, James. 1979. *Their Chastity Was Not Too Rigid: Leisure Times in Early Australia*. Melbourne: Reed.

Curry, Lisa. 1990. *Lisa Curry's Total Health and Fitness*. Sydney: Collins/Angus & Robertson.

Daley, Caroline. 2003. *Leisure & Pleasure Reshaping & Revealing the New Zealand Body 1900–1960*. Auckland: Auckland University Press.

Davis, Fred. 1992. *Fashion, Culture, and Identity*. Chicago: University of Chicago Press.

Dyer, Richard. 1991. 'A Star is Born'. In *Stardom Industry of Desire*, edited by C. Gledhill. London: Routledge.

Eco, Umberto. 2005. *History of Beauty*. 2nd ed. Translated by Alastair McEwan. New York: Rizzoli.

Eicher, Joanne Bubolz. 1995. *Dress and Ethnicity: Change Across Space and Time*, edited by J.B. Eicher. Oxford: Berg.

Entwistle, Joanne. 2007. 'The Dressed Body'. In *The Fashion Reader*, edited by L. Welters and A. Lillethun. New York: Berg.

Erdman, Andrew L. 2004. *Blue Vaudeville: Sex, Morals and the Mass Marketing of Amusement, 1895–1915*. Jefferson, NC: McFarland & Co.

Featherstone, Mike. 1991. 'The Body in Consumer Culture'. In *The Body: Social Process and Cultural Theory*, edited by M. Featherstone, M. Hepworth, and B.S. Turner. London: Sage.

Felderer, B. 2001. 'Fashion Will Go Out of Fashion'. In *Rudi Gernreich: Fashion Will Go Out of Fashion September 15–November 11, 2001*, edited by R. Gernreich. Philadelphia: The Institute of Contemporary Art.

Fields, Armond. 2006. *Women Vaudeville Stars: Eighty Biographical Profiles*. Jefferson, NC: McFarland.

Gibson, E., and B. Firth. 2005. *The Original Million Dollar Mermaid*. 1st ed. Sydney: Allen & Unwin.

Glynn, Prudence. 1978. *In Fashion: Dress in the Twentieth Century*. London: George Allen & Unwin.

Green, Alan. 2006. 'How We Got Started'. In *The Mountain and the Wave: The Quiksilver Story*, edited by P. Jarratt. Huntington Beach, CA: Quiksilver Entertainment.

Grimshaw, Jean. 1999. 'Working Out with Merleau-Ponty'. In *Women's Bodies: Discipline and Transgression*, edited by J. Grimshaw and J. Arthurs. London: Cassell.

Gundle, Stephen. 2008. *Glamour: A History*. Oxford and New York: Oxford University Press.

Harcourt, Tim. 2008. *The Airport Economist*. Crows Nest N.S.W.: Allen & Unwin.

Healy, Robyn, Susan Dimasi, Paola Di Trocchio, and National Gallery of Victoria. 2003. *Fashion and Textiles in the International Collections of the National Gallery of Victoria*. Melbourne: National Gallery of Victoria.

Hellmrich, Dudley. 1929. *How to Swim Correctly*. Sydney: Caxton Printing Works.

Hochswender, Woody. 1993. *Men in Style*. New York: Rizzoli.

Hollander, Anne. 1993. *Seeing through Clothes*. Berkeley: University of California Press.

Hollander, Anne. 1994. *Sex and Suits*. Brinkworth: Claridge Press.

Jarratt, Phil. 2006. *The Mountain and the Wave: The Quiksilver Story*. Huntington Beach, CA: Quiksilver Entertainment.

Jennings, Dare. 1998. *Mambo: Still Life with Franchise*. Rushcutters Bay, N.S.W.: Mambo Graphics.

Joel, Alexandra. 1984. *Best Dressed: 200 Years of Fashion in Australia*. Sydney: Collins.

Joel, Alexandra. 1998. *Parade: The Story of Fashion in Australia*. Sydney: Harpers Collins.

Kaplan, Joel H., and Sheila Stowell. 1994. *Theatre and Fashion: Oscar Wilde to the Suffragettes*. Cambridge and New York: Cambridge University Press.

Kee, Jenny, and Samantha Trenowith. 2006. *A Big Life*. Melbourne: Penguin Group.

Kellerman, Annette. 1918. *Physical Beauty—How to Keep It*. New York: George H. Doran Company.

Kellock, Jo-Anne. 2010. 'The Business of Fashion'. In *Australian Fashion Unstitched: The Last Sixty Years*, edited by B. English and L. Pomazan. Melbourne: Cambridge University Press.

Kennedy, Sarah. 2007. *The Swimsuit*. London: Carlton Books Limited.

Kerper Jr., Robert E. 2002. *Splash! Aquatic Shows from A to Z*, edited by M. Zielinski. Philadelphia: Self-published.

Kidwell, Claudia B. 1969. 'Women's Bathing and Swimming Costume in the United States'. *United States National Museum Bulletin 250* 64:32.

Killoren Bensimon, Kelly. 2006. *The Bikini Book*. New York: Assouline Publishing.

Koda, Harold, and Kohle Yohannan. 2009. *The Model as Muse: Embodying Fashion*. New York and New Haven: Metropolitan Museum of Art Yale University Press.

Kunz, Grace I., and Myrna B. Garner. 2006. *Going Global: The Textile and Apparel Industry*. New York and London: Fairchild.

Lenček, Lena, and Gideon Bosker. 1989. *Making Waves: Swimsuits and the Undressing of America*. San Francisco: Chronicle Books.

Lenček, Lena, and Gideon Bosker. 1998. *The Beach: The History of Paradise on Earth*. New York: Penguin Books.

Lipovetsky, Gilles. 1994. *The Empire of Fashion: Dressing Modern Democracy*, *New French Thought*. Princeton, NJ: Princeton University Press.

Longhurst, Robert. 1995. *Gold Coast: Our Heritage in Focus*. Brisbane: State Library of Queensland.

Mackay, Elina. 1984. *The Great Aussie Fashion Book*. Sydney: Kevin Weldon and Associates.

McKercher, Bob, and Hilary Du Cros. 2002. *Cultural Tourism: The Partnership Between Tourism and Cultural Heritage Management*. New York: Haworth Hospitality Press.

McKnight, Bob. 2006. 'How the Surf Industry Began'. In *The Mountain and the Wave: The Quiksilver Story*, edited by P. Jarratt. Huntington Beach, CA: Quiksilver Entertainment.

Markula, Pirkko. 2001. 'Firm but Shapely, Fit but Sexy, Strong but Thin: The Postmodern Aerobicizing Female Bodies'. In *Contemporary Issues in Sociology of Sport*, edited by A. Yiannakis and M.J. Melnick. Champaign, IL: Human Kinetics.

Martin, Richard. 1998. *American Ingenuity: Sportswear, 1930s–1970s*. New York: Metropolitan Museum of Art.

Martin, Richard, and Harold Koda. 1990. *Splash! A History of Swimwear*. New York: Rizzoli.

Martyn, Norma. 1976. *The Look: Australian Women in Their Fashion*. Melbourne: Cassell Australia.

Maynard, Margaret. 1994. *Fashioned from Penury: Dress as Cultural Practice in Colonial Australia*, *Studies in Australian history*. Cambridge: Cambridge University Press.

Maynard, Margaret. 2000. *Out of Line: Australian Women and Style*. Sydney: UNSW Press.

Maynard, Margaret. 2004. *Dress and Globalisation*, *Studies in Design*. Manchester: Manchester University Press.

Meares, Peter. 2003. *Legends of Australian Sport: The Inside Story*. St Lucia: University of Queensland Press.

Milbank, Caroline Rennolds. 2009. *Resort Fashion: Style in Sun-drenched Climates*. New York: Rizzoli Publishers.

Moffitt, Peggy, William Claxton, and Marylou Luther. 1999. *The Rudi Gernreich Book*. Koln: Taschen.

Nead, Lynda. 2005. 'Response to Paper: Ambiguous Role Models: Fashion, Modernity and the Victorian Actress'. In *Fashion and Modernity*, edited by C. Breward and C. Evans. Oxford: Berg.

Polhemus, Ted. 1994. *Streetstyle: From Sidewalk to Catwalk*. New York: Thames & Hudson.

Polhemus, Ted. 2005. 'What to Wear in the Global Village?'. In *Global Fashion Local Tradition*, edited by J. Brand and J. Teunissen. Arhem: Uitgeverij Terra Lannoo BV.

Probert, Christina. 1981. *Swimwear in Vogue since 1910*. New York: Abbeville Press.

Ribeiro, Aileen. 2003. *Dress and Morality*. Oxford: Berg.

Roessler, Patrick. 2006. *Viewing our Life and Times: American and German Magazine Design in the 20th Century: A Cross-Cultural Perspective on Media Globalization*. Dresden: University of Erfurt.

Salazar, Ligaya. 2008. *Fashion v Sport*. London: V&A Publishing, Victoria and Albert Museum.

Sandow, Eugen, and G. Mercer Adam, eds. 1894. *Sandow on Physical Training*. New York: J. Selwin Tait & Sons.

Saunders, Kay, and Julie P. Ustinoff. 2005. *A Crowning Achievement: A Study in Australian Beauty, Business and Charitable Enterprise*. Canberra: National Museum of Australia Press.

Schoumann, Helene. 2006. *Gottex Swimwear Haute Couture*. Paris: Assouline.

Schweitzer, Marlis. 2009. *When Broadway Was the Runway: Theater, Fashion, and American Culture*. Philadelphia: University of Pennsylvania Press.

Seid, Roberta P. 1994. 'Too "Close to the Bone"': The Historical Context for Women's Obsession with Slenderness'. In *Feminist Perspectives on Eating Disorders*, edited by P. Fallon, S. C. Wooley, and M. Katzman. New York: Guilford Press.

Slessor, Kenneth. 1983. *Backless Betty from Bondi*. Sydney: Angus & Robertson.

Steele, Valerie. 1985. *Fashion and Eroticism: Ideals of Feminine Beauty from the Victorian Era to the Jazz Age*. New York and Oxford: Oxford University Press.

Steele, Valerie. 1992. 'Chanel in Context'. In *Chic Thrills: A Fashion Reader*, edited by J. Ash and E. Wilson. New York: New York University Press.

Steele, Valerie. 1997. *Fifty Years of Fashion: New Look to Now*. New Haven: Yale University Press.

Tapert, Annette. 1998. *The Power of Glamour*. London: Aurum Press.

Tatar, Maria. 2002. *The Annotated Classic Fairy Tales*. 1st ed. New York: Norton.

Taylor, Lou. 2000. 'The Hillfiger Factor and the Flexible Commercial World of Couture'. In *The Fashion Business*, edited by N. White and I. Griffiths. Oxford: Berg.

Walding, Murray. 2008. *Surf-o-rama: Treasures of Australian Surfing*. Carlton: Miegunyah Press.

Walsh, G. P. 1979. 'Charlton, Andrew Murray (Boy) (1907–1975)'. In *Australian Dictionary of Biography*. Melbourne: Melbourne University Press.

Walsh, G. P. 1983. 'Annette Kellerman'. In *Australian Dictionary of Biography*, edited by B. Nairn, G. Serle, and C. Cunneen. Melbourne: Melbourne University Press.

Warner, Patricia Campbell. 2006. *When the Girls Came Out to Play: The Birth of American Sportswear*. Amherst: University of Massachusetts Press.

Watson, Linda. 2008. *Vogue Fashion*. Camberwell: Penguin Group (Australia).

Watts, Diana. 1914. *The Renaissance of the Greek Ideal*. London: William Heinemann.

Wells, Lana. 1982. *Sunny Memories: Australians at the Seaside*. Melbourne: Greenhouse Publications.

Wheaton, Belinda. 2004. *Understanding Lifestyle Sports: Consumption, Identity and Difference*. London and New York: Routledge.

Wilson, Elizabeth. 2003. *Adorned in Dreams: Fashion and Modernity*. Rev. ed. New Brunswick, NJ: Rutgers University Press.

Woollacott, Angela. 2001. *To Try Her Fortune in London: Australian Women, Colonialism, and Modernity*. Oxford: Oxford University Press.

EXHIBITION CATALOGUES AND MUSEUM COLLECTION NOTES

Cuthbert, Penny. 2009. *1930s Swimwear in the Australian National Maritime Collection*. Sydney: Australian National Maritime Museum.

Rainbird, Stephen. 1988. *Paula Stafford and the Bikini*. Gold Coast: Centre Gallery.

Ward, Lindy, and James Cockington. 2004. Itsy *Bitsy Teen Weeny: A Brief History of the Bikini*. Sydney: Manly Art Gallery & Museum.

GOVERNMENT AND INDUSTRY REPORTS

Austrade (Australian Trade Commission). 2003. 'Productivity Commission Inquiry into Post-2005, Textile, Clothing and Footwear (TCF) Assistance Arrangements'. www.pc.gov.au/__data/assets/file/0009/28197/sub085.rtf.

Da Silva, Josue Gomes. 2006. 'Brazilian Fashion Takes the World'. www.dc.mre.gov.br/imagens-e-textos/Industry10-BrazilianFashion.pdf.

Department of Health and Ageing, Australian Commonwealth Government. 2009. 'Evaluation of Skin Cancer Campaign'. [cited 8 December 2009]. http://www.skincancer.gov.au/internet/skincancer/publishing.nsf/Content/42DA1BE1B409955DCA25766D001531A2/$File/ev092.pdf.

Gattorna, John, and Deborah Ellis. 2008. 'Supply Chain Considerations for the Australian TCF Industries'. In *Building Innovative Capability*, edited by R. Green. Canberra: Commonwealth of Australia.

Harcourt, Tim. 2006. 'Quiet Achievers and Celebrity Success Combine to Make Australia's Day'. [cited 13 October 2009]. http://www.austrade.gov.au/Quiet-achievers-and-celebrity-success-combine-to-make-Australia-s-day/default.aspx.

Harcourt, Tim. 2009. 'Whether its Bikinis or Budgie-Smugglers—Australian Beachwear Exports Are Going Swimmingly'. http://www.austrade.gov.au/Whether-its-Bikinis-or-Budgie-Smugglers/default.aspx.

Newbery, Malcolm. 2005. 'Global Market Review of Swimwear and Beachwear—Forecasts to 2012'. Bromsgrove: Aroq Limited.

Newbery, Malcolm. 2007. 'Global Market Review of Swimwear and Beachwear—Forecasts to 2013', edited by A. Limited. Bromsgrove: Aroq Limited.

Zehntbauer, J. A. 1927. 'Proposed Jantzen Factory in Australia'. Portland: Jantzen.

Zehntbauer, J. A. 1955. 'History of Jantzen Knitting Mills'. Portland: Jantzen.

INTERNET SOURCES

Abraham, Tamara. 2010. 'Paris Fashion Week: Elle Macpherson and Laetitia Casta Return to the Catwalk for Louis Vuitton's Celebration of Womanly Curves. [cited 15 May 2011]. http://www.dailymail.co.uk/femail/article-1257001/Paris-Fashion-Week-Elle-Macpherson-Laetitia-Casta-return-catwalk-Louis-Vuittons-celebration-womanly-curves.html.

Adidas. 2007. 'Impossible is Nothing'. [cited 14 February 2008]. http://www.press.adidas.com/au/DesktopDefault.aspx/tabid-11/212_read-7995/.

AntBlog701. 2004. 'Speedos v Board Shorts'. [cited 16 February 2010]. http://ant.sillydog.org/blog/2004/000473.php.

Australian Screen. 2007. *Bondi Rescue* (2005–current). Australian Film Commission. [cited 19 July 2007]. http://australianscreen.com.au/series/bondi-rescue.

Berkes, Howard. 2008. 'China's Olympic Swimming Pool: Redefining Fast'. [cited 4 January 2010]. http://www.npr.org/templates/story/story.php?storyId=93478073.

Bittemann, Jim. 2010. 'France Moves Toward Partial Burqa Ban'. [cited 25 February 2010]. http://www.cnn.com/2010/WORLD/europe/01/26/france.burqa.ban/index.html.

Coiacetto, Eddo. 2009. 'Gold Coast Development: A Special Case or Same Old City Factories?' Urban Research Program. [cited 28 February 2010]. http://www.fbe.unsw.edu.au/cf/staff/peter.rickwood/soac2009/PDF/Coiacetto%20Eddo.pdf.

Cook, Joanne. 2007. 'Collaborations Between Sports and Fashion 2007'. [cited 23 August 2007]. http://www.wgsn-edu.com/members/active-market/features/am2007jun27_020076_a?from=search.

'Craig's Swimwear Scene a Close Call'. 2006. [cited 14 January 2008]. http://www.moono.com/news/news03468.html.

de Brito, Sam. 2008. 'Cossies v Boardshorts'. *Brisbane Times*. [cited 22 February 2010]. http://blogs.brisbanetimes.com.au/executive-style/allmenareliars/2008/10/03/cossiesvboard.html.

Fair Sport. 2006. [cited 31 October 2007]. http://www.indianlink.com.au/?q=node/967.

Flotsam & Jetsam. 2002. [cited 15 May 2005]. http://www.music.princeton.edu/~juliet/flotsam.html.

Fraser, Dawn. 2007. [cited 15 November 2007]. http://www.dawnfraser.com.au/profile.htm.

Gruendl, Martin. 2007. 'Beautiful Figure'. [cited 17 January 2010]. http://www.uni-regensburg.de/Fakultaeten/phil_Fak_II/Psychologie/Psy_II/beautycheck/english/figur/figur.htm.

Gwynn. 2003. 'What We Wear Down-under!' [cited 4 April 2005]. http://www.anu.edu.au/andc/ozwords/October_2003/speedos.html.

Hanson Sports Media. 2008. 'Speedo Launches "Space Age" Swimsuit in Worldwide First'. [cited 13 February 2008]. http://www.hansonsportsmedia.com/article.asp?id=2212.

Hotel Bondi Swim. 2008. [cited 20 March 2009]. http://www.hotelbondiswim.com.

Hourigan, Peter. 2008. 'They're a Weird Mob'. [cited 11 March 2010]. http://archive.sensesofcinema.com/contents/dvd/08/47/theyre-a-weird-mob.html.

Hudson, Louise. 2003. 'Rosa Cha Brazil's Leading Luxury Swimwear Brand'. WGSN. [cited 23 August 2007]. http://www.wgsn-edu.com/members/trends/track/intimate/ti007484/main.htm.

Huntington, Patty. 2011. 'Robyn Lawley Strikes Again—In *Vogue* Australia's First Ever Plus Size Fashion Shoot 2011' [cited 1 August 2011]. http://frockwriter.blogspot.com/2011/07/robyn-lawley-strikes-again-in-vogue.html.

Kenrick, John. 2003. 'A History of the Musical' [cited 18 March 2007]. http://www.musi cals101.com/vaude4.htm.

Liza Bruce Biography. [cited 13 November 2011]. http://www.lizabruce.com.

Longman, Peter. 2003. 'Britain's Hippodrome Theatres Making a Splash' [cited 20 March 2007]. http://www.arthurlloyd.co.uk/Archive/Jan2003/Hippodromes.htm.

Mitchell, Rob. 2005. 'Is Fashion Design a Team Sport? Brand Channel' [cited 14 February 2008]. http://www.brandchannel.com/features_effect.asp?pf_id=262.

MultiChannelNetwork. 2008. 'Sarah Murdoch Joins Foxtel'. [cited 1 February 2010]. http:// www.mcn.com.au/New/NewsArticle.aspx?IdDataSource=87.

National Gallery of Victoria. 2008. 'Advertising and Popular Culture' [cited 6 June 2008]. http:// www.ngv.vic.gov.au/australianimpressionism/education/insights_cviews.html.

Next Eco-Warriors, The. 2009. 'Eco-Warrior: Hannah Fraser'. [cited 29 February 2010]. http:// www.nextecowarriors.com/2009/08/eco-warrior-hannah-fraser.html.

Noveck, Jocelyn. 2008. *Harshest Words Saved for Britney's Body*. Associated Press 2007 [cited 19 January 2008]. http://www.usatoday.com/life/music/2007-09-10-355617165_x.htm.

OMG. 2011. 'Britney Spears Makes Comeback: No Longer Toxic'. http://omg.yahoo.com/ news/britney-spears-makes-comeback-no-longer-toxic/54161.

Petersen, Freya. 2008. 'Aussiebum: Down Under Designs in More Ways Than One'. *International Herald Tribune*. [cited 8 June 2008]. http://www.iht.com/articles/2008/01/21/style/raus. php.

Ragtrader. 2010. 'Roxy and Rowley United'. [cited 13 April 2010]. http://www.ragtrader.com. au/news/roxy-and-rowley-unite.

Raszeja, Veronica. 1993. 'Clare Dennis (1916–1971)'. *Australian Dictionary of Biography*. [cited 3 January 2010]. http://adbonline.anu.edu.au/biogs/A130687b.htm.

Rose, Ian. 2007. 'Elle Macpherson: Super Business Model'. [cited 16 January 2010]. http:// news.bbc.co.uk/2/hi/business/6479635.stm.

Rushall, Brent S. 2008. 'Bodysuits—Deja Vu?'. [cited 4 January 2010]. http://coachsci.sdsu. edu/swimming/bodysuit/2008suit.htm.

Smith, Amanda. 2001. 'Dawn Fraser'. ABC, June 8 [cited 16 October 2007]. http://www.abc. net.au/rn/talks/8.30/sportsf/stories/s444345.htm.

Speedo. 2011. 'Unforgettable Swims'. [cited 9 May 2011]. http://www.speedo.com/en/unfor gettableswims/unforgettableswims_2.html.

Sporting Pulse International. 2007. 'Sporting Pulse Take Out Australian Sport Award for IT'. 2007. [cited 19 January 2008]. http://www.sportingpulseinternational.com/index.php?id= 170&tx_ttnews%5Btt_news%5D=103&tx_ttnews%5BbackPid%5D=152&cHash=c5d297 b3a1.

Starr, Steve. 2005. 'Starrlight: Esther Williams'. Windy City Media Group. [cited 7 January 2010]. http://www.windycitymediagroup.com/ARTICLE.php?AID=7300#.

Superbrands. 2007. '100% Mambo'. [cited 17 February 2010]. http://www.superbrands.com. au/BrandDetails.aspx?id=21.

Surf Life Saving Australia Limited. 2007. 'Surf Lifesaving: Our History'.. [cited February 3 2007]. http://www.slsa.asn.au/?s=ourhistory&year=1920.

Trendletter by Fashionoffice.com. 2007. 'Adidas by Stella McCartney Spring/Summer'. [cited 31 November 2007]. http://www.fashionoffice.org/collections/2007/mccartney10–2007.htm.

Watchpaper.com. 2010. 'Olympic Legend Ian Thorpe Partners with TW Steel'. 2010. [cited 18 January 2010]. http://www.watchpaper.com/2010/01/14/olympic-legend-ian-thorpe-partners-with-tw-steel/.

Waverley Library. 2007. *The Great Aussie Cossie*. [cited 19 February 2007]. http://www.waverley.nsw.gov.au/library/localstudies/historical/cossie.htm.

WGSN. 2000. 'Fast Track Intimate/Swimwear: Interview Nicole Zimmermann'. [cited 23 August 2007]. http://www.wgsn-edu.com/members/trends/track/intimate/zimmerman-6012/main.htm?from=search.

Who Magazine. 2009. 'Sarah Murdoch Fights the Good Fight'. http://au.lifestyle.yahoo.com/who/latest-news/article/-/6190726/sarah-murdoch-fights-the-good-fight.

Wilson, Brent. 2007. 'The Devil Wears Speedos' [cited 28 May 2011]. http://blogs.smh.com.au/suitsyou/archives/2007/05/the_devil_wears_speedos.html.

Zahn, Paula. 2005. 'The Hidden Jane Fonda Revealed'. CNN. [cited 28 January 2010]. http://transcripts.cnn.com/TRANSCRIPTS/0510/31/pzn.01.html.

INTERVIEWS AND PERSONAL CORRESPONDENCE

Fuller, Damion, and Fern Levack. 2010. Hotel Bondi Swim. Email correspondence. 14 March.

Jones, Lloyd, AussieBum. 2010. Email correspondence. 25 March.

McCann, Edwina. 2007a. Email correspondence. 28 June.

McKinney, Warren. 2010. Sunseeker. Email correspondence. 20 and 30 March.

Milnes, Julie. 2012. Flamingo Sands Company Update, May 5.

Rochford, Brian. 2007. Email correspondence, Sydney. 23 May.

Rochford, Brian. 2009. Email correspondence. 5 March.

Rowsell, Nicky. 2010. Email correspondence. 17 March.

Smythe, Gloria. 2005. Personal interview, Sydney. 25 August.

Stafford, Paula. 2005. Personal interview, Gold Coast. 8 August.

Stanley, Amelia. 2010. Tigerlily. Email correspondence. 27 February.

Travis, Peter. 2008. Telephone interview. 14 January.

Utz, Julia. 2007. David Jones. Email correspondence. 19 June.

Walkom, Genelle. 2010. Seafolly. Telephone interview. 23 March.

JOURNAL ARTICLES AND PAPERS

Barron, Lee. 2007. 'The Habitus of Elizabeth Hurley: Celebrity, Fashion, and Identity Branding'. *Fashion Theory: The Journal of Dress, Body & Culture* 11 (4): 443–61.

Booth, Douglas. 2001. 'From Bikinis to Boardshorts: Wahines and the Paradoxes of Surfing Culture'. *Journal of Sport History* 28 (1): 3–22.

Craik, Jennifer. 2009. 'Is Australian Fashion and Dress Distinctively Australian?'. *Fashion Theory: The Journal of Dress, Body & Culture* 13 (4): 409–43.

Griffin, Grahame. 2004. ' "The Man Has Gone—The Dream Lives On": The Palazzo Versace and the Re-branding of the Gold Coast'. *Queensland Review* 11 (2): 75–88.

Hartley, John. 2006. 'Sync or Swim? Plebiscitary Sport, Synchronized Voting, and the Shift from Mars to Venus'. *The South Atlantic Quarterly* 105: 409–28.

Moore, Keith. 2005. 'Embracing the Make-believe—The Making of Surfers Paradise'. *Australian Studies* 18 (1): 187–210.

Sinclair, John. 2008. 'Branding and Belonging'. *Journal of Cultural Economy* 1 (2): 217–31.

Stewart, Bob, James Skinner, and Allan Edwards. 2008. 'Cluster Theory and Competitive Advantage: The Torquay Surfing Experience'. *International Journal of Sport Management and Marketing* 3 (3): 201–20.

van Acker, Elizabeth, and Jennifer Craik. 1996. 'Effects of Restructuring the Australian Fashion Industry: From Industry Policy to Cultural Policy'. *Journal of Fashion Marketing and Management* 2: 21–33.

Wilson, Elizabeth. 2007. 'A Note on Glamour'. *Fashion Theory: The Journal of Dress, Body & Culture* 11 (1): 95–107.

MAGAZINES ARTICLES

British *Vogue*. 1980. 'A Month of Sundays'. July. 73.

British *Vogue*. 1990. 'Blue Belles'. July. 142.

Cahill, Tim. 1973. 'Mark and the Seven Wisemen: Everybody Needs Milking'. *Rolling Stone*. March.

Clements, Kirstie. 2010. Editor's Letter. *Vogue* Australia.

Coffey, Debbie. 1996. Fashion News. *Vogue* Australia.

Cooper, Rosemary. 1959. Letter to the Vogue Reader. *Vogue* Australia.

Cordaiy, Hunter. 2007. '"H2O: Just Add Water": A Fairytale in a Real World'. *Metro Magazine: Media & Education Magazine*.

Curlewis, Jean. 1929. 'The Race on the Sands'. *The Home*.

Gawenda, Michael. 1989. 'The Big Elle'. *Time Australia*.

Goatly, Erica. 1999. 'Leading the Way'. *Vogue* Australia, 129–35.

The Home. 1926. 'A Place in the "Sun"'.

The Home. 1927. 'Where Paris Wets Her Feet'. 28.

The Home. 1930. 'Crocus Knitting Wool'. 95.

Kelly, Eugene. 2009. 'Gaga for Tahnee'. *Harper's Bazaar*.

McCann, Edwina. 2009. Editor's Letter. *Harper's Bazaar*.

Maglia. 1966. 'Escape to Adventure in Maglia'. *Vogue* Australia.

marie claire UK. 2009. 'Karl Lagerfeld Says People Prefer Skinny Models'. [cited 1 March 2010]. http://www.marieclaire.co.uk/news/health/400998/karl-lagerfeld-says-people-prefer-skinny-models.html.

Morton, Camilla. 2003. 'The Biggest Splash of All'. *Pop Magazine*.

Nelson, Judy. 1991. 'The Forgotten Mermaid'. *ITA*.

Pegley, Rob. 2007. 'Alpha Females: The Hot 20 Australia's Most Beautiful Sports Stars'. *Alpha*.

Sproat, Muffie. 2007. 'Bathing Beauties'. *Vogue* Australia. December. 85–9.

Vogue. 1961. 'Bilgola Beach, Sydney.' January.

Vogue. 1980. Christian Dior Advertisement. January.

Vogue. 1991. 'Fitness Special'. April. 276.

Vogue. 1995. 'Good Sports'. May. 268.

Vogue. 1996. 'The Bikini Sets Sail'. May. 250.

Vogue. 2001. 'Bound for Glory'. May. 272–277.

Vogue Australia. 1960. 'Brief Beach Flowerings'. Summer. 66.

Vogue Australia. 1974. 'Summer Starts Here'. September.

Vogue Australia. 1976. 'Robin Garland'. August. 54.

Vogue Australia. 1983. 'Ripper Looks'. November.

Vogue Australia. 1986. 'The Print'. September. 211.

Vogue Australia. 1989. 'Swim'. August. 222.

Vogue Australia. 1992. 'The Strong Suit'. November. 128.

Vogue Australia. 1993. 'Out in Front'. 119–25.

Vogue Australia. 1996. 'Two-timing'. July. 118.

Vogue Australia. 2009. 'Water Baby'. September.

Weiss, Philip. 1999. 'Return of the Curve'. *Vogue* Australia.

NEWSPAPER ARTICLES: HARD COPY AND ONLINE

AAP. 2009. 'PM Not Keen on Abbott's Budgie Smugglers'. *The Sydney Morning Herald*. [cited 5 May 2012]. http://news.smh.com.au/breaking-news-national/pm-not-keen-on-abbotts-budgie-smugglers-20091203-k88w.html.

Addington, Tim. 2007. 'The Australian Goes for the Nation's Heart Campaign' [cited 19 May 2011]. http://www.bandt.com.au/news/the-australian-goes-for-the-nation8217s-heart-in-a.

The Age. 2002. 'Thorpe Takes Gold with Undercover Angels'. [cited 3 November 2007]. http://www.theage.com.au/articles/2002/05/13/1021002427789.html.

The Age. 2005. 'Bare Necessities'. http://www.theage.com.au/articles/2004/09/08/10945 30689479.html.

The Age. 2009. 'Sorry, Minister, Beauty Trumps'. http://www.theage.com.au/opinion/sorry-minister-beauty-trumps-20091027-hj1y.html.

Armstrong, Lisa. 2004. 'Wannabe Weeks'. *The Australian*. December 3. 12.

Bremmer, Charles. 2006. 'Bikini Shots Expose a Sea Change in Politics' [cited 3 April 2011]. http://www.timesonline.co.uk/tol/news/world/europe/article603568.ece.

Bunting, Madeleine. 2011. 'Nigella Lawson and the Great Burkini Cover-up'. *The Guardian*. [cited 27 May 2011]. http://www.guardian.co.uk/lifeandstyle/2011/apr/23/nigella-lawson-burkini-bikini-swimming.

Campbell, Melissa. 2003. 'Sexy Nation'. *The Age*. http://150.theage.com.au/view_bestofarticle.asp?intid=932&inttype=1&straction=update.

Chadakoff, Rochelle. 1989. 'Williams Plunges into Swimwear Fashion'. *Ocala Star-Banner*. June 19. 49.

Chrisafis, Angelique. 2011. 'Muslim Women Protest on First Day of France's Veil Ban'. [cited 22 May 2011]. http://www.guardian.co.uk/world/2011/apr/11/france-bans-burqa-and-niqab.

Cogdon, Kamahl. 2008. 'Libby Trickett, Grant Hackett Are Marketing Gold'. *Herald Sun*. http://www.news.com.au/entertainment/celebrity/trickett-hackett-are-marketing-gold/story-e6frfmqi-1111117862816.

Connolly, Kate. 2009. 'Karl Lagerfeld Says Only "Fat Mummies" Object to Thin Models'. *The Guardian*. http://www.guardian.co.uk/lifeandstyle/2009/oct/12/lagerfeld-size-zero-thin-models.

David Jones Limited. 1931. 'David Jones Surf Suit Dept Advertisement'. *The Sun*. November 17. 7.

Gordon, Briony. 2011. 'Nigella's Burkini Proves Women Can't Win on a Beach'. [cited 25 May 2011]. http://www.telegraph.co.uk/foodanddrink/8464398/Nigellas-burkini-proves-women-cant-win-on-a-beach.html.

Gosper, Sophie, and Damien Woolnough. 2011. 'Never Too Old to Wear the Great Aussie Cossie'. *The Australian*. August 20–21. 8.

Gotting, Peter. 2003. 'Rise of the Metrosexual'. *The Age*. http://www.theage.com.au/articles/2003/03/10/1047144914842.html.

Hume, Marion. 2002. 'Up, Up and Away'. *The Sun Herald*. July 7. [cited 5 May 2012]. http://www.smh.com.au/articles/2002/07/06/1025667076767.html.

Hunter, Tim. 2007. 'Set the Budgie Free'. *The Age*. [cited 15 January 2008]. http://www.theage.com.au/news/style—grooming/set-the-budgie-free/2007/03/01/1172338779390.html#.

Huntington, Patty. 2006. 'Once Were Critics: Fashion Week's Golden Tickets'. [cited 14 October 2006]. http://www.smh.com.au/news/fashion/once-were-critics-fashion-weeks-golden-tickets/2006/04/21/1145344277851.html.

Kennedy, Maev. 2009. Alton Towers Bans Men in Speedos. *The Guardian*. August 17. [cited 5 May 2012]. http://www.guardian.co.uk/lifeandstyle/2009/aug/10/alton-towers-speedo-ban.

Krum, Sharon. 2010. 'Prada Ditches Teenage Zombies for Aussies'. *The Australian*. http://www.theaustralian.com.au/news/prada-ditches-teenage-runway-zombies-for-aussies/story-e6frg6n6–1225834931790.

Levine, Bettijane. 1976. 'New Speedo Swimsuit Big Winner at Olympics'. *Los Angeles Times*, August 1. 6.

Loucas, Anthea. 2003. 'Sisters on the Springboard, with Designs on a Ripple Effect'. *The Sydney Morning Herald*, May 5. 3.

McCann, Edwina. 2007b. 'Style'. *The Australian*, December 8–9. 71.

Meacham, Steve. 2009. 'Muscle Beach Party'. *The Sydney Morning Herald*. http://www.smh.com.au/articles/2009/01/08/1231004167858.html.

Menkes, Suzy. 1996. 'Redefining Beauty: Women Muscle Into a Fashion Revolution'. *International Herald Tribune*. http://www.iht.com/articles/1996/07/16/fash.t_6.php.

Munro, Peter. 2008. 'How Flesh Became the New Black'. *The Sydney Morning Herald*. November 17. [cited 5 May 2012]. http://www.smh.com.au/lifestyle/fashion/how-flesh-became-the-new-black-20090403-9odm.html.

O'Brien, Katrina. 2009. 'Smarty Pants'. *The Australian*. March. 34.

Parnell, Sean. 2008. 'Slippery Business'. *The Australian*. May 31–June 1.

Robbins, Glenn. 1976. 'We're on the Olympic Map'. *Daily Mirror*. March 9.

Robinson, Georgina. 2009. 'Burqini Creator Pours Water on French Ban'. http://www.smh.com.au/national/burqini-creator-pours-water-on-french-ban-20090813-eiyk.html.

Safe, Georgina. 2006. 'Golden Girls' Gear Surfs Celebrity Wave'. *The Australian*. August 11. 18.

Safe, Georgina. 2007. 'For the Record That's . . . 1010 Bikini Babes on Bondi Beach. *The Australian*, September 27. 3.

Safe, Georgina. 2008. 'Designing Duo Splash into Vogue'. *The Australian*. March 13. 7.

Safe, Georgina. 2010. 'Lapping Them Up'. *The Australian*. January 30. 24.

The Sydney Morning Herald. 2004. 'Grant Eyes Off the Record'. http://www.smh.com.au/ar ticles/2004/03/09/1078594354750.html.

Totaro, Paula. 2009. 'Aussie Burqini Sparks Religious Storm in France'. *The Sydney Morning Herald*, August 13. [cited May 5 2012]. http://www.smh.com.au/world/aussie-burqini-sparks-religious-storm-in-france-20090813-eim9.html.

Toy, Naomi. 2008. 'Former Miss Universe Jennifer Hawkins Launches "Cozi" Swimwear Label'. *The Daily Telegraph*, July 28. [Cited May 5 2012]. http://www.news.com.au/entertainment/ fashion/hawkins-dives-in-with-own-cossie-label/story-e6frfn7i-1111117032544.

Tucker-Evans, Anooska, and Marie-Christine Sourris. 2009. 'Rebecca Gibney Feels Like a Million Dollars for Logies Bid'. *Courier Mail*. http://www.news.com.au/couriermail/ story/0,23739,25417879–953,00.html.

Walshaw, Nick. 2007. 'Libby Lenton on love, fame and life outside the pool'. *The Telegraph*. http://www.dailytelegraph.com.au/sport/more-sports/libby-my-life-after-beijing/story-e6frey6i-1111114769065.

Wells, Rachel. 2009. 'Designers Swim with the Tide as Offshore Siren Sings'. *The Age*. http://www.theage.com.au/news/national/designers-swim-with-tide-as-offshore-siren-sings/2009/02/28/1235237990210.html.

Wilson, Eric. 2008. 'The Sun Never Sets on the Runway'. [cited 14 May 2011]. *New York Times*. http://www.nytimes.com/2008/09/08/fashion/shows/08WEEKS-1.html.

THESES

Herlihy, Mark. 2000. 'Leisure, Space, and Collective Memory in the "Athens of America" A History of Boston's Revere Beach'. Department of American Civilization, Brown University, Rhode Island.

Johns, Maxine James. 1997. 'Women's Functional Swimwear, 1860–1920'. Iowa State University, Ames, Iowa.

Raszeja, Veronica. 1992. 'A Decent and Proper Exertion. Sports History'. Faculty of Arts and Social Sciences, University of Western Sydney, Macarthur, Sydney.

Vaughan, Laurene. 1998. 'An Investigation into the Success of the Australian Apparel Product in the Area of Swim, Surf and Resort Wear in the International Market'. Department of Fashion and Textile Design, RMIT University, Melbourne.

TRADE JOURNALS AND MAIL-ORDER CATALOGUES

Blum, Stella. 1981. *Everyday Fashions of the Twenties as Pictured in Sears and Other Catalogs*. New York: Dover Publications.

Blum, Stella. 1986. *Everyday Fashions of the Thirties as Pictured in Sears Catalogs, Dover Books on Costume*. New York: Dover Publications.

David Jones Summer Catalogue. 1972. 'Minimates by Speedo'.

Olian, JoAnne. 1992. *Everyday Fashions of the Forties as Pictured in Sears Catalogs*. New York: Dover Publications.

Olian, JoAnne. 1995. *Everyday Fashions, 1909–1920, as Pictured in Sears Catalogs*. New York: Dover Publications.

Olian, JoAnne. 2002. *Everyday Fashions of the Fifties as Pictured in Sears Catalogs*, *Dover Books on Fashion*. Mineola, NY: Dover Publications.

Sears, Roebuck and Company. 1902. Catalogue no. 111. 341, 1068.

Sears, Roebuck and Company. 1915. Spring/summer catalogue.

Sears, Roebuck and Company. 1922. Spring/summer catalogue.

Sears, Roebuck and Company. 1936. Spring/summer catalogue.

Sears, Roebuck and Company. 1944. Spring/summer catalogue.

Sears, Roebuck and Company. 1945. Spring/summer catalogue.

Sears, Roebuck and Company. 1950. Spring/summer catalogue.

Sears, Roebuck and Company. 1955. Spring/summer catalogue.

Sears, Roebuck and Company. 1958. Spring/summer catalogue.

Sears, Roebuck and Company. 1961. Spring/summer catalogue.

Sears, Roebuck and Company. 1965. Spring/summer catalogue.

The Draper of Australasia. 1914. 'Buyers' Notes'. August 27. 368.

The Draper of Australasia. 1924. 'Parisian Shops Feature Holiday Wear'. 581–2.

The Draper of Australasia. 1933. 'Knitwear'. May 31. 36.

The Draper of Australasia. 1934a. 'Knitted Beach and Parade Suits'. May 22. 33.

The Draper of Australasia. 1934b. 'The Miracle Yarn'. November 30. 20–21.

The Draper of Australasia. 1935. 'Black Lance'. 13. December 31. 13.

The Draper of Australasia. 1936. 'Revelations in 1937 Swimsuits'. May 30. 48.

The Draper of Australasia. 1939. 'Swim Suits'. June 30. 43.

The Draper of Australasia. 1946. 'New Season's Beachwear Styles'. September 30. 68.

The Draper of Australasia. 1947. 'Beach and Sports Wear Preview'. July 31. 49.

The Draper of Australasia. 1952. 'Jantzen Review of Summer Fashions'. June 10. 26–8.

The Draper of Australasia. 1953. 'Cole of California Visits Australia'. June 10. 30–1, 42.

The Draper of Australasia. 1956. 'New 'Watersun' Swimsuits Are Exciting'. May 10. 24.

The Draper of Australasia. 1960. 'Helanca in the News for 1960'. January 1. 26.

The Draper of Australasia. 1963. 'Bri-nylon Swimsuit for Eartha Kitt'. October 10. 6.

Index